Fundamentals of Data Base Systems

S. M. Deen

*Department of Computing Science,
University of Aberdeen*

First edition 1977
Reprinted 1979, 1980, 1981, 1982 (twice), 1983

Published by
THE MACMILLAN PRESS LTD
Companies and representatives
throughout the world

ISBN 0 333 19738 0 (hard cover)
    0 333 19739 9 (paper cover)

Typeset by Reproduction Drawings Ltd., Sutton, Surrey
Printed in Great Britain by The Pitman Press Bath

W 20356 /6·95·.10·83

to my mother

Contents

Preface

In 1973 we decided to offer a course on data bases to our final-year honours students in computing science. The duration of this course was to be 24 lecture hours, and we felt that it was more important for the students to develop the basic understanding of Data Base Systems (DBSs) in general rather than to be tied down to the narrow confines of a particular package, which they may or may not have the opportunity to use in their working life. Accordingly I sat down to prepare a course of lectures on the general principles, objectives and characteristics of DBSs, and descriptions of major models with examples of some well-known products. The implementation aspects of data bases were also included in the syllabus. The first problem I faced was the total lack of any material that could serve as a text for the course. Information on data bases was scattered over various reports, articles and conference proceedings in a form not particularly acceptable for a beginner. This led me to prepare a set of detailed notes for the students to use as text, and this book is primarily based on those notes. The secondary contributions come from the lectures I gave to industry.

However, the book is not a series of lecture notes. It is intended as a text on the subject consistent with the course objectives, both for the students and the new users of data bases. By now a number of books have appeared on the market, but most of them do not offer any comprehensive treatment of the subject; instead they mostly concentrate on data organisations and the details of specific DBSs. There still remains the need for explaining thoroughly the basic principles and problems involved, how they are tackled in the existing and the proposed systems, and how a data base fits into a user environment. In this book I have attempted to cover these topics, among others, in sufficient detail so as to be interesting and use- ful to learners. As the title might suggest, the book is intended to provide the understanding of the basic issues; for advanced studies the reader should consult the references given at the end of each chapter.

Each topic in the book is developed from an elementary level within the under- standing of readers with only a basic knowledge of data processing. Exercises are given at the end of each chapter. In chapter 1, the evolution of data bases is traced and their advantages and disadvantages are discussed. Data and more traditional file structures along with pointer organisations are reviewed in chapter 2 to provide the necessary background information for the appreciation of data bases. The issues and problems of DBSs are discussed in chapters 3 and 4. Both the CODASYL model (chapter 5) and the relational model (chapter 6) are treated in depth, since in my opinion they form the foundations of all major DBSs of the future. In the CODASYL model all the main clauses are covered, partly to unfold to the reader the extent of complexities in a DBS and partly to provide the reader with some initial preparation for the understanding of the CODASYL Journals of Development. Examples of a CODASYL Schema, Subschema and application programs are also given, but all along stress is on the semantics rather than the syntax of any clause, since the understanding rather than the ability to write programs is the purpose of the book. Since the CODASYL model is evolutionary, the likely future changes are indicated along with a brief note on the Fortran facilities. Please note that in the text 'Codasyl' is used rather than 'CODASYL', for convenience.

In developing the concepts of the relational model, I have tried to avoid the usual mathematical jargon and to explain it in simpler terms for the understanding of people with a non-mathematical background. The second and third normal forms are explained both with and without using the concept of the functional dependency, which, therefore, the reader does not need to understand in order to appreciate the model. The state of the art is presented to enhance the appreciation of the issues involved by showing how they are handled in the major packages. IBM's IMS is discussed in greater detail owing to its complexity and wide-scale usage. In chapter 8 attention is turned to the data base users, and there the implementation problems, DBS selection techniques and the impact of data bases on data-processing departments are discussed. To complete the picture the book concludes with a discussion and some speculation on the future development of data bases including the issues of standardisation.

I hope the book is useful to all learners of data bases—be they students, programmers, systems analysts, data base administrators or data-processing managers.

Department of Computing Science,   S. M. Deen
University of Aberdeen

Acknowledgements

A number of people assisted me during the writing of this book. First I would like to express my deep gratitude to Mr Stephen Knowles of the Aberdeen University Computing Centre and Miss Anne Meredith of the Medical Computing Centre (Grampian Health Board), Aberdeen; in addition to giving encouragement, both read through the manuscript and corrected, criticised, suggested improvements and supplied material. I am also grateful to Mr David Bell of the Aberdeen University Computing Centre for going through part of the manuscript and for suggesting improvements. I gratefully acknowledge the comments and suggestions of my students, who acted as the guineapigs. I would also like to express my appreciation to Dr Alexander Murray, Head of the Computing Science Department for allowing me to make use of the departmental facilities. Miss Nan Keith of this department deserves a special mention for her diligence and professionalism in producing the draft manuscript from the jungle of my handwriting; I am particularly indebted to her. Thanks are also due to Miss Ann Collie (soon to be Mrs Milne) for typing the final manuscript.

Finally I must thank my wife Rudaina for her keen interest and constant encouragement throughout. I should also perhaps mention the names of two very young men, Rami (3) and Alvin (1), who are lovely people to be with and whose daddy had to forgo their company during the writing of this book.

1 *Introduction*

Essentially a data base is a mass storage of data. Its concept is not a sudden break-through in computer technology, rather it is brought about gradually through experience and requirements. Many organisations contributed to the development of data bases; the list is long and includes computer manufacturers, software houses, user organisations and professional bodies. In this chapter we shall first briefly describe the role of data bases, tracing the history of their development. Later sections will be used to clarify some basic concepts and to discuss the advantages and disadvantages of a data base.

1.1 THE EVOLUTION OF DATA BASES

A data base may be regarded as the most modern technique of data storage, which started with the invention of punched cards by Dr Herman Hollerith[1] of the U.S. Bureau of Census in the 1880s. Dr Hollerith was confronted with the problem of completing the 1880 census of 13 million Americans before 1890, when the next census was due. In 1886 it was clear that the job could not be completed in time using the existing manual means of counting. Necessity was the mother of invention: from his knowledge of the use of punched cards in Jacquard looms, Dr Hollerith invented a method of storing information on them, thus introducing the era of mechanised card files, which was to remain the leading information storage medium for the next 60 years.

The first electronic computer, ENIAC, was operational in 1946. It was designed by Professors Eckert and Mauchley of the University of Pennsylvania for the U.S. Defense Department mainly to calculate trajectories and firing tables. In those early days, computers were largely used for scientific calculations where the facility for the storage of data did not feature as an important requirement—the speed of arithmetic calculation was all that was needed. But when the use of computers was subsequently extended to data processing, the limitations of card files began to be felt. One of the organisations that became seriously concerned by such limitations was the U.S. Bureau of Census. Faced with the approaching 1950 census, the Bureau became particularly anxious to have a faster storage device. In 1951 a new computer—later to be called Univac-1—designed by Eckert and Mauchley, was delivered to the Bureau to cope with the 1950 census data. It had a unique device called a *magnetic tape system*, which could read a magnetic tape both forwards and backwards at high speed.[2] The necessity of the Census Bureau thus mothered two major inventions in 70 years—the punched card and the magnetic tape files.

The impact of magnetic tape on data storage was overwhelming. Those of us involved in some early card file processing can still recall the frustration of finding mispunched, slightly off-punched and screwed up cards scattered in large card files produced by a computer. The fear of accidentally dropping a box of cards and getting them out of sequence was also considerable. With the advent of the magnetic tape system all these nightmares were over. Here was a medium that was light, reliable and neat; its storage capacity and speed compared with a card file were phenomenal. However, the magnetic tape did not alter the processing mode substantially. The file organisation was still sequential, although it allowed the representation of variable length records in a more convenient form. All terminologies of card file systems such as files, records and fields were carried over to the magnetic tape system.

The data-processing systems used in the 1950s were mostly simple payroll subsystems designed in isolation, that is, independent of other related subsystems. A typical payroll subsystem would consist of a large number of small programs with many files each containing fragmented information. The situation changed when the subsequent attempt to computerise more complex systems brought in a new breed of experts—the systems analysts. They took a global view and introduced the concept of integrated files to be shared by a number of programs in more than one subsystem. These shared files were relatively large, and the problem of writing long data descriptions in each program for each file was resolved by the Cobol COPY verb, which allowed a program to copy a prewritten general data description of a file. From then on the evolution of data base became the history of the progress from less to more integrated storage of data.

The introduction of magnetic discs in the mid 1960s gave a further boost to this integration. To access a record on a magnetic tape it is necessary to scan all the intervening records sequentially, but on a disc it is possible to access a record directly, by-passing the other records, and thus gaining an overall retrieval speed of 2 to 4 orders of magnitude over magnetic tape. Disc storage thus provided the much needed hardware support for the large integrated files.

By the mid 1960s, the concept of Management Information System (MIS) gained currency. The basic approach was to run the programs of the MIS package on the output files of all the relevant subsystems. However, it was soon found that for a large organisation the number of input files to the MIS package was excessively high, with the attendant problems of extensive sorting and collating. Moreover, the failure of one system could easily wreck the whole operation. Data duplication in the files leading to update inconsistencies posed yet another problem. Thus these MIS packages turned out to be unreliable, cumbersome and generally unsatisfactory. This highlighted the need for still greater integration and led many organisations to opt for development in this direction.

One of the outstanding products of that time was the Integrated Data Store (IDS) introduced by General Electric (now owned by Honeywell) in 1965. As the name suggests, IDS was used to create large integrated files that can be shared by a number of applications. It was a forerunner of the modern Data Base System and can support a number of data structures. Its pioneer, Charles W. Bachman, subsequently played a very active role in the development of the Codasyl data base proposal, which incorporated many of the features of IDS.

IDS was soon followed by other MIS packages based on integrated files for major systems. Many organisations invested large sums of money in them only to discover that their MIS packages were not as effective as they would like. The problem was the lack of coordination between the files of the major systems. It was soon realised that what was needed was a data base containing a generalised integrated collection of data for all the systems of an organisation serving all application programs. It was recognised that such a data base should be both program- and language-independent if it was to serve all applications; in particular, a change in the data should not require a change in the application program. If a data base is to respond efficiently to the conflicting needs of all the application programs, then it must support a variety of data structures from simple to complex, providing multiple access paths. This concept of a data base crystallised only in the early 1970s although the term data base or data bank had been used loosely since the mid 1960s to refer to almost any integrated file.

A number of Data Base Systems have appeared on the market in the last few years which give variable performance and hardly any compatibility. Codasyl became interested in data bases in the late 1960s and set up a task group to provide a common framework for all data base designs. Since the publication of its draft specifications a few years ago, there has been a noticeable movement away from diversity, converging on the Codasyl model (chapter 5). Now all major computer manufacturers except IBM, are committed to implement the Codasyl proposal. A few Codasyl type data bases are already available. In 1972, the American National Standards Institute (ANSI) set up a working group to standardise data bases (section 9.3); its proposals are likely to lead to a standard model based on the Codasyl specifications.

Parallel to these developments the IBM research laboratories produced two new models for future data base design, in addition to the one on which their present Data Base System IMS is based. One of these is the Relational Data Base Model and the other is the Data Independence Accessing Model (DIAM). The first of these is more widely known than the second; both of them are discussed in this book.

1.2 ORGANISATIONS INVOLVED

We shall briefly describe here the role played by some of the major organisations.

Codasyl

Codasyl or CODASYL is an international organisation of computer users, manufacturers, software houses and other interested groups. Its principal objective is
the design, development and specification of common user languages. It has
produced the Cobol language and is still continuing work on its future development.
Codasyl's involvement in data bases is a direct consequence of its interest in the
extension of the Cobol language facilities. In 1967 it created a Data Base Task
Group (DBTG) whose draft proposal of April 1971[3] laid the foundation of the
Codasyl model. A fuller description of Codasyl and its activities is given in
chapter 5.

Guide and Share

GUIDE and SHARE are American user organisations of large IBM computers for
commercial and scientific users respectively. They set up a joint Data Base Requirement Group (DBRG), which in November 1970 produced a report known as the
Data Base Management Systems Requirements.[4] As the name suggests, this
report analysed the objectives and functions of data base management and listed
facilities that should be provided for the users. The report did not discuss the
implementation problems of these facilities, nor did it allocate priorities on the
requirements. Some of these facilities, cannot be provided by present-day technology, but the report nevertheless represents a set of user objectives which should
be the goal of all data base design. The report stressed data independence and the
need and functions of a data base administrator. It is widely quoted and has
influenced the Codasyl specifications.

GUIDE has subsequently established a study group to investigate the various
data base requirements. SHARE is working independently of GUIDE, but in close
cooperation with Codasyl, and it held a conference on data base management
systems in July 1973.[5]

BCS, ACM and Other Organisations

Both the British Computer Society (BCS) and the Association for Computing
Machinery (ACM) have taken an active interest in the Codasyl proposal. The BCS
held a conference in October 1971[6] to discuss the DBTG report of April 1971,
and has subsequently established a number of subcommittees to study the various
aspects of data bases. In October 1974 BCS arranged a symposium[7] on implementations of the Codasyl proposal. ACM convened a conference on data bases in
1971;[8] it has also set up several special interest goups to study data base requirements, and their reports are published annually. In the United Kingdom, the
United States and Europe BCS, ACM and IFIP (International Federation of
Information Processing) have published various data base proposals on behalf of

Codasyl. Both the U.S. and Canadian Governments financed some of these publications.

The contributions of the computer manufacturers and software houses in the evolution of data bases cannot be overstated. Without their keen participation, there would not be a data base facility today. IBM in particular has conducted, and is still conducting, expensive research in data bases.

1.3 CONCEPTS AND DEFINITIONS

As stated earlier, the term *data base* has been used loosely since the mid 1960s to indicate any large integrated collection of data. In some circles it is still used in this sense, and this leads to a certain amount of confusion. We shall use the term only in its present concept following the reasoning developed earlier. More specifically, we can define a data base as

> a generalised integrated collection of data which is structured on natural data relationships so that it provides all necessary access paths to each unit of data in order to fulfil the differing needs of all users.

This definition can be analysed as follows.

(1) A data base is a generalised collection of data.
(2) The collection is integrated to reduce redundancy.
(3) Data structure is based on natural data relationships to provide all necessary access paths. The required access path to a unit of data is really a consequence of its relationship to other data. If there are records for father and children, then the access paths likely to be used are from the father to a child, from a child to the father and from a child to a child. To achieve this, a data base has to employ complex data structures. This ability to represent the natural data relationships with all necessary access paths is the fundamental distinction between a data base and a conventional file.
(4) A data base must fulfil the differing data needs of all users in an efficient and effective manner.

A diagram showing a computer configuration for a data base is shown in figure 1.1. A data base is normally stored on direct-access devices such as discs. The system can include remote terminals for the data base users, and it can be operated in both batch and on-line modes depending on the need. The minimum computer memory required for average data bases varies from 30K to 160K bytes. A major part of the memory is occupied by the routines and tables required for the run-time management of the data base. These routines act as an interface between the operating system of the computer and the application programs using the data base.

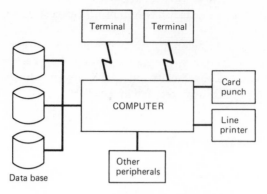

Figure 1.1 A hardware configuration for a data base

Definitions

Defined here are some of the terms used in the text.

(1) *Data Base System* (DBS) A system that generates, runs and maintains data bases; as such the system must include all the software needed for the purpose. Thus IMS of IBM is a DBS, DMS 1100 of Univac is another.

(2) *Data Base Control System* (DBCS) The software required for run-time control, that is, management of a data base. It is therefore a component of DBS.

(3) *Data Base Management System* (DBMS) The software that manages a data base; the word 'management' is often interpreted to include the function of creation as well as that of maintenance. It is therefore used in either sense as a DBS or DBCS.

(4) *Implementor* Implements a specification to produce a DBS; for instance, Univac is the implementor of the Codasyl proposal on which the DMS 1100 is based.

(5) *Manufacturer* Refers to computer manufacturers.

(6) *Application Program* The program that uses the data base; alternatively known as a *user program*.

(7) *Run-unit* One execution of a job step which would normally be a part of an application program. The concept is used in concurrent usage, but for this book the difference between an application program and a run-unit can be ignored.

(8) *Host language* The language in which an application program is written; depending on the languages permitted by a DBS, it can be Cobol, Fortran, PL/1 and so on.

(9) *Data Base Administrator* (DBA) The person responsible for the data base in the organisation.

(10) *User* There are several types of user in a data base environment; the application programmer, the systems analyst, the DBA are all users; the user department is a user and the organisation as a whole is a user, but the problem faced by each is different. The term *user* is employed in this book as a common name for all users; the meaning will be apparent from the context.

Two Basic Models

Data bases can be classified into two groups—formatted and relational. In formatted data bases a variety of data structures is used to represent relationships. These structures are complex and usually involve pointers to relate records logically. A range of data structures from simple to complex is supported to facilitate the required access paths, which must be specified explicitly. Therefore a data structure can support only a limited number of predefined access paths and, unless an access path is specifically provided, a given unit of data cannot be accessed.

In relational data bases all data structures are reduced to two dimensional tables of specified characteristics, which in mathematics are called relations. Access is provided to each data item directly by value through algebraic operations on relations; access is universal.

The relational model is discussed in chapter 6. The rest of the book concentrates on formatted data bases, unless otherwise stated. All available Data Base Systems, including the Codasyl model, belong to the formatted class.

1.4 FACILITIES AND LIMITATIONS

As indicated earlier, there are a number of Data Base Systems currently available. The facilities offered by them vary a great deal depending on the level of sophistication. However, in general, a good DBS should provide the following advantages over a conventional system.

Independence of Data and Program

This is a prime advantage of a data base. Both the data base and the program can be altered independently of each other. This saves time and money spent on modifying them to retain consistency.

Ease in Systems Design

A systems designer in a data base environment is not concerned with extensive file design, data duplication, data inconsistency, maintenance and backup facilities of a conventional system. In a data base, data exist in a form suitable for all applications; the designer has only to select what he needs. The systems design is therefore easier.

Ease in Programming

The programming task is significantly reduced because the programmers are relieved of the details of file processing, file updates and extensive sorting. The level of programming skill required is generally lower for a data base.

Multiple Host Languages

Language independence is another virtue of a data base. A data base can support a number of host languages, and the user can choose the one most convenient for a particular application.

Consistent and Up-to-date Data

A data base reduces data duplication and provides consistent and up-to-date data. In a conventional system, data duplication in various files often leads to chaos and inconsistency.

Concurrent Usage

A data base permits more than one program to access the data base at the same time, thus maximising resource utilisation.

Data Protection

In a data base, privacy and the integrity of data can be controlled.

Terminal Facilities

A data base can be used from remote terminals. A query language is available for non-programmer users interested in some straightforward retrieval of data from a terminal.

Evolutionary System

Data bases are regarded as evolutionary systems. The user can build up his data base, gradually learning from his experience. Facilities for reorganising the data base to optimise the overall performance are provided. Because of data independence, the changes in the data base do not affect the application programs.

The disadvantage of a data base is the cost. It is expensive to install, run and maintain. The major cost factors are as follows.

Large Memory

In addition to the operating system, data bases need large memory to house the DBCS routines, application programs, the data base tables, directories and system buffers.

Storage Device

A data base requires a large number of storage devices, a good part of which is consumed as overheads.

Channel Capacity

Additional input/output channel capacity can be required to cope with the increased data traffic between the data base on the physical devices and the computer memory.

Slow Processing Speed

The processing speed, particularly the update speed, is very slow in a data base.

Staff Overhead

A data base needs a data base administrator. In most cases it is a full-time job. Additional staff are also required depending on the size of the system.

Implementation

The implementation of a data base is a major and expensive undertaking. Nothing like this happens in the conventional systems.

Incompatibility

The incompatibility of the available Data Base Systems is a disadvantage for the user; once he has implemented one DBS, it becomes very difficult and expensive for him to change to another.

The advantages of a data base are in most cases intangible; they are conveniences which cannot easily be quantified. This makes an objective cost-benefit study of a data base almost impossible. The value assigned to a convenience largely

depends on what a person expects. Having installed and used a data base satisfactorily for some time, an organisation is likely to forget the cost. The level of
justification required to change from a conventionally computerised system to a
data base system is similar to that required for changing from a manual to a computerised system. If we regard the manual operation as the first stage in information processing, then the use of a data base is the logical third stage.

EXERCISE

1.   Discuss the impact of magnetic tapes on data processing. Compare their ad-
      vantages with discs.

REFERENCES

[1] S. H. Hollingdale and G. C. Tootil, *Electronic Computers* (Pelican, London,
      1970) p. 59.
[2] S. Rosen, *Computg Surv.,* 1 (1969) p. 7.
[3] CODASYL DBTG Report, April 1971.
[4] Joint GUIDE-SHARE Report on Data Base Management System Requirements,
      November 1970.
[5] SHARE Conference Data Base Management System. *Proceedings of the Share
      Working Conference on DBMS 1973* (North Holland).
[6] BCS October 71 Conference on April 71 Report.
[7] *Proceedings of the Symposium on Implementations of CODASYL Data Base
      Management Proposals,* October 1974 (BCS).
[8] ACM Conference, *Proc. 1971 ACM-SIGFID.*

2 Data and File Structure

As a collection of data, a data base uses the concepts of data items, records and files in one form or another, and it employs the techniques available for their representations in a computer environment. The knowledge of these concepts and techniques therefore forms a prerequisite for a proper understanding of data base technology. This chapter is intended to satisfy this prerequisite. In section 2.1 the characteristics of data items are examined. A general discussion on records and files is given in section 2.2. Indexed files are described in section 2.3 and direct files, along with various hashing techniques are given in section 2.4. Inverted files are presented in section 2.5, with list-structured files and techniques for pointer organisation in section 2.6.

2.1 CHARACTERISTICS OF DATA ITEMS

A *data item* is defined as the smallest unit of data that can take part independently and meaningfully in processing. Apart from its indivisibility, a data item displays a number of other characteristics, some of which are logical or machine-independent while others are physical- or machine-dependent. The name given to a data item is a *data item name*. In Fortran a data item is often referred to as a *field*, and in Cobol it is referred to as an *elementary item*. Another associated term is a *data unit*, that is, a unit of data that can stand for anything from a data item to a collection of sets of records. The name given to a data unit is a *data name*.

2.1.1 Logical Characteristics

Every data item contains a particular value out of a set of possible values. The user is principally concerned with the value and with the change in the value which occurs from time to time. The value itself can be *numeric, alphabetic* or *alphanumeric*, thereby grouping data items into classes. If the class is numeric, the unit in which a data item is expressed becomes a relevant characteristic, although the unit may not necessarily be a part of the data item. The class of a data item is obvious from the value, but the unit generally is not; for instance, a value of 1450 may stand for pounds sterling, pence or miles.

The meaning of a data item is an external characteristic imposed by the user, although it can be partly clarified by the value and the unit. Consider, for instance, three data items containing the following values

LONDON AVENUE
WASHINGTON
1240

From the value we could be tempted to assume LONDON AVENUE to be a street name, but it could equally well be the name of a shop. WASHINGTON could be a person or a city, but 1240 could be anything, even if we knew its unit. (For instance, if the unit is pounds sterling, the data item for 1240 could still represent such items as salary, bank balance or tax.) We cannot know its meaning unless some additional external information is supplied.

2.1.2 Physical Characteristics

The machine representation of a data item imposes certain physical characteristics on it. The first is the physical size, commonly expressed in units of *bytes*. A *byte* is defined as the smallest individually addressable unit of storage, usually consisting of 8 binary positions or *bits*. In most large computers, 4 bytes make a *word*, which is used as the basic functional unit for arithmetical operations. In more recent machines, computer memory is divided into physical blocks known as pages, each page containing around 1000 words. Although there are machines that do not use the concept of bytes, most large computers do use it, so we shall base our discussions of the physical characteristics of data items on this concept.

Normally a data item in the store occupies the next available bytes, which may spread across word boundaries, but since a word is the basic unit for arithmetic operations, calculations are slower on straddling data items. For faster arithmetic calculations, data items involved can be stored in complete words, aligning them on the right-hand word boundary. This is known as *alignment* or *synchronisation*. Alignment on the left is also available for non-numeric data. An alignment naturally wastes storage space as is shown below. Consider two data item values

RAY 524

Normally we require 6 bytes for their storage as follows

Bytes	1	2	3	4	5	6
	R	A	Y	5	2	4
Words		1			2	

If we wish to use the value 524 in calculation, we should synchronise it on the right, resulting in the following storage layout

Bytes	1	2	3	4	5	6	7	8
	R	A	Y			5	2	4

Words   1   2

thus using 8 instead of 6 bytes.

We have assumed above that only one character per byte can be stored, but this is not always true; the storage required really depends on the mode in which the value of a data item is represented. The standard modes of representation are shown by the tree in figure 2.1.

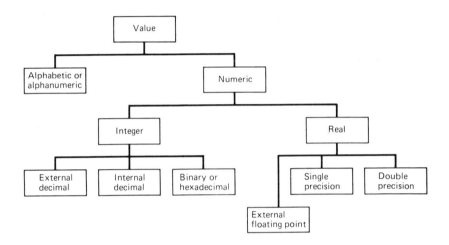

Figure 2.1 Value Representation

Alphabetic and alphanumeric characters are represented as one character per byte. A number can be integer or real — an integer does not have a decimal fraction, but a real number does. In external or unpacked decimal form an integer is stored as one digit per byte, whereas in internal or packed decimal form 2 digits are packed to a byte. For instance, an integer 3405 will be stored in external decimal form as

Unused	3	Unused	4	Unused	0	+	5

Bytes   1   2   3   4

and in internal decimal form as

0	3	4	0	5	+

Bytes   1   2   3

All integers intended for printing have to be in external decimal form, but arithmetical operations can be performed only on integers in internal decimal or binary form. All external decimal numbers are converted by the system to the internal form when needed for calculation. However, arithmetical operations are faster in binary or hexadecimal form where, depending on the size, an integer is stored as a string of binary bits occupying 2 to 8 bytes. The binary mode is the most economical method of storing integers.

Real numbers are broken down into two parts — a mantissa and an exponent — using either 10 or 16 as the base

$$\text{real number} = \text{mantissa} \times \text{base}^{\text{exponent}}$$

In external floating point mode the base is 10, and both the mantissa and the exponent are stored in external decimal form with one digit per byte. In internal floating point form 16 is used as the base and a normalised hexadecimal fraction is used as the mantissa, both the mantissa and the exponent being stored in pure binary form. When needed for calculation, all external floating point numbers are converted into internal floating point form. Generally this conversion is not exact— the system truncates the mantissa somewhere, depending on the precision specified. In the single precision mode of an internal floating point number, one word of 4 bytes is allocated to the number, yielding an accuracy of up to 6 hexadecimal digits for the mantissa, whereas in the double precision mode 2 words each of 4 bytes are allocated to the number, giving an accuracy of up to 14 hexadecimal digits.

2.1.3 Format of a Data Item

It is evident that the physical size of the storage required for a data item is not the same as its logical size, that is, the size of its value. The alignment and the mode of representation can and do affect the physical size. Report symbols such as £ signs, commas, blanks and cheque protection characters can be attached to the value of a data item; they need not be permanently stored, only generated as necessary. We shall use the term *format* to mean the characteristics of a data item, namely, class (numeric, alphabetic or alphanumeric), type (integer or real), mode of representation (external, internal, binary, single or double precision), alignment (left or right), report symbol, and so on. Two users may wish to use the same data item value in two different formats, for instance, one as an integer and the other as a real number.

The identification of a data item is a *need,* but not a *property.* The need arises because the data items appear in association with others. The principal method of identification of a data item is by its relative position (within a record) to which a data name is given.

2.2 RECORDS AND FILES

Records

A named collection of data items is known as a data-aggregate[1], and a named collection of data-aggregates constitutes a record. In Cobol data-aggregates are known as *group items* or *group fields*. An example of a record, say a customer record, is given below.

Description	*Data Names Used*
Record name	CUST-REC
Account number	ACN
Customer name	CNAME
Balance for the last	
three months (data-aggregate)	BALANCE
in month 1	MONTH1
in month 2	MONTH2
in month 3	MONTH3

This record can be represented by a tree structure as shown in figure 2.2.

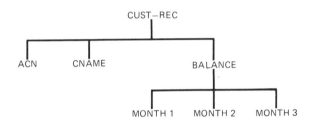

Figure 2.2

A record can be either logical or physical. A logical record is a collection of data items in which the user is interested, but the collection need not occupy contiguous space in the storage device. A physical record does occupy contiguous storage and may contain, besides the data items, additional information such as the physical record size and the pointer to the next record in key sequence. It is normal to store one logical record to a physical record, but this need not always be true. In fact in a data base we might wish to construct logical records with data items selected from several physical records.

A logical record has two parts — key and data. A key is the collection of data items used to identify the record. The remainder of the record is data. A record is characterised by its type, there being many records within each type. The customer record represented in figure 2.2 is a record type, which shows the type of information held for each customer. In this case, the set of information for one customer constitutes a single customer record or one occurrence of the record type CUST-REC; each record is identified by the value of a key, which in this case can be the account number.

Files

A file is a named collection of records containing the occurrences of one or more record types. Usually the term *file* is associated with the physical organisation of the records in one or more contiguous areas of the physical device purported to maximise the retrieval and storage speed of records for a particular application. We therefore need a separate term to refer to a collection of related records as viewed by a particular user without any consideration of their storage organisation. In this book the term *logical file* or *dataset* will be used for such a purpose. A particular record may belong to only one physical file but to many logical files. Ideally each user should be free to define his dataset as a collection of the records in which he is interested, irrespective of their storage organisation. In fact a major objective of a Data Base System is to provide facilities to construct such datasets and to define access paths to the records of the datasets (see also section 3.2.4).

   In general we can group files into the following six categories

> serial
> sequential
> indexed
> direct
> inverted
> list

   A serial file is simply a collection of records in one physical area without any reference to the key. They are usually temporary files waiting to be sorted according to a key order. A sequential file is a sorted serial file, that is, a file where records are stored in ascending or descending order of a key. If the file is on a magnetic tape, the records are accessed solely by scanning sequentially. However, if the records are on a disc, access can be obtained by a method known as binary chop, where the middle record of the file is examined to determine whether the key of the wanted record is up or down. By using binary chops successively, the wanted record is found. Sequential files are used for those applications where most of the records are required in every computer run. A common example is a payroll master file holding information on employees, which is needed to calculate their salaries every month. The update of such a file involves copying the old file and incorporating the new information in the copy.

   The other types of file listed above can be supported only by direct-access devices. Their organisations are more complex and will therefore be dealt with individually in detail.

2.3 INDEXED FILES

The essential feature of an indexed file is an index table containing a list of the keys and the addresses of the corresponding records on disc. An index table can be constructed in three different ways: *implicit, basic* and *limit.* In implicit index, the table maintains a list of all possible keys, and as a result the keys are always in order. An address can be found quickly by using the binary chop method for scanning, but the size of the table is usually too large for the average user. Basic index leads to what is known as an indexed random or an indexed non-sequential file, and limit index leads to an indexed sequential file. The former is less commonly used than the latter which is supported by standard Cobol software.

2.3.1 Indexed Random Files

The basic index table used for this file looks somewhat like this

Entry No.	Key	Record Address	Chain (Entry No.)
1	1	6	5
2	3	26	0
3	4	15	0
4	5	25	6
5	2	40	2
6	6	100	0

A chain contains the entry number for the next higher key. If the next key is the next higher key, then its chain is set to zero, all chains being initially at zero. During subsequent amendment runs, when records are deleted or new records are inserted out of sequence, the chains are updated, a deleted record being bypassed by chaining. To find a record, the index table is searched for the record address, either sequentially or by using some other technique.

2.3.2 Indexed Sequential Files

Limit index used in indexed sequential files is rather a compromise system. Records are grouped into blocks, each block having an exclusive range of keys represented by the highest key, as shown below

Block No.	Key	Range Represented
1	6	1-6
2	12	7-12
3	24	19-24
4	18	13-18

Within a block records are chained, each chain indicating the location of the next higher record. To access a record, a block with the next higher key is searched through. For instance, in this example, to find the key number 14, the block 4, which has the next higher key 18, will be read by the computer. The correct record will be made available by matching the key. This type of indexing system is very compact and reasonably efficient, and hence popular.

The storage used for an indexed sequential file is divided into three areas which we shall refer to as the *primary data area* (PDA), the *cylinder overflow area* (COA) and the *independent overflow area* (IOA), each being divided into blocks. Every cylinder contains a number of PDA blocks for the original records and a number of COA blocks to accommodate the overflows from these PDA blocks. The overflows from COA are absorbed in IOA. While a PDA block is designed to contain a number of records for efficient storage utilisation, a COA or an IOA block is usually restricted to holding a single record. If needed for overflows, one or more COA blocks are allocated to a PDA block, all COA blocks belonging to a PDA block being chained. The IOA blocks are also chained. In large files, two levels of index are maintained: a cylinder index to indicate the cylinder for the record, followed by a block index within every cylinder to locate the block of the record (figure 2.3).

The first IOA cylinder

Cylinder Index
Independent Overflow Area
As many cylinders as specified
(All IOA blocks are chained)

Cylinder index occupies part of the first cylinder followed by IOA.
More cylinders for IOA are used if required

A PDA cylinder

Block Index
Cylinder Overflow Area
As many blocks as specified
(All COA block belonging to the same PDA block are chained)
Primary Data Area blocks as specified.

As many cylinders as necessary each containing Block Index, COA and PDA.

Figure 2.3 Indexed sequential file

When a file is created, all records within every block are in sequential order. It is possible to reserve space in the PDA blocks for new insertions. If a PDA block is full, a record belonging to this block is placed in a COA block, which is chained to the other COA blocks of this PDA block. The block index maintains an additional entry showing the address of its first COA block. The actual process can be illustrated by the following example. Suppose a PDA block, capable of holding 6 records has the following 5 records

1	2	3	5	10

If, in a subsequent run, records 4, 6 and 8 are inserted, the PDA block will be reorganised as

1	2	3	4	5	6

and two COA blocks will be allocated to this PDA block for records 8 and 10. The block index will keep an entry for record 8 and its location in COA. If record 9 is inserted in a later run, it would be stored in a COA block, updating the chains there; but if COA is full, the record will be placed in an IOA block. To retrieve a record, the appropriate PDA block or COA block is searched as indicated by the index; if the record is not found, the IOA blocks are scanned. Deletions of records are permitted, but the technique varies from ignoring the record to physically removing it.

An indexed sequential file can be processed both sequentially and randomly. In sequential processing the chains are used, while in random processing only the wanted records are accessed. Variations of the indexed sequential technique described are possible, but will not be discussed here.

2.4 DIRECT FILES

Directly organised files are held on discs where records are grouped into blocks called buckets, with one or more buckets per track of a disc. No index table is maintained; instead the user is required to provide an algorithm—known as a hashing or an address-generation algorithm—in his program to calculate the bucket address from a record key. The user must also provide adequate means to deal with overflow problems. Once the address is known, the bucket concerned is accessed directly. The system then produces the wanted record from those in the selected bucket by matching the key. No pointers or chaining are required. Compared to an indexed sequential file, access is much faster here, since searching through a lengthy index table is avoided. However, it is difficult to design a hashing algorithm which will take care of all future insertions and overflows efficiently. The additional advantage of sequential processing permitted in indexed sequential files is not available in direct files, but there are a number of applications—such as real-time systems with fast response times—where direct files provide the only means of support.

The factors affecting the efficiency of a direct file are

> bucket size
> treatment of overflows
> hashing technique

Small buckets tend to increase storage overheads, and large buckets lead to long scanning time to find the appropriate record from the bucket. It is therefore important to select a suitable bucket size. The user must also design an efficient system for the treatment of overflows. The most important of these factors—the hashing technique—is discussed below.

Hashing involves the generation of the bucket address from a key, and it is carried out in three steps. First all non-numeric characters of the keys are converted to numeric form, a convenient method being the replacement of letters A to Z by numbers 10 to 35. In the second step the numeric keys obtained from the first step are transformed into another set of numbers which is evenly distributed over the range of interest. In the final step the transformed set of keys is normalised to fit the range of the addresses. The most difficult part is the selection of an appropriate key-transformation technique for the second step. A number of methods is available, some of which are more efficient than others, depending on the applications; a complete randomisation is not really possible. Discussion of the major techniques used follows.

Key Organisation

This is a simple method and involves organising the keys into suitable groups which can be used to generate an address. Consider for example a file with 5 groups of keys, each group having 100 records to be distributed over 50 buckets with 10 records per bucket. Suppose the groups are

> CB100–CB199, XM300–XM399, LA700–LA799
> ZL500–ZL599, MK800–MK899

This set does not need any conversion to numerical values; all that is necessary is simply to use the last two digits 00–99 as the transformed keys, thus giving a range of 100. We calculate the normalisation factor, NF, as

$$\text{NF} = \frac{\text{total number of buckets}}{\text{range of the transformed key}}$$

$$= \frac{50}{100} = 0.5$$

By multiplying a transformed key by NF, we shall find its bucket number. The key 0 and 1 of each group will go to bucket 0 (10 records), key 2 and 3 of each group to bucket 1, key 98 and 99 of each group to bucket 49, and so on.

This method is suitable only if the records are evenly distributed within each group.

Quotient

Let us assume that we have 1000 records with keys 0 to 999 to be distributed over 50 buckets, with 20 records per bucket. We divide a key by 20 and take the result as the transformed key. Thus for record key 855

$$\frac{\text{key}}{\text{total number of records per bucket}} = \frac{855}{20} = 42.75$$

The range of the transformed key set is 0 to 49 and therefore normalisation in this case is 1. The bucket number for record key 855 is then 42.

This method can be used only if the keys are evenly distributed over the range.

Remainder

We shall now use the previous example of 1000 records still to be distributed over 50 buckets, but taking as the transformed key the remainder of the key divided by the total number of buckets. Thus for record key 855

$$\frac{\text{key}}{\text{total number of buckets}} = \frac{855}{50} \text{ with remainder 5}$$

The range of the transformed keys is 0 to 49 and hence the normalisation factor is 1. Therefore the record with key 855 will be stored in the fifth bucket.

This method is convenient if the keys are randomly distributed over a part or the whole of the range. However, it breaks down if the keys are clustered in groups leaving gaps at equal divisor distances, as would be the case for gaps at 42–47, 92–97, 142–147, and so on in our example.

Radix Transformation

In this method the key is changed into a number base other than its own. For example 52419 can be transformed to, say, base 11 as

$$5 \times 11^4 + 2 \times 11^3 + 4 \times 11^2 + 1 \times 11^1 + 9 \times 11^0 = 76371$$

Buckets numbers can be found by multiplying this transformed key 76371 by the appropriate normalisation factor. This method can be used to break down clusters and produce an evenly distributed set.

Midsquare Method

Here the value of the key is squared and the central digits of the square are used as the transformed key. Assume that we have a 5 digit key for a file with 2000 buckets. Then, if the key under consideration is 25312, we have

$$25312 \times 25312 = 0640697344$$

Selecting the central 4 digits 0697 as the transformed key, then the bucket number for this key is

$$\frac{\text{total number of buckets}}{\text{the range of the transformed key}} \times 697 = \frac{2000}{10000} \times 697 = 139.4$$

Therefore 139 is the bucket number.

Shifting

Let us assume that the key is 64012418. Now split the key in the middle into two parts, 6401 and 2418. We can now add these to the middle of the key to yield the transformed key as follows

$$
\begin{array}{r|l}
6401 & 2418 \\
64 & 01 \\
24 & 18 \\
\hline
\end{array}
$$

$$\text{transformed key} = 89 \quad 43$$

Now we can normalise the value of the transformed key to give the address.

Folding

In this technique the key is partitioned into a number of parts, each equal to the address length, and then folded over along the partition boundary like a piece of paper. The digits falling into the same position are added. Assume, for example, an 8-digit key with 3-digit address length. Then

$$\text{Key} = \boxed{1 \;|\; 2 \;\|\; 3 \;|\; 4 \;|\; 5 \;\|\; 6 \;|\; 7 \;|\; 8}$$

Fold   Fold
here   here

So we have

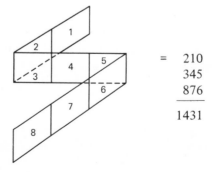

$$
\begin{array}{r}
= \quad 210 \\
345 \\
876 \\
\hline
1431 \\
\end{array}
$$

Now take 431 as the transformed key and adjust as necessary to fit the range of the addresses. Note that the last part of the fold has only two significant digits since the key is 8 digits long. The folding and shifting methods are useful for large keys.

Polynomial Method

In this method, each digit of the key is expressed as the coefficient of a polynomial. For a key 25312 therefore

$$2x^4 + 5x^3 + 3x^2 + x + 2$$

The polynomial is divided by another invariant polynomial and the remainder is taken as the transformed key.

Investigation shows that the remainder method gives best overall performance, with the polynomial and the midsquare methods coming next. Other complex methods such as digit analysis or Lin's method are found to be poor[2] in performance, and hence are not described above.

2.5 INVERTED FILES

The files discussed so far are commonly used in data processing and are referred to as the *regular files*. Their organisation is simple, each record being characterised by a single key by means of which any of the records can be related. Departure from this involves a complex organisation where a record can be accessed either through multiple keys or through pointers linking the related records. The first of these is the inverted file organisation which permits multiple keys per record. Essentially there are three ways of organising an inverted file, as follows.

Fully Inverted File

In a fully inverted file, every data item of a record is represented as a key, and an index table is maintained for all their values. Since a data item value could be common to more than one record, the index table consists of entries for every data item value followed by the addresses of all the relevant records. Similarly, since all the data item values of each record appear in the index table, there is no need to store data records in the conventional sense; hence the file is inverted.

Partially Inverted File

In a partially inverted file, data records are stored explicitly in addition to an index table for the keys. It is not necessary to represent all the data items as keys.

Secondary Indexed File

This is a modified version of a partially inverted file where one key is selected
as primary and the others as secondary. Two index tables, one for the primary
keys and the other for the secondary keys, are maintained. The primary
indices give the record addresses, whereas the secondary indices refer to the
primary keys. The data records are stored in the primary key sequence. Although
records can be selected on secondary keys, actual retrieval has to be made
through the primary index.

An inverted index table, that is, the index table for an inverted file, is
very large. In fact it is itself a file, complete with storage and retrieval problems.
In a fully inverted file, the data item values belonging to a record are distributed
throughout the inverted index table, and therefore, in the absence of any explicitly
stored records, additional facilities are needed to recreate the records as and when
necessary. This is done by maintaining, at the record locations, the pointers for
the relevant data item values indicating their positions in the inverted index table.

Inverted files are often used for document retrieval in large libraries. We shall
use here an example of document retrieval to illustrate some of the points discussed earlier. Consider a small example involving three records on three books
as follows.

INFORMATION	MANAGEMENT	SYSTEMS	Other information

INFORMATION	SYSTEMS	ANALYSIS	TECHNIQUE	Other information

INFORMATION	SYSTEMS	DESIGN	TECHNIQUE	Other information

We assume it to be an inverted file where the data items containing the words
of the title are represented as the keys—or *descriptors* as they are called. The file
maintains an index table for these descriptors, but not for other information
such as author, publisher, year of publication and shelf-mark. The inverted index
table can be as shown in figure 2.4. At the record location we may have a situation
as shown in figure 2.5

Instead of storing other information items at the record locations, we can
replace them by pointers showing the locations of other information. To find the
location of a book (shelf-mark) or other information, the user may supply some
or all of the descriptor values. The inverted filing system would then search
through the indices and select only those records which share these descriptor
values. The selected list would be smaller if more descriptor values were supplied.
The principle can be illustrated by means of a Venn diagram for the title
Information Systems Design Technique (figure 2.6). If all the four descriptor

Address	Descriptor values	Pointers to records		
A1	ANALYSIS	P2		
A2	DESIGN	P3		
A3	INFORMATION	P1	P2	P3
A4	MANAGEMENT	P1		
A5	SYSTEMS	P1	P2	P3
A6	TECHNIQUE	P2	P3	

Figure 2.4 Inverted index table

P1	A3	A4	A5	Other information	
P2	A3	A5	A1	A6	Other information
P3	A3	A5	A2	A6	Other information

Figure 2.5 Record locations

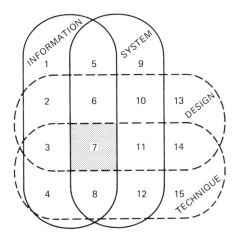

Figure 2.6 Venn's diagram

values are supplied, the selected list will correspond to the area 7 (shaded) in the diagram. On the other hand, if only one descriptor value, say, information, is supplied, the list will correspond to all the areas 1 to 8, producing the list of all the books which have 'information' in their titles.

The main advantage of an inverted file is the flexibility of access to the records it permits through multiple keys. However, locating a particular entry in the inverted index has its own problems. For example, variable length of the index entry records makes the application of the binary-chops method difficult, although the use of indexed random or indexed sequential techniques can be considered. Updating an entry in the inverted index is another serious problem, since a change in one entry might affect many records. Finally, the reconstruction of records using auxiliary indices in a fully inverted file is very time consuming.

Data structures of some modern Data Base Systems are based on partially inverted files, with additional facilities for supporting tree structures of the related records.

2.6 LIST STRUCTURED FILES

In list structured files[3] records are related by pointers, which can support a variety of logical sequences of records, independent of their physical locations. The pointers themselves can be logical or physical as will be discussed later. Lists can be divided into two categories: *open list* or *chain* and *closed list* or *ring*. In a chain, the end record does not point back to the header record, but in a ring it does. We shall discuss both of these shortly, but first we note the conventions used in the illustrations.

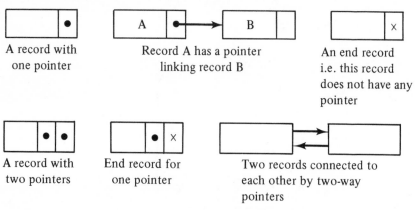

A record with
one pointer

Record A has a pointer
linking record B

An end record
i.e. this record
does not have any
pointer

A record with
two pointers

End record for
one pointer

Two records connected to
each other by two-way
pointers

2.6.1. Chains

It is possible to construct a number of chain structures by linking the records in a number of ways. A few of the more important structures are as follows.

One-way Chains

A one-way chain is a list of records connected either in the backward or in the forward direction (figure 2.7).

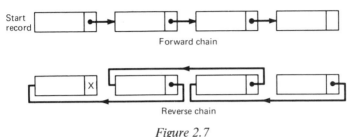

Figure 2.7

Two-way Chains

In a two-way chain, records are connected in both forward and backward directions. This facilitates bidirectional search (figure 2.8).

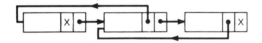

Figure 2.8 Two-way chain

Trees

A tree is used to represent a hierarchical data structure in the form of nodes and branches, a node or a branch being a record. A branch may become a node generating further branches, thus giving rise to successive levels of hierarchy. A node is often known as the *owner* or the *father*, and the branches from it as its *members* or *children*. A tree is identified by its topmost node (root) which is known as the *root record*. An example of a tree is given in figure 2.9. The

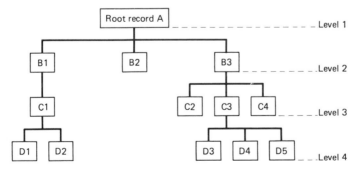

Figure 2.9 A tree structure with four levels of hierarchy

records in the tree could be the components and subcomponents of a product **A** which is made up of part numbers B1, B2 and B3. Part number B1 is made up of part number C1, which is composed of D1 and D2. Likewise, part number B3 consists of C2, C3 and C4, C3 itself being constructed from D3, D4 and D5. We thus have a tree showing four levels of hierarchy.

An owner and its members can be connected to each other through a one-way or a two-way ring.

2.6.2 Rings

Rings are extensions of chains where the last record is allowed to possess a pointer for the first, thus forming a closed configuration. Processing can start at any record and continue through the ring. Thus one-way and two-way rings appear as shown in figure 2.10.

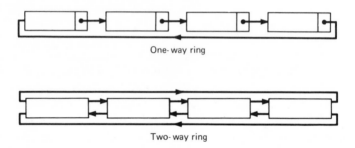

One-way ring

Two-way ring

Figure 2.10

We shall consider below two interesting ring structures.

Ring with Owner and Member Pointers

This is an important structure used to represent a dataset consisting of an owner and its members. Figure 2.11 shows such a structure with bidirectional links between the adjacent members, each member having a pointer to the owner. It is possible to search through this ring in both directions, and in addition the owner can be reached directly without having to trace through the whole ring. The structure can be made more flexible if the owner is also provided with member pointers, one for each member, thus providing a direct access facility. Although access is fast, the updating of such structures can be costly due to the multiplicity of pointers—but then we cannot expect to get flexibility without paying for it.

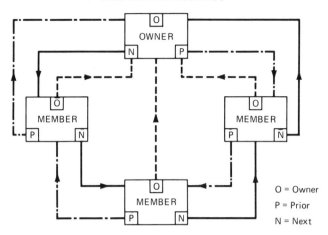

Figure 2.11 A two-way ring with pointers to the owner

Coral Ring

This is a somewhat simplified version of the bidirectional ring structure with
owner pointer. Here all the members are connected in the forward direction by
a one-way ring, but in the reverse direction only the alternate (even or odd)
members are linked; the other alternate (odd or even) set of members have
owner pointers (figure 2.12). This technique reduces the number of pointers
per record from 3 to 2, but it increases the update problem if a new member
is inserted in the middle. The structure is fairly stable, since, if a record is
destroyed, the others can still be accessed.

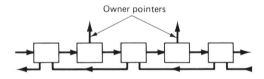

Figure 2.12 Coral ring

2.6.3 Pointer Organisation

The pointers used in a list structured file, or for that matter in any file, fall into
any one of the following four categories

> hash key
> internal pointer
> absolute pointer
> relative pointer

A hash key of a record is the key used in a hashing to find the address of the record, while an internal pointer is an entry in an index table providing the address of the record concerned, but both are independent of the physical address. An absolute pointer, as the name suggests, is the absolute physical address of a record, while a relative pointer is the relative physical address. Relative pointers are partly device-independent and allow the records to be moved up or down in the storage space. Reorganisation is required only if the relative position of the record is affected.

The hashing technique to calculate the physical address directly is not very practicable for list structured files since it can become obsolete by future alterations in the file. Of the three remaining techniques, the absolute pointers provide the fastest access, closely followed by the relative pointers. In the context of a data base, internal pointers are preferred because they offer independence from the storage device. Hashing techniques can be used to find an internal pointer. In this book the term *logical pointer* will be used as a synonym for *internal pointer* unless otherwise stated. The pointers can be embedded or not embedded in the records.

Embedded Pointer

Embedded pointers are maintained as part of the record in the form of an array. We can illustrate this by representing the records of figure 2.9 as shown in figure 2.13.

Records	Pointers		
Record A	B1	B2	B3
Record B1	A	C1	
Record B2	A		
Record B3	A	C2	C3	C4
Record C1	B1	D1	D2
Record C2	B3		
Record C3	B3	D3	D4	D5
Record C4	B3		
Record D1	C1		
Record D2	C1		
Record D3	C3		
Record D4	C3		
Record D5	C3		

Figure 2.13 Representation of the tree of figure 2.9

To retrieve a record through embedded pointers, the system must retrieve every record in the chain linking the wanted record. This is clearly a time-consuming process.

Non-embedded Pointers

In this case the pointers are stored separately from the record, therefore the search time for a record is reduced because it is not necessary to retrieve the intervening records. The search speed can be improved if during processing the non-embedded pointers are stored in a relatively faster device—for instance, in the memory. The update of non-embedded pointers is also less complex because the main file with the records remains unaltered.

Non-embedded pointers can be stored in the form of pointer arrays or bit maps. As the number of pointers associated with a record will vary, so will the length of the pointer array. To minimise the effect of the uncertain size of a pointer array, it might be divided into a series of fixed-length pointer arrays chained together as shown in figure 2.14.

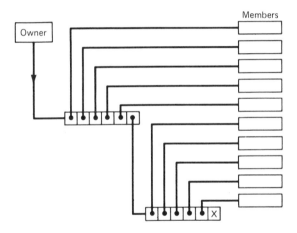

Figure 2.14 Multi-extent pointer array

A bit map is a table of pointers between two sets of records, entries in the table being 1 or 0 for the presence or absence of a relationship respectively. The example of figure 2.9 involves four levels of hierarchy and hence three sets of relationships. These can be represented by three bit maps as shown in figure 2.15 instead of pointer arrays as in figure 2.13.

The advantage of one over the other depends on the requirements. For a limited number of records, bit maps offer a compact form of representation and easy updates, but the advantage evaporates if too many records with too few

	A
B1	1
B2	1
B3	1

	A	B1	B2	B3
C1	1			
C2				1
C3				1
C4				1

	A	B1	B2	B3	C1	C2	C3	C4
D1				1				
D2				1				
D3						1		
D4						1		
D5						1		

Figure 2.15 Bit maps representing the relation of figure 2.13;
1 if the relation is true, space otherwise

relationships are entered. Also the representation of directional relationships, such as those of figure 2.11, is arduous in a bit map since it shows only the existence of a relationship but not its direction. This problem can be overcome by defining the direction externally, say, in terms of the record keys.

We shall end this chapter with an example of how we can represent the structure of figure 2.9 by a two-way ring with owner pointer for the records of each node. There are 5 nodes in the tree, giving rise to 5 datasets each with an owner and a number of members. We shall use a set of 3 pointers—owner, prior and next, per record per dataset—that is, a record belonging to n number of datasets must have n triple pointers. The owner pointer of an owner record will be assumed null. We have then the representation shown in figure 2.16. (Note that each record here participates at most in two datasets.)

Figure 2.16 is not the only possible configuration. We might, for instance, associate a pointer array with each dataset for all its records in such a way that it can be processed both forwards and backwards, and replace the triple pointers in a record by a doublet—one pointer for the owner and the other for the location of its own pointer in the pointer array of the dataset. As mentioned before, the representation of this structure by bit maps would be cumbersome due to the difficulty of indicating a pointer as owner, prior or next.

Records	First dataset	Second dataset
Record A	0 B3 B1	
Record B1	A A B2	0 C1 C1
Record B2	A B1 B3	
Record B3	A B2 A	0 C4 C2
Record C1	B1 B1 B1	0 D2 D1
Record C2	B3 B3 C3	
Record C3	B3 C2 C4	0 D4 D3
Record C4	B3 C3 B3	
Record D1	C1 C1 D2	
Record D2	C1 D1 C1	
Record D3	C3 C3 D4	
Record D4	C3 D3 D5	
Record D5	C3 D4 C3	

Figure 2.16 Representation of the datasets
of figure 2.9 as two-way ring
with owner pointer

EXERCISES

1. Describe the three main types of indexing technique for disc files and explain with diagrams the mechanism of record retrieval in an indexed sequential file.

2. Discuss the relative merits of three commonly used filing techniques—sequential, indexed sequential and direct.

3. Design a library information system based on inverted files for 100 titles.

4. Show with diagrams how you can represent the tree of figure 2.9 with non-embedded pointers to provide direct access to the owner and bidirectional sequential access to the members of each A-set there. What precaution would you take against the accidental damage of the pointer array?

REFERENCES

[1] Codasyl Data Base Task Group, April 1971 Report.

[2] V. Y. Lum *et al.*, *Communs Ass. comput. Mach.*, 14 (1971) p. 228.

[3] J. Martin, *Computer Data-Base Organisation* (Prentice-Hall, Englewood Cliffs, N. J., 1975). This is highly recommended for advanced reading in logical and physical data structures.

3 *Data Base Organisation*

Within the context of an organisation, data are related to one another in a rather complex manner. At any given time, an individual user is concerned with only a subset of these relationships, but a data base, wishing to serve all users, must represent all their facets. This can only be achieved by using complex data structures. In fact the performance of a data base is critically dependent on the data structures it can support and the flexibility such structures can provide. This is why data organisation is such a key issue in data base design. In this chapter we shall discuss the basic problems of data base organisation and examine their solutions.

The plan of the chapter is as follows. In section 3.1 we develop the concept of entity as the representation of the world of reality and discuss its relationships to the traditional concepts of data processing. In section 3.2 we examine natural data relationships and the techniques of representing them, including their access paths. The architecture of data bases is discussed in section 3.3 followed by a discussion on data independence in section 3.4.

3.1 THREE REALMS IN DATA PROCESSING

In data processing we are concerned with three successive realms[1,2] of interest. These can be identified as the world of reality, the world of information and the world of machine (figure 3.1). These realms are connected in series, each realm being the representation of the realm that it precedes. Things, and their characteristics as they really are, exist in the first realm. Our ideas and information in our mind about them constitute the second. The third is the representation of our mental information as data in a suitable form so that they can be processed by a machine. In this context, the data representation ideally implies the construction of a model that can *mirror faithfully the world of reality into the world of machine through our ideas and information in the world of information.* As we shall see later, it would be impracticable—if not impossible—to represent the world of reality in its entirety; we are able to view only a part at a time with any degree of efficiency, and this leads to a trade off between flexibility and efficiency.

Before proceeding further into the properties of the three realms, we need to define a few new terms, starting with *entity. The Concise Oxford Dictionary* defines this as

> A thing's existence as opposed to its qualities or relations; thing that has real existence.

For our purpose we shall define an entity as anything of interest and, if the thing is interesting, we are likely to collect data about it. An entity can be real or abstract, animate or inanimate, tangible or intangible. It can be a person, a place, an event, an object or an organisation. An entity is characterised by its properties, which are manifest in information we collect about it, such as the name of an employee or his job title. Using the concept of entity, we can, for the purpose of this book, redefine the world of reality as *the realm inhabited only by entities and their properties.*

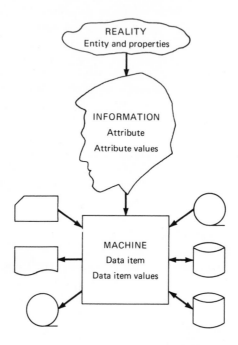

Figure 3.1 Three realms in data processing

Consider an entity called 'employee' whose name is George Brown, whose employee number is 802 and who is employed as a systems analyst for the project P27 led by James Watson. Then the properties of the employee are George Brown, 802, systems analyst, P27 and James Watson, the corresponding property classes being employee name, employee number, job title, project number and project leader. The properties include both intrinsic characteristics such as the name George Brown and relationships to other entities such as James Watson. This set of information is the data collected on the entity George Brown, but it could equally represent data collected about other entities such as project P27, project leader James Watson, or even job title systems analyst, if we so define. Therefore a collection of facts does not automatically identify the entity; we have to define it. For an entity employee we can use either his name or employee number to identify him uniquely. However, in practice we shall use the employee number rather than employee name since there can be more than one employee with the same name. This unique identifier is known as the *entity name*, which in this case can be 802.

Entities with similar properties are entities of the *same type*, and a collection of entities of the same type forms an *entity set*. A set of employees, a set of part numbers or a set of cities will each be an entity set.

In the world of information we use the word *attribute* to represent property class, the *attribute values* being the properties. Thus employee name is an attribute and George Brown is an attribute value. Clearly one of the attributes that we shall refer to as the *identity attribute* will be used to identify the entities, its values being the entity names. For instance, the attribute employee number will be the identity attribute if its values are used to identify the entities employees. These values are known as the *unique identifiers* or the *entity identifiers*. For the other attributes we shall use a common term *role attribute*, since they play a role in describing the identified entity.

To each entity we allocate a set of attributes, consisting of one identity attribute and a number of role attributes; the collection is called an *entity record*. Corresponding to an entity set, we have a set of entity records; the collection is known as an *entity record set*. An entity record set contains information on the entities of the same type.

In the world of machine we impose structure on the attributes and represent them as data items whose values correspond to attribute values. The terms used in this realm and their equivalences in the other two realms are shown in figure 3.2. Note that some of the terms are not directly equivalent, for instance, a record key can consist of several attributes or none at all, since it can be just a serial number.

We pointed out earlier that data collected on the employee George Brown could equally be data on project P27 or project leader James Watson. In fact every attribute is a potential identity attribute, and it is up to the user to decide on the entities of interest so that data can be represented in the world of machine to facilitate easy access to each chosen entity. If every attribute of an entity record is an entity of interest, then we may use inverted file structure to represent the data; on the other hand, for a single entity of interest, a more economical file structure would be advisable. The presence of multiple entities of interest in an entity record reflects the complexity of the relationships among the entities, since complex relationships require complex data structures to represent them.

World of Reality	World of Information	World of Machine
Entity and properties	Entity record	Record
Entity type	Identity attribute	Key
Entity name	Entity identifier	Key value
Property class	Attribute	Data item
Property	Attribute value	Data item value
Entity set and properties	Entity record set	A collection of all the occurrences of the same record type or a file

Figure 3.2 Terms used in the three realms

3.2 DATA RELATIONSHIP AND REPRESENTATION

Entity relationships are usually referred to as natural data relationships. They exist in the context of an organisation and define the purpose, scope and relevance of data in its usage. Some examples of related entities are

> invoice numbers and customers payment
> product code and product description
> suppliers and supplies
> superior part number and its subordinate part numbers
> project numbers and parts required
> sales and profit
> stock ordered and stock received
> employee number and department number

The characteristics of such relationships are discussed below.

3.2.1 General Characteristics

Data relationships often show a certain amount of hierarchy such as that between the superior and subordinate part numbers or that between a manager and employees. A hierarchy can have many levels, since a subordinate part number may consist of other part numbers thus forming a tree structure (see section 2.6.1). In a hierarchy, the relationship between an owner and one of its members is *vertical* or *directed* and the relationship between two members of the same owner is *lateral* or *nondirected* (figure 3.3).

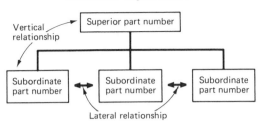

Figure 3.3 A hierarchy of relationships

Within a hierarchy the elements at a higher level can be directly or indirectly related to those at a lower level. Consider the following two examples relating some part numbers named A, B, C, and so on.

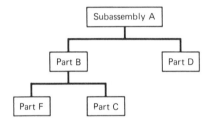

Figure 3.4 A and B are intransitively (directly) dependent on B and C respectively, but A is intransitively (indirectly) dependent on C

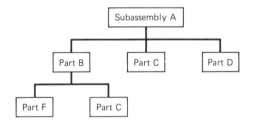

Figure 3.5 Both A and B are intransitively dependent on C

In figure 3.4, part B is a direct component of subassembly A and part C is a direct component of part B, but part C is not a direct component of subassembly A. Subassembly A is therefore directly or *intransitively* dependent on part B, but indirectly or *transitively* dependent on part C, part B being intransitively dependent on part C. However, in figure 3.5 part C is made a direct component of both subassembly A and part B, and therefore subassembly A is now intransitively dependent on both part B and part C, the relationship between part B and C remaining unchanged.

The extent of an entity relationship can be one to one, one to many and many to many, denoted by 1:1, 1:N and M:N relationships; the related entities belong to one or more entity sets. Since the relationships exist in the world of reality, we use the concept of entity to describe them; but they are mirrored in the world of machine, so we can describe them equally well in terms of record occurrences and record types, instead of entities and entity sets. Thus in the following pages the terms entity and record occurrence, and entity set and record type may be assumed to be interchangeable. We should perhaps note that the data structures used to represent these relationships are logical data structures, independent of the physical locations of the records, and the same record is able to participate in more than one such data structure.

A one-to-one relationship is a simple association between two records and, for all practical purposes, it can be regarded as a single collection of data divided into two groups. The relationship can be represented by cross-linking the two groups as shown below.

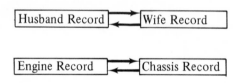

The representations of the other two relationships are more complex, and therefore we shall describe them separately.

3.2.2 1:N Relationship

Tree and Net

One-to-many relationships lead to hierarchical structures where 1 record in a level is related to N records in the next lower level. Figures 3.3, 3.4 and 3.5 are examples of such relationships, figure 3.3 showing a two-level relationship and figures 3.4 and 3.5 three-level relationships. A tree structure can be used to represent figures 3.3 and 3.4 but not figure 3.5 since part C belongs to two nodes: nodes A and B. Logically A is the father of B, B is the father of C, but A is also a father of its own grandson C. To represent this relationship, we use a *net structure* which allows the same branch to belong to several nodes. Figure 3.6 shows an example where F is owned jointly by B and D, and G by A and B.

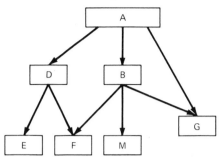

Figure 3.6 Net structure

In a tree or net structure, the nodes and branches are often used to represent record types rather than individual records. Structure thus has many occurrences, each occurrence showing the actual relationships among a group of records belonging to the record types at the nodes and branches. For instance, a 1:*N* relationship between managers and their employees can be viewed as a relationship between record type Manager and record type Employee as shown in figure 3.7a. The arrow flows from the owner to the member. If there are 5 managers there will be 5

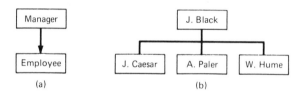

Figure 3.7 (a) A tree structure; (b) one occurrence of the tree

occurrences of this structure, each owned by a manager and having none, one or many employees belonging to this manager. One such occurrence is shown in figure 3.7b (see also figures 7.1 and 7.2a).

Cyclic Net

A series of 1:*N* relationships constitute a *cyclic net*, or *cycle*, if a later branch of a tree is allowed to own some former owners. Consider the relationships between Doctor, Patient and Drug records which can be diagrammatically represented as

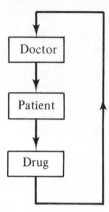

where the arrows point from the owners to the members. Each doctor treats many patients, each patient takes many drugs and each drug is prescribed by many doctors. We thus have three sets of 1:N relationships among these three record types such that they form a cycle.

3.2.3 *M:N* Relationship

This is the most general type of relationship and it can exist among the occurrences of the same record type, or between the occurrences of two or more record types, being known as loop, network and cyclic network respectively. Of these, the network is the most commonly occurring relationship and it will be considered first.

Network: Direct Representation

A network relationship between the occurrences of the two record types can be illustrated by the relationship between courses and students where each course has many students and each student takes many courses. By using course records and student records, this relationship can be diagrammatically represented as

where each occurrence of one record type owns many occurrences of the other. Suppose that the explicit relationship is

Course 1 is taken by Student 1, 2, 3 and 4

Course 2 is taken by Student 2 and 3

Course 3 is taken by Student 1, 2 and 4

Student 1 takes the Course 1 and 3

Student 2 takes the Course 1, 2 and 3

Student 3 takes the Course 1 and 2

Student 4 takes the Course 1 and 3

This relationship can be tabulated as in figure 3.8, where 1 signifies the presence and space the absence of a relationship.

	Student 1	Student 2	Student 3	Student 4
Course 1	1	1	1	1
Course 2		1	1	
Course 3	1	1		1

Figure 3.8 Bit map for a network

We may define 7 datasets, each with an owner record and a variable number of member records to represent these relationships, as shown in figure 3.9. It

Datasets	Owner	Members
Dataset 1	Course 1	Student 1, Student 2, Student 3, Student 4
Dataset 2	Course 2	Student 2, Student 3
Dataset 3	Course 3	Student 1, Student 2, Student 4
Dataset 4	Student 1	Course 1, Course 3
Dataset 5	Student 2	Course 1, Course 2, Course 3
Dataset 6	Student 3	Course 1, Course 2
Dataset 7	Student 4	Course 1, Course 3

Figure 3.9

should be noted here that the representation of an *M:N* relationship by a group of datasets as in figure 3.9 requires (1) the same record type to provide both owner and member records, and (2) the same record occurrence to appear more than once in the datasets. This complicates pointer representation discussed below.

A network can be represented in the world of machine either by a bit map as in figure 3.8, or by a multitude of pointers as shown in figure 3.10. As discussed in the last chapter, the efficiency of one method over the other will depend on

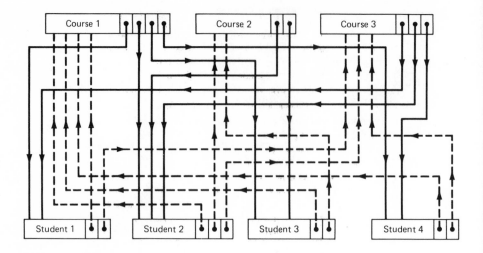

Figure 3.10 Pointer representation of the network of figure 3.8

many factors, in general though both are tedious for updates, particularly for insertion and deletion due to the large and variable number of pointers required. This is why many Data Base Systems, including the Codasyl model do not allow the direct representation of a network structure; instead a network is divided into two 1:N relationships, one owned by the first record type and the other by the second record type as described below.

Network: Representation by Link Records

We may resolve an $M:N$ relationship into two 1:N relationships as

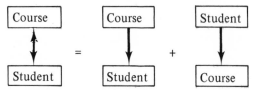

However, this resolution does not reduce the pointer requirements of figure 3.10 —we still need the same 7 datasets to represent them, and hence all the pointers of figure 3.10. All we have done is to divide the 7 datasets into two types of

group, one type being owned by the occurrences of the Course records and the other type by the occurrences of the Student records. This alone does not simplify the representation required. To do this we introduce the concept of *link records*.

From the table of figure 3.8 we pick out the related pair of entities, using C*i* and S*j* as the key for Course record *i* and Student record *j* respectively in the world of machine as

C1S1	C1S2	C1S3	C1S4
	C2S2	C2S3	
C3S1	C3S2		C3S4

We can construct an intermediate record type, called link records, each containing a pair of those keys and allow the link records to be jointly owned by both Course and Student records as

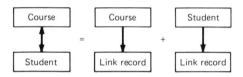

Figure 3.11

where the link record for C*i*S*j* is owned by Course record *i* and Student record *j* as

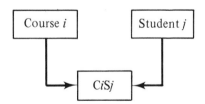

This technique makes the course and student records independent of each other, and it reduces the number of pointers per record. We can now represent the relationship by two dataset types, say, 1 and 2. Type 1 is owned by the Course records and type 2 by the Student records, the link records being members in both the dataset types, but the same link record appearing only once in the datasets of the same type as shown in figure 3.12. This technique also prevents a record type from contributing both owner and member records to the datasets of the same type (see section 5.2.4).

Dataset Type	Datasets	Owners	Members (Link Records)
1	Dataset 1	Course 1	C1S1, C1S2, C1S3, C1S4
1	Dataset 2	Course 2	C2S2, C2S3
1	Dataset 3	Course 3	C3S1, C3S2, C3S4
2	Dataset 1	Student 1	C1S1, C3S1
2	Dataset 2	Student 2	C1S2, C2S2, C3S2
2	Dataset 3	Student 3	C1S3, C2S3
2	Dataset 4	Student 4	C1S4, C3S4

Figure 3.12 Representation of the network of figure 3.10 by link records; note that a link record is represented here by a pair of keys

In addition to storing the keys of the related pair, the link records can be designed to contain information on the relationship itself such as the marks obtained by a student in a course examination. A relationship between entities is an object of interest to us and as such it is also an entity. We may even collect data about this entity, for example, a student's performance in a course examination. Therefore, like other records, link records can also be regarded as entity records.

Cyclic Network

As stated earlier, in a cyclic network more than two record types are involved, the occurrences of each record type having an *M:N* relationship with those of another. It is the counterpart of the cyclic net and it represents *M:N* instead of 1:*N* relationships. This can be illustrated by the same example of Doctor, Patient and Drug given earlier.

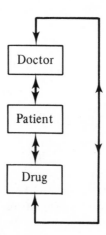

Each doctor treats many patients, each patient takes many drugs and each drug is prescribed by many doctors. If we also allow a patient to be treated by many doctors, a drug to be taken by many patients and a doctor to prescribe many drugs, then we have *M:N* relationships between doctors and patients, patients and drugs, and drugs and doctors, thus forming a cyclic network instead of a cyclic net. The cyclic networks are not usually represented directly; they are broken down into 1:*N* relationships using link records.

Loop

In a loop an occurrence of a record type owns its other occurrences. The problem can be illustrated by the relationship between three cousins (figure 3.13). Using

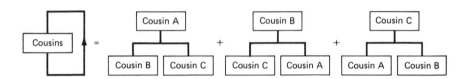

Figure 3.13 Loop

link records jointly owned by the cousins the problem can be resolved as

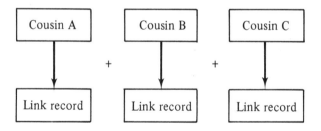

Most Data Base Systems do not permit a direct representation of a loop, but using link records they can be represented as 1: *N* relationships (see section 5.2.4).

3.2.4 Access Paths

In this subsection we shall examine access paths that need to be supported for data structures discussed earlier. It is clear from the examples presented that the basic building block of all 1: *N* and *M:N* data structures is a data unit containing one owner record and none, one or more member records belonging to one or more record types. For convenience we shall refer to such a data unit as an *Atomic data-*

set, or *A-set* for short. One or more A-sets constitute a dataset, which can be defined as an occurrence of a dataset type described by one data structure representing relationships among record types. A dataset type may consist of one or more A-set types depending on the DBS. For instance, IBM's IMS permits a single data structure to describe a 15-level tree, thus allowing a dataset type to contain up to 14 levels of A-set types, while in contrast the Codasyl model restricts the size of a dataset type to a single A-set type. In developing the concept of link records in the last subsection, we defined datasets as consisting of single A-sets—we could have described them equally well in terms of A-sets. The concept of A-set can be used to describe even a sequential collection of records, provided a dummy owner is defined for it.

Given a dataset type, the following major access paths are useful.

(1)   Direct access to all datasets
(2)   Direct access to all A-sets (or their owners) of a given dataset
(3)   Direct access to the members from an owner of an A-set
(4)   Sequential access to the members of an A-set in the forward and in the backward directions
(5)   Direct access to the owner from a member record of an A-set

Access to an owner or to an A-set may be assumed identical. We may wish to access a member record of an A-set directly, either by some keys or by position such as the first, last or nth member of the A-set, provided that the relative logical position of the members in the A-set is defined. Direct access to member records by one or more keys usually requires a separate index table for each such key of an A-set, whereas direct access by position can be facilitated by a non-embedded pointer array (see section 2.6.3) for the members of an A-set, so that the member can be found quickly from the array. These access facilities could be required for all the member records of an A-set irrespective of member record types, and also separately for the member records of a given record type to the exclusion of the members of the other record types belonging to this A-set. This is also true for sequential processing where we might wish to access the member records irrespective of their record types or those of a given record type only. Like direct access by position, sequential access to member records also assumes a predefined logical order—the order is logical since an A-set, and for that matter a dataset, is a logical collection of records, the same record appearing in more than one A-set. The facility for accessing the owner record directly from a member record is necessary for speedy access to related A-sets where this owner is either the owner or a member. Some of these access facilities—(4) and (5) above—are shown in figure 2.11.

In addition to these, direct access facilities by multiple keys to any record of the data base irrespective of datasets should also be supported.

As far as practicable, all access paths should be hidden from the application programmer who should request access according to his requirements. For instance, if he wishes to access a member record of an A-set directly by a key, and if this facility is not provided in the data structure, then the DBCS should scan all the relevant member records, sequentially if need be, and deliver the required record.

Data structures supported by a DBS can be considered flexible, if it is permissible to specify according to particular requirements either one or more access paths out of a total number available. The structure is simple or complex, depending on the number and the type of access paths specified for it. For a given application, complex structures with multiple access paths are naturally more expensive to process than simple structures with a single access path specifically provided for this application. It would be up to the DBA to estimate the usage of data and to provide appropriate access paths to minimise the cost of overall performance, rather than that of a single application.

3.2.5 Data Redundancy

Data integration is generally regarded as an important characteristic of a data base. It implies that a data base should be an integrated collection of data without having any redundancy. There is no doubt that the avoidance of redundancy should be an aim, but the extent to which this can be achieved in practice is open to cost-benefit analysis. Direct data redundancy can be avoided by employing very complex data structures involving a multitude of pointers which will link the records concerned to their common data items. The high processing cost of such complex structures has to be weighed against the principal advantage of data integration, namely, the ease in maintenance of the data base due to reduction in update problems associated with data redundancy. On the other hand, data redundancy provides faster access to data, which is denied in an integrated collection. A balance between the two conflicting requirements has to be struck by the DBA, but the DBMS can assist him in identifying the redundant data and accumulating relevant statistics on their access and update performance.

Apart from direct data redundancy, indirect redundancy can also occur. This will arise if a data item can be derived from other data items, such as the content of a control record containing the totals of the various quantities from the detailed records. Some indirect redundancy, which we may regard as *controlled indirect redundancy*, has to be introduced in a data base deliberately for data validation, but other forms should be avoided wherever possible by using what are known as *virtual data*.

Virtual data do not exist, but can be seen, whereas *transparent* data exist, but cannot be seen. The terms are borrowed from optics, where an image is virtual if it can be seen although it does not exist; a material is transparent if it exists but cannot be seen as light passes through it without being reflected or absorbed. In the context of a data base, data that do not exist in the store but can be obtained from other data are virtual. By contrast a physical record in a data base is transparent, since the application programmer does not get it, being constrained to receive logical records only. The term *data transparency* is often used to mean data independence (see section 3.4) where a programmer at the local level need not know the data structure at the global or physical levels, although they exist.

Returning to the problem of indirect redundancy, a Data Base System should provide facilities to declare as virtual such data items that can be derived from other data items, which, by definition, would not be stored but would be generated and presented by the DBCS to the application programmer. A record may consist of only real or only virtual data items or a mixture of them both.

3.3 DATA BASE ARCHITECTURE

In this section we shall present the general structure of a data base, including the means necessary to support it. We shall also discuss the flexibility that should be built into the structure to enable a data base to respond efficiently to changing and differing user needs.

3.3.1 Five Views of Data

We have discussed earlier the realms associated with data processing and have commented that data processing takes place in the third realm—the world of machine. But data in the world of machine can be viewed from several levels, in fact, as far as a data base is concerned, we can identify five distinct levels (figure 3.14)

> physical or device level
> storage or Storage-schema level
> global or Schema level
> local or Subschema level
> terminal or end user level

It is easier to understand these levels if we begin their explanation from the global level. This level refers to the overall logical description of the entire data base, without considering its storage representation. This description is known as the Schema where, in the main, entries are made for data items, record types and dataset types. How the data should be organised for storage in the physical device is specified in the Storage-schema, which will consist of entries for overflows, physical block sizes and record placement techniques. Access paths could also be specified here (see section 3.4.1). The device level is the view of the actual physical data—the data that can be seen if a dump of the data base is printed. In this sense, we may refer to this as the *dump view*. This view would not make any sense to us unless interpreted in conjunction with the provision of the Storage-schema. The data base is stored on physical devices in conformity with the specification of the Storage-schema intended to optimise the overall performance of the data base whose logical description is given in the Schema.

A particular application program is unlikely to use all the record and dataset types in the Schema, which would represent a vast amount of data. Even when the program is using a record type, it may require only a few specific data items, leaving the rest of the record type untouched. Thus an application programmer is interested only in a subset of the data described in the Schema: his need is local and his view is partial. To save him the inconvenience of invoking the whole global Schema to satisfy his local need, Subschemas are provided. A Subschema is the application programmer's view of the data base; it is a logical description of the part of the data base (not necessarily a physically contiguous part) in which he is interested, and it consists of entries for data items, record types, dataset types and so on as necessary. Two application programs could be using the same part of the data base, each describing it as its own Subschema. The variations that should be permitted among three schemas—the Storage-schema, Schema and Subschema—are discussed in the next section.

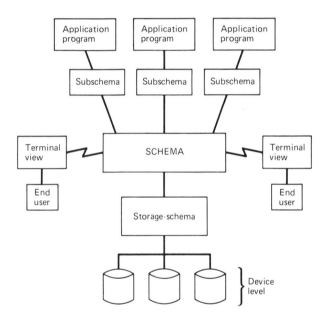

Figure 3.14 Architecture of a data base; the same Schema may support more than one Storage-schema with its own data base, Subschema, application programs and end users

The physical level is the physical data base, whereas the Schema and the Sub-schema are logical descriptions. The Storage-schema lies somewhere in between since it describes the placement of the logical data base on to physical devices. A data base has only one Schema, usually supported by a single Storage-schema at a given time. However, there are situations where it might be desirable to use more than one Storage-schema simultaneously for the same Schema.[3] For instance, a large enterprise with many branches, each branch having a data base of its own, may like to maintain a single central Schema with many Storage-schemas, each supporting a data base with its exclusive Subschemas, application programs and end users. Given a Schema, the Storage-schema may be changed from time to time to reorganise the data base for improving its performance. There is no limit to the number of Subschemas that can be supported by a Schema.

The fifth level is the view of the data base as seen by an end user from a remote terminal using a query language. The user's requirements cannot be catered for by a Subschema, since he is likely to insist on unrestricted use of the whole data base. We shall discuss this in section 4.5.1. Since the view of data at the physical level is not of particular interest, we shall exclude it from subsequent discussions, concentrating only on the Storage-schema, Schema and Subschema views.

To describe the three schemas, three languages are needed. More accurately these are sublanguages—a *Data Strategy Description Language* (DSDL) for the Storage-schema, a Schema *Data Description Language* (DDL) for the Schema and a Subschema DDL for the Subschema. Each Schema consists of entries in its own language, each being independently compilable. The name *Device Media Control Language* (DMCL) has been used in the past instead of DSDL, but this new name is now adopted by a Codasyl working group.[4] Although the Subschema DDL is independently compilable, it is usually based on a host language, each host language having its exclusive Subschema DDL.

To manipulate data in the data base by the application program we need a *Data Manipulation Language* or DML—one for each host language. The DML acts as an interface language with the data base. Its major functions are

> to select a record from the data base

> to present it to the application program

> to add new records and relationships to the data base

> to change existing records and relationships in the data base

> to remove existing records and relationships from the data base

Finally we should mention that the currently available DBSs do not provide any Storage-schema; their Schemas (or equivalents) usually include some storage specifictions. However, the concept of a separate Storage-schema is adopted in the ANSI-SPARC model (section 9.3) and it will almost certainly appear in a future Codasyl model.

3.3.2 Flexibility

The term *map* is used to represent the correspondence between two sets of objects. *Data map* will be used here to represent correspondence between the values of two related sets of data. A data map showing the relationship between an entity set for employees and a set of attributes for employee number, employee name, salary, job title and date of birth can be represented as shown in figure 3.15.

Entities	Employee Number	Employee Name	Salary	Job Title	Date of Birth
Entity 1	2403	E. Browings	3012	Programmer	4.05.49
Entity 2	2414	S. Hanif	3415	Analyst	2.08.50
Entity 3	2809	J. Kennedy	2500	Operator	25.11.48
.	.	.	.	.	.
.	.	.	.	.	.
.	.	.	.	.	.
Entity-n	4533	H. Wilson	2600	Mechanic	18.03.46

Figure 3.15

Specific entries for entity names are not necessary since they can be identified by the entity identifiers. Nor do we need entries for *attribute names*, such as employee number and employee name to identify the attribute as long as the attributes are kept in the same order. The content of this table is an entity record set, that is, a collection of the occurrences of a record type.

This data map shows a logical relationship between entities and their properties. Each entity record is self-identified by the entity identifier; hence the order in which they appear is not important. We can store this table on a physical device in a variety of ways, depending on our requirements. Since this table represents the relationship of the entity set employee with the other attributes, it can be stored as it is, using the employee number as the key. But these entity records can also be used to represent the relationship of the entity set job title with the other attributes. In this case we can store this set of records using job title plus employee number as the key (more than one employee can have the same job title, hence the need for the employee number in the key). If both the entity sets are relevant to the user, then the records can be stored in an inverted file with two sets of keys. If the records are stored in employee number order only and we subsequently want to access them in job title order, the processing cost will be high. Since it is not generally possible to predict the future needs, a data base is required to facilitate insertion, deletion and amendments of data maps.

It might be argued that, in the absence of information on future requirements, the Schema and the Storage-schema of a data base should be so designed that they can satisfy all possible future requirements. Apart from the problem of identifying all possible requirements, a data base built on this approach will probably be prohibitive both in terms of storage space and processing cost. A trade off is therefore called for between cost and flexibility. A DBS can adopt a four-pronged approach to overcome this problem, as follows.

(1)   Flexible data structures for representing data relationships leaving it to the DBA to choose those access paths that suit his requirements.

(2)   Facility to define Subschema independent of the Schema.

(3)   Facilities to evaluate the performance and to carry out reorganisation of the data base to optimise its performance without affecting the Schema and the Subschema.

(4)   Facility to restructure the Schema permitting insertion, deletion and alterations of record types and dataset types without disturbing the existing Subschemas.

Some of these points are covered in the next section. Points (2) and (4) overlap to some extent. Currently no DBS exists that allows Schema restructuring and, as mentioned earlier, the Storage-schema facility is not available either, but a number of DBSs permit some degree of storage reorganisation. The Subschema independence to be discussed in the next section also varies widely from one DBS to another. As regards data structures, the Codasyl model permits the construction of A-set types, which the user can then employ to create net structures. All access paths discussed in section 3.2.4 are supported. The direct representation of $M:N$ relationship is not allowed—it is represented through link records. IMS uses tree structures supporting up to 15 levels of hierarchy. A dataset (one occurrence of a tree) can be accessed directly, but the A-sets within it and their members are usually accessed only by following specified hierarchical paths from the root of the tree. ADABAS of Software A.G. is built on a partially inverted file structure with somewhat restrictive facilities for the construction of A-sets and datasets. The members can be accessed directly and sequentially from the owner through index tables. TOTAL of Cincom Systems Inc. uses two-level net structures with cumbersome provision for the representation of hierarchies. Direct access to the owner record and bidirectional sequential access to the members are permitted. In the relational model, data are structured in the form of two-dimensional tables as in figure 3.15; direct access is permitted to any data item value irrespective of its physical location. No specific access paths need be provided, and therefore the comments made earlier about the difficulty of satisfying all possible future access requirements do not apply.

3.4 DATA INDEPENDENCE

Data independence in the context of a data base implies the independence of one view of data with respect to others. This permits the DBA to make changes in one view of data, when necessary, to improve certain aspects of data base performance without disturbing the other views. The main areas of interest are as follows.

(1)   Schema. Conceptually the Schema is independent of other views. It is specified, at least in principle, before the other views; it is written in an independent DDL and is compiled independently.

(2)   Storage-schema. This view cannot be independent of the Schema since its purpose is to organise the storage of data in conformity with the Schema specification, but every single change in the Schema should not necessarily force a change in the Storage-schema. The Storage-schema need not be dependent on the physical devices. These points are discussed under storage independence in the next subsection.

(3)   Subschema. Although the Subschema is the logical description of a subset of the data, it need not be a subset of the Schema; some variations can exist between the two views. The Subschema independence refers to the ability to define a Subschema independent of the Schema and also the Storage-schema if relevant and, once defined, its stability against the subsequent changes in those views. These two aspects are described as *logical data independence* and *logical binding* in sections 3.4.2 and 3.4.3, respectively.

3.4.1 Storage Indpendence

Given a Schema, the data can be organised on a physical device in a variety of ways and, depending on the use of the data base, one of these ways will provide an optimum performance; but this optimal way can only be found by trial and error. Furthermore since the usage of the data base is likely to change with time, what is optimal performance at one time may not remain so at another time. Therefore we need good facilities for optimising performance by reorganising the storage without affecting the Schema. The Storage-schema provides the basis for this facility[4].

Ideally a Schema should consist of entries for data items, records and datasets only, leaving the other characteristics of data—even the format of the data items —to the Storage-schema. Currently it is being debated whether the access paths should be specified in the Schema or in the Storage-schema. The argument in favour of the Schema is that the access paths can be specified logically as part of the Schema data structure. The opposing viewpoint rests on the ground that,

for a given Schema, the access paths can be used as tools to improve the performance of a data base, and that as such they should belong to the Storage-schema
and should be transparent to the application programs (see the next subsection).

Given a global record type in the Schema, it could be that some of its data
items and record occurrences are more frequently used than others. If so the
DBA should be able to split a global record type into a number of storage record
types and if it improves the overall access performance, store some or all of their
occurrences on a particular physical storage area of the data base. The other
features that the Storage-schema should control are block sizes, overflows and
pointer organisations. To ensure the independence of the Schema, its mapping on
to the Storage-schema should be included in the compiled version of the Storage-
schema. In the event of a change in the Schema, the Storage-schema need not
necessarily be changed. For instance, if a Schema record type is split into two
new record types along some existing storage record boundary, then it should be
enough to recompile the Storage-schema. Moreover, if more than one Storage-
schema is supported by the same Schema, the changes in the Schema may need
to be reflected in only one Storage-schema and not necessarily in the others.

The dependence of the Storage-schema on the physical devices can be eliminated
if storage allocation in this level is made in terms of pages rather than tracks and
cylinders, and if logical pointers rather than physical addresses are used for the
internal reference of the storage records within the Storage-schema; for if the data
base is reloaded into another type of disc, it would then be necessary to change
only the lookup table relating the internal pointers and the physical addresses for
the new device. These logical pointers—to be referred to as the *storage keys*—are
transparent to the application program and should not be confused with the
logical pointers for the Schema records—known as the *data base keys* in the
Codasyl model (see section 5.2.1).

3.4.2 Logical Data Independence

The freedom to define an independent Subschema depends on the variations
that can be permitted in the definition of data items, records, datasets and access
paths from those in the Schema and the Storage-schema, the Storage-schema
being relevant if the data item formats and access paths are described there rather
than in the Schema. We examine here these four aspects.

Data Item

The Subschema definition of the data item formats should be permitted to be
different from those in other views. For instance, if a data item is described as
an internal decimal number in the Storage-schema, we should be able to define it
as a binary number in the Subschema, should it be useful in the applications for
which this Subschema is intended. The DBCS should carry out the necessary
conversion.

Record

We should be able to define a Subschema record type with only a subset of data
items from a Schema record type. Permission should be given to reorder and
regroup the data items, with new group names if necessary. Ideally we should be
allowed to construct a new Subschema record type from data items belonging to
more than one Schema record type. To provide this facility the DBS would need
to maintain complex mappings to match the correct occurrences of the record
types, and this can lead to heavy overheads. At present no DBS provides this
facility. Honeywell was once interested[5] to introduce it (with certain restrictions
to reduce the mapping overheads) in IDS-II.

Dataset

In the Subschema we should be able to define a new dataset type independent
of the Schema definitions. The freedom allowed in the DBSs marketed today
usually restricts the Subschema definition of a dataset type to a subset of the
Schema definition. This is satisfactory so long as it is possible to foresee all future
requirements and include them appropriately in the Schema; this is obviously an
unrealistic expectation, and therefore a case for supporting new dataset types
exists, but due to the heavy overheads involved, this facility is not provided in
currently available systems.

Access Paths

The actual access paths provided in a data structure should be transparent to the
application programmers, who should be permitted to request for data using
any of the access procedures supported by the DBS, some of which might need
to be specified in the Subschema, while others could be provided by standard
DML commands, irrespective of the actual access paths specified for the data
structures. For instance, it should be possible to access the owner record from a
member record of an A-set by using an appropriate DML command, even if owner
pointers are absent in the data structure (if necessary the DBCS will have to scan
sequentially to find the owner).

The system should provide facilities for using different names for the Subschema data units—this is particularly important if the Schema names are illegal
in the host language. We mentioned earlier the need for Schema restructuring. To
protect the existing application programs (and Subschemas) from changes in the
Schema, we would presumably maintain the old record types (where necessary
by using virtual data items) and data structures. The need for Subschema compilation in the event of such restructuring will depend on binding, discussed below.

3.4.3 Binding

Binding is the process of converting one view of data to that of another view. If a program requests for some records from a file, then the program reference (record name, and so on) of the records must be converted into the machine reference, and the request itself must be formulated in terms of machine instructions to locate the records. Once this conversion process is established, the two views—the programmer's view and the physical view—are bound together. Without this binding, the physical data of the file cannot be accessed, and once bound the program is no longer independent of the file. Suppose a program is being run in a computer for updating an indexed sequential file originally created with 100 overflow blocks per cylinder. Now if someone by some means reorganises the file, changing the number of overflow blocks after the update program is bound, then the result will be catastrophic, since the program could be using directories which are no longer valid. The binding is thus a firm association between a program and its data, neither of which can be changed independently without losing validity once they are bound. In the context of an application program using a data base, we are concerned with four views of data. These lead to two types of binding—the logical binding for converting the programmer's view to the view of the Storage-schema, and the physical binding for converting the Storage-schema reference to the physical level. The physical binding is largely provided by the operating system (being initiated by the DBCS in the case of a data base). It is not of interest to the data independence problem and hence we shall not discuss this further.

Because of the presence of three views, the logical binding is a two-step process, namely, the Subschema binding for the conversion of the Subschema data and the DML commands to their Schema equivalent, and the Schema binding for the conversion between the Schema and the Storage-schema. Since the record definitions can vary between the Subschema and the Schema, the only common factors between them are the data items. To establish the transformation process between the two views, the DBCS has to scan various Schema and Subschema tables in the data base and specify the Schema data items and the path to be followed for accessing them by means of tables and pointers. A similar process takes place for the Schema binding. The stability of a Subschema against the changes in the other two views depends on the timing of the binding, which can take place as follows.

On Execution

The binding routines are invoked as each DML command is executed. All the relevant Schema and Subschema tables have to be present for the analysis to be carried out. The process is time consuming and requires extra memory, and it is therefore inefficient.

On Loading

When the application program is loaded for running, the binding can be carried out before execution begins.

On Composition

When the compiled application program is composed (that is, link-edited or consolidated), the precompiled DML commands can be included as a part of the composed program.

On Compilation

The DML commands can be compiled along with the compilation of the application program. However, this will necessitate an extended host language compiler.

The Subschema and the Schema binding need not take place at the same time, in fact any binding can use a combination of the above methods. The degree of data independence varies inversely with the efficiency in binding. The first method—also known as the *dynamic binding*—provides maximum independence, permitting changes in the Schema and the Storage-schema at any time prior to the execution of the DML commands. But owing to high processing overheads this method is not generally favoured. The other three methods come in the category of *static binding* as opposed to dynamic binding. As we go down the list, the efficiency increases at the expense of data independence. The second method restricts changes to the Schema and Storage-schema once the application program is loaded, since binding occurs at each loading. There is not much to choose between the third and the fourth method except that the fourth method requires an extended host language compiler. If the third or the fourth method is used, the application program must be recomposed or recompiled and recomposed at every instance of the Schema or Storage-schema change. Currently most Data Base Systems employ compilation time binding.

The restrictions imposed on data independence by binding do not create an impasse; after all at worst we only have to recompile the program after each change in the global and storage descriptions. However, complete logical data independence with the unrestricted freedom to define any new data structure with any required access paths irrespective of the Schema and the Storage-schema structure is a different matter, and it is unlikely to be provided by any formatted DBS, due to excessive overheads. As we shall see later, the cost consideration applies even to the relational model where data independence is the avowed purpose. In practice it is necessary to weigh the benefit of data independence against the cost of providing it, and accept a compromise. Complete data independence is likely to remain an unattainable luxury.

EXERCISES

1. A net structure, such as the one in figure 3.6, also shows many-to-many relationship between two sets of records; for F is related to D and B while D is related to E and F, and B to F, M and G. How is this type of many-to-many relationship distinguished from a network and why is its representation easier?

2. In figure 3.10 we have assumed only direct representation between the members and the owners. Draw a diagram showing only the backward and forward link of each A-set there.

3. We have stated that loops can be represented using link records. If we consider the relationships among cousins in figure 3.13, how many link records should we have? (See section 5.2.4 for answer).

4. In section 3.2.4 we have listed a number of important access paths for a data base. Discuss their relative importance and indicate other types of access paths that can be useful. (See sections 5.3.4 and 5.4.3 for ideas.)

5. Consider a Schema with three record types as follows

> Employee records (key employee number)
>
> Project records (key project number)
>
> Machine records (key machine number)

Assume that they form a cyclic network. Describe a Schema-to-Subschema mapping for Subschema record types to be constructed with data items from any two or all three of these record types in the Schema. (*Note* Mapping would be easier if each record contained the keys of the occurrences of the other two record types to which it is related—consider the situation both with and without such keys.)

6. In the above example assume that the record-type project owns the other two record types in the Schema. Design a Schema-to-Subschema mapping for a new Subschema relationship where the record-type Employee owns the other two record types. Assume that the records of one type do not contain the keys of the other types.

REFERENCES

[1] G. H. Mealy, *Proc. AFIPS,*   (1967) p. 525.
[2] R. W. Engles, *A. Rev. autom. Progmg*, 7 (1974) p. 1.
[3] Proceedings of Data Base Administration Working Group, 1976 (unpublished).
[4] Data Base Administration Working Group, June 1975 Report (BCS).
[5] F. E. Johnson, *Proceedings of Implementation of CODASYL Data Base Management Proposals* (BCS) October 1974, p. 114.

4 *Features and Requirements*

In the last chapter we discussed data base organisation, which forms the foundation of a data base. Certain key features, such as data independence and the flexibility of data structures, follow directly from this foundation, but there are other features that must be built on the foundation to transform it into a viable data base capable of offering the full range of the expected advantages. These features provide the following facilities. (1) Performance optimisation: facilities to evaluate performance and tune the data base from time to time to optimise its performance. (2) Concurrent usage: the use of the data base by more than one application program at the same time. (3) Data protection: the protection against loss or damage of data in the data base and the protection of the confidentiality of the data from unauthorised persons.

These facilities, along with data independence and flexible data structure, may be regarded as constituting the major features of a Data Base System, and as such they should form the main basis in its critical study. Data independence, as discussed in detail in the last chapter, essentially implies the independence of the global logical structure or the Schema from the storage organisation or the Storage-schema, and the independence of the local structure or the Subschema from the Schema. The first is usually achieved by removing all storage considerations from the Schema, but the second poses some serious problems. Although absolute Subschema independence may not be available, largely because of unacceptable processing cost, a high degree of independence can nevertheless be secured, and this should be aimed at in all Data Base Systems. Facilities should exist so that the data base administrator can choose the degree of independence he needs depending on his own cost-independence criteria.

In the last chapter we also established the need for a range of data structures, from simple to complex, reflecting access path requirements and the complexity of data relationships. We pointed out that complete data integration, although desirable, is not feasible mainly owing to the high processing cost involved in dealing with complex data structures which must be used to avoid direct redundancy. Some indirect redundancy is essential for data validation, while some others can be avoided by replacing them with *virtual data*.

In this chapter the first three sections are devoted to the topics listed earlier, followed by sections on the other aspects of a DBS including its software and operational requirements.

4.1 PERFORMANCE OPTIMISATION

A data base is often described as an evolutionary system, so much so that some data base vendors even advertise the evolutionary aspect as a strong selling point. The reason is that a data base is a complex system requiring considerable experience to derive the full benefit from it. The usual practice is to develop a data base gradually by adding one subsystem to it at a time in such a way that it is possible to learn from experience. As each new subsystem is added, the Schema requires changes and it becomes increasingly more complex. For a given Schema it is necessary to find an optimal Storage-schema by trial and error. This is a continuous process because the usage of a data unit changes with time, even after the Schema is stabilised; thus periodic tuning of the data base is required on the basis of the usage statistics accumulated on the past performance.

4.1.1 Performance Evaluation

Performance evaluation consists of collecting usage statistics from the parameters of interest and analysing them to find inefficient use of resources, to pinpoint bottlenecks and to identify inefficient data and storage structures. The parameters of interest are as follows.

Global Data Structure

The global data structure is usually determined by the relationships of interest, and the DBA would presumably know them without having to collect usage statistics on them.

Storage Structure

The usage characteristics of data units, their volume, volatility and access frequency, will affect the record placement technique and the access path allocation in the Storage-schema. Other interesting parameters would be pointer organisation, overflows, packing density and data compression.

Memory Utilisation

Computer memory will be used to hold the DBCS routines and tables, application programs and the input–output buffers. Depending on the technique of memory allocation supported by the operating system, the user may have to

(1)   overlay the DBCS routines, which will increase the processing time
(2)   decrease the number of application programs in the memory, thus under-utilising the data base

(3)   decrease the buffer size, which will reduce the data that can be held in the buffer, and consequently increase the accesses to the data base, thereby decreasing the efficiency of the operation.

The requirements here are conflicting and the DBA should make the choice. If the dynamic memory allocation (see section 4.3.1) is permitted, some of these problems would disappear.

4.1.2 Usage Statistics

Statistics generated for tuning would vary from one Data Base System to another, depending on the requirements. However, it should cover the following.

(1)   Device and channel activity
Number of input messages per channel per unit time.
Number of output messages per channel per unit time.
Number of transaction errors per channel.
(2)   Memory utilisation: memory used by and the frequency of the usage of each
application program
system buffers (section 4.6.2)
DBCS routines (section 4.6.2)
DBCS tables (section 4.6.2).
(3)   Data usage: frequency of access to and update of each
dataset
record
data item.
(4)   Response time and privacy breach: response time to access individual records and datasets, and number of attempts to privacy breach (for example, wrong password leading to failure) in each protected data unit.
(5)   Application program error: in order to improve the standard of the application programs, for each application program
data base access errors
data base update errors
number of times involved in deadlocks (see later).

This is not an exclusive list of statistics; it only shows the nature of information required.
    The generation of usage statistics is a continuous operation to be undertaken by the DBCS with the help of special routines. The analysis of these statistics should be carried out regularly at fixed intervals by using system-provided utilities. Tuning or optimising performance is a rather complicated function which involves finding or guessing the best configuration for the parameters of interest and changing the Storage-schema accordingly, followed by the reorganisation of the data base to reflect the changes. The routines to carry out these should of course be provided as part of the DBMS.

4.2 CONCURRENT USAGE

The basis for concurrent usage is the ability to share the data base with several run-units (or application programs) at the same time. If this facility is not available, only one run-unit can be allowed in the machine at any given time, resulting in the underutilisation of both the data base and the computer facilities. On the other hand, if concurrent usage is permitted, the system would run into a series of problems, mainly concerning concurrent updates as illustrated below.

4.2.1 Concurrent Update

Let us consider two concurrent run-units A and B, both updating accumulated sales to a customer in the following record

D715	A. SMITH	180

where D715 is the customer's account number, A. Smith is the customer and 180 is the total sales. The following sequence of events may take place.

(1) Run-unit A reads the original record as given above.
(2) Run-unit B also reads the original record as given above.
(3) Run-unit A updates the total sales by adding 50 to it, and writes the record back to the data base as

D715	A. SMITH	230

(4) Run-unit B updates the sales by adding 270 to it in the original record it read and returns the record to the data base as

D715	A. SMITH	450

overwriting the updated version generated by run-unit A.

This final version is incorrect, since it should have been

D715	A. SMITH	500

To prevent this happening, run-unit B must be forced to read or reread the record after it was modified by run-unit A. In other words, the concurrent update of a record cannot be permitted. This restriction can be enforced by introducing a system of locking and unlocking of records whereby a record during the process of update is locked out to the other run-units. This means that no run-unit can access a record until it is unlocked or released by the updating run-unit. If this scheme is used, run-units A and B in the above example will be required to declare their intention to lock the record during reading, whereupon the record will be locked as soon as it is read by any one of them, say, by A. The run-unit B, and others if any, wishing to access this record must then wait in a queue until the record is released by A.

Locking at record level as discussed above is very effective for controlling concurrent updates. But due to the large overheads involved in providing a locking mechanism for individual records, many Data Base Systems permit locking only for larger units of data such as a dataset or a physical block. In the subsequent discussions, the term *data resource* will generally be used to denote the unit of data where locking is allowed, although at times we may for convenience give the example of records.

4.2.2 Deadlock and Rollback

However, the basic system of locking and unlocking referred to above has a serious flaw, leading to what is known as *deadlock* or *deadly embrace*. Deadlock is a general logical problem which can arise whenever two or more contending processes wish to exercise exclusive control over common resources. Consider the following sequence of events where run-units A and B need exclusive control over both of the two resources 1 and 2.

(1) Run-unit A gets the exclusive control of resource 1.
(2) Run-unit B gets exclusive control of resource 2.
(3) Run-unit A requests for resource 2, but A must wait in a queue until B releases resource 2.
(4) Run-unit B requests for resource 1, but B must wait in a queue until A releases resource 1.

We have now reached a deadlock, because A will not succeed in getting resource 2 nor will B succeed in getting resource 1.

We have used the term *resource* rather than *data resource* in the above example mainly to emphasise that in a concurrent environment data is only one of several resources, such as memory, buffers and control tables, which need to be shared, and can give rise to deadlock. In fact deadlock in resource allocation is recognised in all multiprogramming operating systems, although its occurrence there seems to be very rare. There is a fundamental difference between data and non-data resources. A data resource or a record can change with time as a record is updated; additionally they do not have duplicates in the sense that, if a run-unit needs a particular record, no other record in the data base can fulfil this need. On the other hand, a non-data resource such as a line printer does not change, and any one of several line printers can do the work. This difference probably makes data bases involving a large number of data resources more vulnerable to deadlock. We do not intend to discuss here the deadlocks involving non-data resources because they are not specific to data bases and they are generally tackled by the operating system of a computer; we may, however, make occasional comments.

Returning to the example of deadlock, involving data resources, if run-units A and B are deadlocked, then all the run-units waiting in the queue for resource 1 and resource 2 will be caught up, and in turn other run-units might also be affected if they are waiting for resources to be released by those in the queue for resource 1 and 2. This may eventually bring the whole data base to a halt. Prevention is certainly better than cure, but if fail-safe prevention proves impossible, the system must provide means of detecting and resolving deadlocks once they occur. This process of resolution is known as rollback, since it involves rolling back to a previous state by allowing one of the contending run-units, selected on the basis of some predefined priority scheme, to proceed after unloading the necessary resources. The priority scheme can, for instance, be built on the number of locked records in the run-unit or on other desirable preferences. As we shall see, the major problem associated with the use of rollback mechanism lies in the efficient detection of a deadlock.

The general conditions for deadlock are laid down by Coffman *et al.*[1] We present them here with some modifications.

(1) Concurrency condition: run-units claim exclusive control of more than one resource.

(2) Hold condition: a run-unit continues to hold exclusively controlled resources until its need is satisfied.

(3) Wait condition: run-units wait in queues for additional resources while holding resources already allocated to them.

(4) Cycle condition: a circular chain of run-units exist such that each run-unit holds one or more resources that are being requested by the next run-unit in the chain.

The fourth condition cycle defines the state of a deadlock, provided that the other three conditions are true. Consider figures 4.1a and b—referred to hereafter as *state graphs*—where each run-unit has an exclusive control of one or more resources and requests the control of an additional resource held by another run-unit pointed by the arrow. In figure 4.1a there is no deadlock because the run-unit A can wait for the resource to be released by B, but figure 4.1b displays a deadlock involving three run-units.

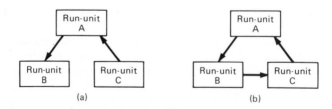

(a) (b)

Figure 4.1 State graphs. the run-unit at the head of an arrow is holding a resource wanted by the run-unit at the tail of the arrow. (b) constitutes a deadlock but (a) does not

In more formal terms the state graph of figure 4.1a does not contain a cycle, but that of figure 4.1b does, indicating the existence of a deadlock. To detect a deadlock, the system must maintain some form of state graph to be updated each time a resource is allocated, requested or released. After every unsuccessful request, the state graph must be examined for cycles and, if they are found, the rollback mechanism must be invoked. In its simplest form, the system may maintain for each run-unit a list of exclusively allocated resources and also one requested resource for which the run-unit concerned will wait in a queue—assuming that a run-unit may not queue for more than one resource at a time. Starting from the last requested resource it is possible to scan through the lists to determine the existence of a cycle. To demonstrate the technique, let us consider lists of resources for four run-units A, B, C and D, where the numerical entries (as shown in figure 4.2) represent the resources. In this case the last entry in each case is the requested resource which, if zero, indicates the absence of a request. Now assume that the run-units B and C are waiting for resources 10 and 8 respectively, and run-unit D has just made a request for resource 15, as shown in figure 4.2.

Run-units	Resource List
A	1 2 0
B	4 15 3 10
C	10 8
D	8 6 15

Figure 4.2 Resource list for run-units A, B, C and D, showing the formation of a cycle as run-unit D requests for resource 15

Scanning the list we find that B is holding resource 15. We now check its requested resource which is 10. Again by scanning we find that run-unit C is holding resource 10, its requested resource 8 being held by the original run-unit D, thus forming a cycle. If the requested resource for C were 2 instead of 8, we would not have had any cycle.

However, scanning through the list after each request for a resource is time consuming. Furthermore updating the resource list after each allocation and release of resources will be complex, because the number of resources per run-unit will vary with time—unless we limit, by using fixed-length records, the maximum number of resources that can be locked by a run-unit. This type of technique is used in the IMS of IBM. The DMS1100 of Univac also uses a detection and rollback strategy, but it waits until all the run-units in the system are in queues before invoking a rollback. As a result, it is unable to detect a deadlock between two run-units A and B, as in our example on p. 65, until the whole data base is brought to a halt (see section 7.1.1 for more details). This does not appear to be an efficient method of detection. Some other Data Base Systems, with variable degrees of efficiency, base their strategy on prevention rather than resolution of deadlocks.

4.2.3 Prevention of Deadlock

In searching for the means of avoiding deadlock, we shall examine here the conditions laid down earlier. If any of the conditions can be relaxed, deadlock can be avoided.[2]

Concurrency Condition

If we limit the exclusive control of resources to one per run-unit at a time, dead-lock can be eliminated. Every run-unit must then release its locked data resource if it wishes to lock another data resource. But this will prevent the joint updating of a set of related records belonging to several data resources where all of them must be locked. Furthermore, locks are meant only for the Schema records of the data base, whereas updating takes place in the Subschema records, each of which can be made up of several Schema records—all of which may in turn, have to be locked to update the Subschema record. Therefore, we cannot relax the concurrency condition.

Hold Condition

We may force a run-unit to release all its locked resources and rollback to a previous state if it subsequently fails to gain exclusive control of a resource. This is known as the *pre-emption* strategy. Return to a previous intermediate state in the update is unsafe for a data resource, because such a state cannot usually be well defined owing to changes that can occur in the data. The best recourse is to fall back to the original state as it was at the start of the update. This can be accomplished by maintaining a copy of the original data resource in the memory during an update. As we shall see later, such copies are required for other purposes as well and therefore no extra effort is involved.

Wait Condition

To offset this condition, we may insist that a run-unit must declare and gain exclusive control of all the resources it needs exclusively for a particular activity before it uses any of them. This technique is known as the *preclaim* strategy.

If a run-unit fails to acquire the exclusive control of a single resource of the declared list, it must release all its locked resources and try again later. While holding some resources exclusively, a run-unit may not request additional resources except those previously declared. This technique can be used satisfactorily for both data and non-data resources, as long as the resources required are known at the beginning. However, if the need for a resource is known only dynamically, that is, through a set of calculations on other resources, all of which require locking, then this technique would fail. User experience suggests that such need exists, and hence the preclaim technique is not very satisfactory. Although a particular record occurrence required is not known, the record type concerned is generally known at the beginning. Therefore, by enlarging the size of a data resource to accommodate all the occurrences of a record type, the problem can be overcome. However, large units of data resources lead to inefficiency in processing, since more run-units are likely to wait in queues for records in those resources. The situation could perhaps be improved if variable-size data resources are permitted, so that the application programmer can lock individual records when the need is known and record types otherwise. Further study is required to ascertain the problems associated with variable-size data resources.

Cycle Condition

It can be shown mathematically that a cycle will not form in a state graph if all the resources are linearly ordered in a specified manner. For a data base this would imply ordering all the data resources and requiring the run-units to request for them in that order. This is clearly unworkable if the requirement of a data resource is only known dynamically. In addition, adoption of this strategy would put severe strain on the freedom of the application programs. Should an application program error occur in locking in the correct order, deadlock can be expected. In ADABAS, it is possible to lock records in a predefined sequence, but the facility for rollback in the event of a deadlock also exists.

4.2.4 Comparison of the Techniques

It is clear from the above that three techniques—detection followed by rollback, preclaim and pre-emption—appear to be good candidates for adoption. We shall show their relative merits below with an example. Let us consider two run-units A and B, each wishing to carry out a consistent series of updates. Here run-unit A requires the data resources R1, R2 and R3, and run-unit B requires data resources R1, R3 and R4 with the sequence of events as given below for each case.

Deadlock and Rollback

(1)   A reads and locks R1 and R2, and modifies them into R1$'$ and R2$'$.
(2)   B reads and locks R3 and R4, and modifies them into R3$''$ and R4$''$.

(3)   A wishes to read and lock R3, which is held by B.
(4)   The DBCS checks for a deadlock.
(5)   B wishes to read and lock R1 held by A.
(6)   The DBCS recognises a deadlock.
(7)   The DBCS invokes the priority routines and decides to rollback A.
(8)   A undoes its update work done so far, returning R1' and R2' to their original states R1 and R2, and then releases R1.
(9)   B reads and locks R1 and completes its updates producing R1", R3" and R4" which are then released.
(10) A now reads and locks R1" and R3", and completes its update subsequently releasing them.

Note that in step (8) R1' and R2' are returned to R1 and R2 for preserving consistency, since B wants R1 and not R1', and R2' produced by A in step (1) is not necessarily consistent with R1" and R3" produced by B in step (9); but R2 forms a consistent set with these R1" and R3" by definition.

Pre-emption

(1)   A reads and locks R1 and R2, and modifies them into R1' and R2'.
(2)   B reads and locks R3 and R4, and modifies them into R3" and R4".
(3)   A attempts, but fails to read and lock R3 held by B.
(4)   A undoes its update work done so far returning R1' and R2' to their original states R1 and R2, and releases them both.
(5)   B reads and locks R1 and completes its update, producing R1", R3" and R4" which are then released.
(6)   A now reads R1", R2 and R3", and completes its update subsequently releasing them.

Preclaim

(1)   A reads and locks R1, R2 and R3.
(2)   B requests for R4, R3 and R1, but it must wait.
(3)   A completes its update producing R1', R2' and R3', which are then released.
(4)   B reads and locks R4, R3' and R1', and completes its update, the resources being then released.

This example shows clearly the simplicity of the preclaim strategy. Such simplicity would be more striking if a larger number of data resources were involved. However, this advantage must be offset against the inefficiency of using large units of data resources (see also the next subsection). The main disadvantage of the pre-emption strategy compared with preclaim is that, in the pre-emption strategy, all updates carried out up to the point of pre-emption are wasted. The deadlock and rollback technique appears far worse, involving four extra steps, (4), (5), (6) and (7), compared with the pre-emption strategy. Of these, steps (5) and (6), for recognising the deadlock are very slow, as discussed earlier. However, the performance there can be improved by reducing the number of state graphs to be maintained. This can be achieved by allowing the application programmer to set an upper limit on the time for which his program may queue for a particular data resource. If the exclusive control of the resource is not gained within the limit, the run-unit will leave the queue and rollback to a suitable previous state.

From the discussions above, it would seem that the pre-emption strategy, and probably the preclaim strategy with variable-size data resources, would be the better choice, although a situation might be envisaged where other techniques could be more efficient. Perhaps the DBS could cater for a number of techniques from which the application programmer may select the one that suits him best, such as the preclaim strategy when the wanted records are known beforehand, and the pre-emption strategy otherwise. However, further investigation is necessary in this area.

None of these techniques would solve the problems of real-time applications with short response time. An extreme example is the control of guided missiles from information stored in a data base. Here, even absolute priority in queues for data resources over other run-units may not yield a quick enough response. The only means of supporting such applications would be the pre-emption of all the data resources required for it at the expense of other run-units processing them. The operational cost would undoubtedly be very high. Perhaps we should not use such a real-time system concurrently or, more probably, we should not use a data base for it.

4.2.5 Time Consistency[3]

The sequence in which alterations are made into a data base does not necessarily reflect the sequence in which events occur in the real world. This may lead to inconsistency in an application program if this sequence happens to be relevant. The responsibility for ensuring such consistency is assumed to lie with the application programmer who, by recording the data and time of the relevant events, can satisfy his requirements. A second aspect of time consistency relates to the protection of the data base against the momentary inconsistencies it will show during a consistent sequence of updates, assuming that the data base is in a self-consistent state both before the start and after the completion of the update sequence. Such a sequence of steps from one consistent state of the data base to the next is known as a *success-unit*. A success-unit can be simple, involving a single-record update, or complex, involving a number of records. It can also be short or long, depending on the time required to complete the update sequence.

The effect of momentary inconsistencies is twofold. Firstly it may provide inconsistent data to the run-unit, entering it at the moment of inconsistency. Secondly, backup files logging the changes in the data base at this instant may receive an inconsistent picture, which will corrupt the data base if it is used for a subsequent recovery in the event of a data base failure. The problem can be resolved if we allow two types of lock for every data resource—a LOCKR for exclusive reading when no update can take place and LOCKU for exclusive updates. The disadvantage of this scheme is that the long success-units will produce long queues for LOCKR, and long exclusive reading processes, such as those required to produce a backup file, will hold up updates. The efficiency can be improved if we delay the consolidation, that is, the writing of updates back into the data base proper until a success-unit is complete. This would imply the division of an update process into two phases—a long update phase under LOCKU where a run-unit will modify the records concerned but will not make the changes in the data base itself, and a short consolidation phase, say under a new lock LOCKC, when the updated version generated in the previous phase will be copied into the data base. Since the data base will remain unaltered in the update phase, exclusive reading with LOCKR can be permitted simultaneously with an update stopping only during the short consolidation phase. A locking system based on these concepts is described in the next subsection.

To facilitate an exclusive consolidation phase, the DBCS should maintain two copies of the data resources concerned—a *before image* and an *after image*. A before image is a copy of a data resource before any modification, and an after image is a copy of the same data resource after modification. A run-unit would update the after image as if it were the data base. At the completion of a success-unit, the after images concerned would be consolidated into the data base under LOCKC, but in the event of a rollback required either for error recovery or for avoiding a deadlock, the system would return to the before images, dropping the after images. If the unit of a data resource is large, larger memory will be required to store the images and the consolidation phase will be longer. This is a point against a preclaim strategy requiring large units of data resources.

4.2.6 Locking System

As indicated above, we need three sets of locks for every data resource. More explicitly we need the following.

(1)   A LOCKR to allow reading of data resources so that they are protected against changes during the reading process. An unlimited number of run-units should be able to issue LOCKR for the same data resource. A LOCKU should not prevent the simultaneous applications of one or more LOCKRs, but if a LOCKC exists either on a data resource or in a queue for it, a LOCKR may not be applied.

(2)   A LOCKU to permit the update of a data resource but not its consolidation into the data base. Only one run-unit may issue a LOCKU for a data resource; the others wishing to update the same data resource must wait in a queue, although a LOCKU may coexist with a number of LOCKRs.

(3)   A LOCKC to allow the copying of the updates into the data base itself to the exclusion of any LOCKR or LOCKU. LOCKC should be transparent to the application programmer, being automatically invoked by the DBCS at the end of a success-unit on behalf of the updating run-unit. If a LOCKR exists on a data resource, the run-unit with LOCKC should wait at the head of the queue for this data resource, disallowing any new LOCKR or LOCKU.

This suggested locking system will provide four modes of access.

(1)   No-lock mode to read any number of records without any locks. A LOCKR or a LOCKU on a data resource may not inhibit it from being read in this mode. A run-unit wishing to read unrelated single records would normally use this mode.

(2)   LOCKR mode to read a consistent set of records under LOCKR. A LOCKR will be held back only if there is a LOCKC on the data resource, or if a LOCKC is waiting at the head of the queue for the data resource.

(3)   LOCKU mode to read a data resource for update. It must wait in a queue if a LOCKU or LOCKC is already there on the data resource.

(4)   LOCKC mode for altering the actual data base when no other process can get access, LOCKC having priorities over other locks.

Locks can be instituted as a three-bit binary pattern, one for each lock type against every data resource in the data base. An additional list of the locked resources can be maintained in the memory for their recovery in the case of a run-unit failure. The solution of the concurrency problem and the locking system suggested here is mainly for the purpose of elucidating the issues involved rather than to offer viable solutions. These suggestions are not implemented anywhere and would require a thorough examination before they could be considered for implementation.

4.3 DATA PROTECTION

The protection of data involves three types of security: physical, operational and authorisational. The physical security relates to the physical loss or damage of storage devices holding the data which must be protected against natural disaster, theft, fire, accident, dust and so on. The installation management is responsible for such protection of all the physical devices used in the installation, therefore we shall not discuss it in this book. The operational security known as *integrity protection* implies the protection of data against loss or damage resulting from failure during the operation of the system, whereas authorisational security refers to the *privacy protection* of data against unauthorised use. They will be considered in this section.

4.3.1 Integrity Protection

Controls for integrity protection can be exercised both at hardware and software levels. Modern computers are designed to provide a number of sophisticated hardware protections to all data, mainly involving data transfer between the computer and its peripherals. The advanced operating systems provide additional protection such as the prevention of interactions among programs in the computer memory in a multiprogramming environment. This facility must exist or should be provided if concurrent usage is to be permitted. Interaction is usually avoided by allocating exclusive areas of the computer memory to each program and its data. The more advanced operating systems allocate memory for each program *dynamically*, as required, in units of pages which are not necessarily contiguous, and provide *virtual machine* facilities where no restriction is imposed on the size of memory and the other services required by each program. In practice each program is allocated only a few pages at a time and queued for all facilities. However, it is difficult for a DBCS to use the paging facility of the operating system because it lies outside the control of the DBCS. Besides the protections mentioned above, there are two other areas where specific controls must be exercised by a combination of software and human intervention to avoid the corruption of a data base. They are[4] update error and system malfunction.

Update Error

A data base is liable to be corrupted by erroneous, incomplete or inconsistent updates. The key control is data validation, including checks for inconsistency jointly exercised by the DBCS and the application program. Controls that can be carried out at a reasonable cost by the DBCS should not be delegated to the application program, which is likely to be less reliable since it will depend on human frailties. The DBCS should check for ambiguities and inconsistencies in relation to the whole data base, such as those that may arise if a request for the deletion of a record is granted. In a data base, a father may not die before his children, that is, the owner record may not be deleted as long as a single member record exists. Similar checks for insertions and amendments should also be instituted, ideally leaving the application programmer to vet for class, range, sign, check-digit and the consistency solely in his own input data. However, it is not feasible for the DBCS to carry out all the checks, partly because of the overheads involved and partly because of the difficulty of defining a foolproof set of validation checks. Consequently some reliance has to be placed on the application programmer, although efforts should be made to minimise his chances of making an error. The data dictionary (see the next section) should stipulate all validations required for each data unit and, where possible, standard routines should be written and incorporated in the system for the application programmer to invoke them.

To avoid data corruption by erroneous programs, a data base must be run in two modes: development mode and production mode.

All program testing must take place in the development mode when either a duplicate copy of the actual data base or a specially prepared test data base is used. The production mode can only be entered by authorised application programs for production runs.

System Malfunction

A data base can be lost or damaged through system malfunction, or through loss or physical damage of the storage devices. The normal protection against this is the retention of the previous copies of the data base, made periodically by dumping it on to magnetic tapes. In an *n tape* cycle, *n* number of copies are maintained at any given time, copy 1 being the current (period 1) data base, while others are the successive copies from the previous periods. In the event of a failure, the data base is recreated from the most recent copy available. The protection system will fail only if all *n* copies are damaged or destroyed. Dumps are time consuming and cannot be attempted too frequently. Therefore to cover the interval between successive dumpings, we need another set of files, which we shall call *changes files*, to record the changes that have taken place since the last dump. There are several types of changes file from which to choose. At the simplest level we can retain the copies of all the transactions that have taken place since the last dump. The recreation of the data base from transactions would involve rerunning the application programs in the correct sequence; hence this is the least attractive option. It is also risky, because it is difficult to ensure the absence of alterations in the application programs since the last dump. The second option is to keep the copies of all the changed records, and the third option is the retention of the after images. There is no reason why a changes file should not keep copies of all three versions of the changes.

A computer malfunction during the execution of the data base can result in the loss of information in the computer memory. To enable the system to initiate an automatic restart, *checkpoints* are useful. A checkpoint is the recording of the state of an application program and its data and other relevant information in the computer memory during run time. Checkpoints can be taken at regular intervals during the running of a program and also at the request of the operator and the program itself. By using checkpoints, the state of the system prior to the failure can be found to initiate a restart.

In addition to checkpoints, both before image and after image mentioned earlier are necessary for simple error recovery and rollback purposes.

To summarise we need the following backup files for a data base.

(1)   Dump file: for large data bases, dump should be taken only rarely.
(2)   Changes files: changes to the data base since the last dump.
(3)   Checkpoint: to be taken periodically and also at the request of the operator and the application programs during a run.
(4)   Images: both before images and after images should be maintained by the DBCS during run-time.

The major Data Base Systems available today provide these backup facilities with some variations.

Restart Facilities

Restarting of a data base will be required if an application program, the data base itself or the processor fails and, so far as practicable, the recovery should be automatic.

(1)   Program failure: at the failure of an application program, the system should automatically return to the before image state and should continue unaffected.
(2)   Data base failure: if a part of the data base fails, the programs not accessing that part should continue uninterrupted. The affected programs should be held at their last checkpoint and should restart automatically as soon as the error is removed.
(3)   Processor failure: processor failure can be avoided by using multiprocessing configuration as used in some real-time systems requiring high reliability. The load is distributed over all the processors in such a way that if one fails the others take over its function automatically by sharing, thus giving reduced but unimpaired performance. Such a system is said to possess a *failsoft* mechanism providing 'graceful degradation of services' and thus making the system *failsafe.*

4.3.2 Privacy Protection

The confidentiality of information in a data base is of utmost importance. Information is power, which can be used to harm others, and therefore rigorous control must be instituted to protect the interests of all concerned. Access to a data base can be sought to extract data, to modify data or to alter the access control codes. No programs should be permitted to use the data base for any of these functions without specific authorisation from the DBA, who should have the facility to exercise control at several levels by means of specific access codes or passwords as indicated below.

Access Control

(1)   Access to terminals: in addition to keeping the terminal under lock and key, special access cards or passwords should be instituted for the DBCS to examine them before granting access to a terminal.

(2)   Access to storage device: access to each physical device such as a disc should be controlled by special codes.

(3)   Access to Schema data units: once a storage device is accessed, further codes should be provided to access the successive hierarchy of data such as data items, record types and datasets. Whether access control should be extended to the data item level appears debatable.

(4)   Access to Subschema: there is a good case for extending access codes to Subschemas as well. In a data base installation the DBA would normally be responsible for the generation of Subschemas, each designed to meet the need of several applications efficiently. To exercise control in their usage, it is clearly necessary to provide for privacy locks for Subschemas and for their lower levels such as datasets and record types. The Codasyl proposal includes specification for such locks.[5]

(5)   Access to special programs: confidential data should be accessible by special programs only. Codes should be instituted not only to access these confidential data, but also to access the relevant application programs.

Sensitive data may be divided into several datasets in the Schema in such a way that individually they do not mean much, but jointly they may reveal explosive information. Consider, for instance, a medical data base where patients' records containing name, address and age are in one record type, and the medical history but not patients' names are in another. Unless the patients' names are related to the medical histories, the confidentiality will not be breached. The ideal would thus seem to be to permit a user to access either record types singly, but not both jointly. Unfortunately there is no effective protection purely against joint extraction of information. We can at best only make it more difficult, for instance, by devising a multilevel access system for such a group of record types, the first level codes for accessing to the record types singly, and the second level codes for accessing a second record type of the group by the same application program. But if an application programmer has authorisation to access the record types singly, he can use two programs to extract the information needed and a third program, or himself manually, to relate them. Therefore there is no special solution to this problem, except to impose rigorous control on each record type individually.

Access Code

The codes to be employed for controlling access require careful consideration. An access code has two parts. The first part can be described as a lock residing on a special area of the data base, and the second part can be described as the key (or the password) needed, as it were, to open the lock to access the relevant data unit. The DBCS will compare the key with the lock and, if a match is obtained, access will be granted.

At an elementary level the value of the key could be the same as that of the lock. In this case the DBCS will simply match the two before allowing an access. The success of this scheme will rather depend on keeping the locks secret from a potential intruder. The DBA is bound to have the list of all the locks and hence the keys which, for highly sensitive information, may not be desirable for him to know. According to Evans and Weiss[6] the protection against such disclosure of keys from locks can be guaranteed if the lock L is made a complex function of the key K such that $L = f(K)$. The DBCS will evaluate the function $f(K)$, granting access if $L = f(K)$. It is possible to design the function $f(K)$ in such a way that it is practically impossible to invert it, even if the intruder knows all the mathematical expressions involved. Therefore if such a scheme is adopted, the locks and the mathematical expressions involved need not be kept secret.

4.4 AUXILIARY FACILITIES

We include in this section three auxiliary facilities that should be provided by a Data Base System as a part of the total package to enchance the scope and effectiveness of the usage of a data base. They are data dictionary, data base procedure and communication interface.

4.4.1 Data Dictionary

The key to the effective usage of the data in the data base is their proper documentation, without which a user is bound to get confused. The data dictionary is used to provide this documentation. The concept is recent and has come into existence only through the excruciating experience of the early users. The need for a data dictionary is felt so strongly now that some recent Data Base Systems are providing this as an integral part. However, the unanimity on the need of a data dictionary has not yet crystallised in any unique definition about its contents. This is perhaps to be expected in view of the limited user experience, each with his own special requirements.

Basically a data dictionary must contain all the relevant information about the data base and its data that can be needed by the user.[7] It should preferably be maintained as a part of the data base in the form of *metadata* (that is, data about data) to avoid the likely confusion with real data. If the concept is extended beyond the immediate user's requirements, the data dictionary could serve as the central reservoir of information on all aspects of the data base, including those generated and required by the data base languages such as DSDL, DDL, DML. It may contain Storage-schema, Schema, Subschema and their compiled versions, including data base directory, data base tables, and user information on Schema, Subschema, datasets, records and data items. A typical set of information for a record can be as follows.

> Name
> Identity (that is, it is a record)
> Its A-sets
> Data items and their formats
> Its number of occurrences
> Validation requirements
> Its meaning and usage
> Duplication if any
> Privacy locks and a list of the authorised users

For a data item one may have

> Name
> Identity
> Format
> Validation including check-digits
> Its meaning and usage
> Duplication
> Privacy lock

From time to time, up-to-date user information on data should be made available (figure 4.3) by printing out the relevant information.

4.4.2 Data Base Procedure

Data base procedures are routines that can be invoked on specified conditions in the Schema to execute a procedure. Some of them can exist as standard facilities of a data base package, while others can be written by the users to suit specific data base requirements. However, their presence in the Schema tends to curtail data independence between the Schema and the Subschema (see section 5.6).

4.4.3 Communication Interface

A communication interface is required to support remote terminals to a data base. In some systems, such as the IMS of IBM, this constitutes an integral part while for some others, such as IDMS, this facility can be acquired at an extra cost. Generally a larger memory is required to support it.

4.5 DATA BASE SOFTWARE

The software required for a Data Base System falls into three categories: *languages* to create, use and maintain a data base, *utilities* to provide support facilities, and *operational routines* for the run-time management of the data base.

4.5.1 Languages

Procedural versus Non-procedural

The controversy on procedural versus non-procedural languages—alternatively known as host language versus self-contained capabilities[8] of a data base—began in the late 1960s. A procedural language is one where the user has full control over the logical flow of his program. All commonly used languages, such as Fortran, Algol, PL/1 and Cobol are procedural, since the user has to lay down the complete logical procedure to follow. A procedural language system for a data base is usually built around a host language such as Cobol. In a non-procedural language system, the user does not spell out the detailed logical procedures. Instead, he sets up the parameters of interest as done when using a Report Generator or a Sort Program. The system is self-contained in the sense that the functions invoked by the user's parameters are preprogrammed or built-in. The parametric user therefore has no control over the detailed logical flow of the processing. Some earlier data base languages were self-contained and designed to provide the following facilities.

(1) Interrogation: allowing data selection, sorting and report formatting. The language for interrogation is sometimes referred to as a *generalised query language.*
(2) Update: permitting selection of data and changing of its value.
(3) Creation: to create a data base.
(4) Restructuring: facilitating modification of a data base to conform to a changed Schema.

    A self-contained system is easier to use and reduces time and effort required for a procedural system. Moreover, the system can be used by non-experts, since it can be treated as a black box. However, the system is inflexible, the range of activities it can support being rather limited. For instance, it will be difficult for a user to make a complex calculation by using a self-contained system. Furthermore, processing in a self-contained system is slower compared with a procedural system, which can be tailor-made to suit user requirements.

    Some languages are more procedural than others. A non-procedural language is problem orientated and its level of procedurality depends on the generalisation that can be achieved in this problem. Of the four self-contained functions listed above, creation and restructuring have been less generalised. The procedurality controversy really hinges around interrogation and update, because they form the programmer's interface with the data base. In a host language system this interface is provided by a host language extended to include a DML, thus offering greater flexibility, which can be used to advantage by expert application programmers. For large-scale processing where execution efficiency is important, the host language system is the only answer.

Self-contained capabilities, on the other hand, would be ideal for a more casual user interested in some straightforward transaction processing. This allows him to process one set of records at a time, whereas DML usually permits him to process only one record at a time. A user of this kind is sometimes known as a terminal user, an end user, a parametric user or even a non-programmer user. He should enjoy a high degree of data independence and should not need to know any Schema or Subschema. His view of data is often known as the fifth or the end-user view (see section 3.3.1).

In an organisation, both types of user will exist, and therefore both the capabilities should be available. Non-procedural capabilities can be provided both as a separate facility and as part of a host language system.

Sublanguages

The languages needed for a data base are really sublanguages, since they purport to serve specific functions only. We identify here seven major sublanguages that should be supported.

(1)   DSDL: a Data Strategy Description Language to describe the Storage-schema as discussed in section 3.4.1. Its compiled version should contain its mapping into the Schema.

(2)   DDL for Schema: as we have defined earlier, this is the Data Description Language for the global description of the data base. A compiled version of the Schema will contain various data base tables containing information such as data definitions and their relationships.

(3)   DDL for Subschema: this is the Data Description Langauge used by the application programmer to describe the local view of data of the data base in accordance with the requirements of the program. The object code Subschema should contain tables showing Subschema data definitions, their relationships and other characteristics.

(4)   DML: we have described Data Manipulation Language as the interface language used by the application programmer to communicate with the data base from the host language in which the application program is coded. DML is essentially a navigational language which enables the application programmer to navigate through the data base with a search strategy defined by the logical relationships of his data in the Subschema. Application programs containing DML statements will either be compiled by an extended host language compiler or by a DML preprocessor followed by a

host language compiler. In either case the DML statements have to be validated. If a data dictionary is used by the system as a central pool of information, as stated in the last section, the compiled versions of the Storage-schema, Schema, Subschema will reside there. Figure 4.3 shows the role played by such a data dictionary.

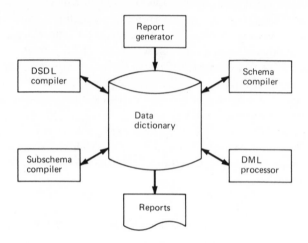

Figure 4.3 Data dictionary

(5)   Non-procedural language: as discussed earlier, a non-procedural language to facilitate simple retrieval and update should be provided. It should provide simplified methods for describing conditions, requests, print format and data entry. Normally data would be keyed and the results displayed on a VDU screen.

(6)   Modification languages: two modification languages are necessary: one to restructure the Schema and the other to reorganise the Storage-schema. Instead of being separate languages, they can form part of their respective base languages—the Schema DDL and DSDL.

(7)   Data base control language: this is equivalent to a job control language for a data base and will be used by the DBA to initiate compilations and modifications of Schema, Subschema and Storage-schema.

4.5.2 Utilities

To operate a data base, a large number of utilities is required. We shall list here only those utilities whose need has been generally recognised.[9]

(1) Dump, edit and print routines: to dump selected parts or the whole data base, to edit the data base and to print the selected parts in a prescribed format.

(2) Load routines: invoked to generate a data base by loading the user data on the physical devices in accordance with the DSDL specifications and to recreate a part or the whole of a data base from the backup files.

(3) Preconditioning routines: it may occasionally be necessary to reload a data base, particularly during the initial stage of evaluation. Preconditioning routines will nullify the effect of a previous load, but will retain the DSDL specification, thus making the data base ready for reloading.

(4) Garbage-collection routines: to remove deleted data and to consolidate the space released on the physical device.

(5) Reallocation routines: to reallocate the space released by garbage collection from the primary and overflow areas to the existing data in an optimum fashion.

(6) Statistics-collection routines: they should be used during run-time to collect statistics required for tuning the data base.

(7) Statistics-analysis routines: to analyse the collected statistics for tuning.

(8) File-conversion routines: to convert conventional user files into data base compatible form according to the record relationships specified by the DBA. However, it is unlikely that it would be possible to create a data base through a general-purpose file conversion package alone, particularly if restructuring of data within records is involved. In fact to exploit the maximum advantage of a data base, the DBA may have to undertake drastic data restructuring, which will be beyond the scope of any general-purpose package. Nevertheless any assistance that can be provided in file conversion, particularly in the early part of the data base development, would be welcome.

(9) Audit routines: utility to create specialised files to record changes in the data base between backup dumps and other information required for auditing.

4.5.3 Operational Routines

During the operation of a data base, a large number of routines is required to be resident in the memory as part of the DBCS. Some examples are as follows.

(1) Data base supervisory routines to supervise the various activities including resource allocation.

(2) Concurrency control routines.

(3) Access control routines for privacy protection.

(4) Data validation routines including checks for duplication and consistency.

(5) Data update routines to organise pointers and their consequences.

(6) Data access routines.

 (7) Integrity protection, including recovery routines.
 (8) Statistics-collection routines.
 (9) Communication routines.
(10) Data base procedures.

These routines are usually written in re-entrant code to avoid core overflow, which is bound to occur if each application program has its own set of routines, particularly in concurrent usage environments involving a large number of application programs.

4.6 DATA BASE OPERATION

In this section we shall briefly discuss the design philosophy of the data base control system, operational concepts and the role of DBCS in the basic operation of a data base.

4.6.1 Design Strategy

The design of a data base control system could in theory be based on any one of the following three strategies.

(1)   As an integrated part of the application.
(2)   As an integrated part of the operating system.
(3)   As an independent system acting as interface with the operating system.

As an integrated part of an application, the DBCS would be more or less a tailor-made system, generated by an extended host language providing faster data transfer than would otherwise be available. However, a major disadvantage is the cost of developing so many tailor-made systems, each application having its own exclusive DBCS. Furthermore, data protection would be problematic since it will be difficult to ensure the absence of incompatibility among these systems. Finally, concurrent usage would be difficult to achieve, because one system would not know what the other is doing and, if concurrent usage is allowed, memory required to accommodate so many exclusive data base control systems will be very large. Thus the first strategy cannot be used.

The second approach could represent an ideal solution from the user's point of view, if it retains a centralised control and yet provides efficient access to the data base. However, the problem is the design of an operating system, which, in addition to its normal function, can manipulate structured information involving hierarchies, cross-links, access codes and so on, as required for a data base. The feasibility of this approach has yet to be ascertained.

The third possibility is a compromise between the first two approaches where the DBCS acts as an interface between the application program and the operating system. However, this is rather inefficient, since the application program cannot directly communicate with the operating system. For the present only this approach offers a viable solution.

4.6.2 Operational Concepts

The operations involved during the running of a DBS are shown in figure 4.5. The diagram is based on the Codasyl model, but it illustrates the general problem well. The data base itself is held on secondary store, which would be discs. The primary store represents the computer memory and contains

(1) the operating system of the computer

(2) DBCS

(3) object Schema and object Storage-schema

(4) object Subschema

(5) application programs

(6) user working area (UWA): this is the space reserved as a part of every application program to hold data described in the Subschema. It is therefore a loading and unloading zone between the DBCS and the application program.

(7) system communication locations: this is a reserved area to store information relating to the outcome of a DML command. For instance, if a request to access a record is successful, information—such as the identifier for its owner and the content of its pointer array showing the relationships with other records—can be stored so that the DBCS can use this information to access the next related record wanted by the application programmer. On the other hand, if the request for access fails, the reason for failure such as 'the record is locked by another run-unit', 'wrong privacy key' or 'the record does not exist' can be flagged out in this area. If an update command is refused by the DBCS because of an inconsistency, this can also be shown there. This set of information is known as the *status information*, and its exact contents depend on the particular DBS used.

(8) system buffer: system buffers are designated areas in the computer memory to hold specific information. For a data base, two types of system buffers can be used, an input–output (I-O) buffer to serve as the loading and unloading area for the operating system and the DBCS, and a reserved area to hold the most frequently used parts of the data base so that the number of physical input-output operations are minimised. The data transfer between the data base and the I-O buffer is carried out by the operating system and that between the I-O buffer and the various UWAs by the DBCS (figure 4.4).

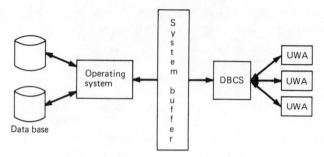

Figure 4.4 Interface of the UWA with the data base

4.6.3 Basic Operations

When a run-unit requests a record from the data base the following operations take place.[9] (The numbers in brackets indicate the links on figure 4.5.)

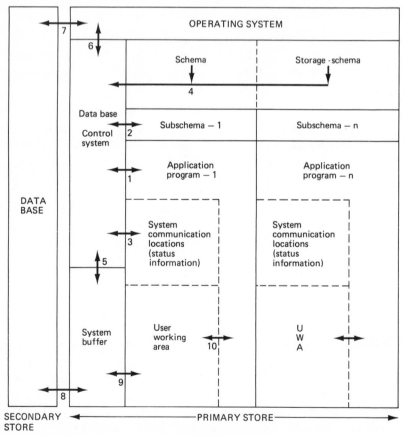

Figure 4.5 A conceptual diagram of data base operations

(1)   The run-unit, using a DML command, makes a call for a Subschema record to the DBCS specifying the required arguments for selection, access codes and so on (1).

(2)   The DBCS analyses the call and checks for its validity against the information present in the object Subschema (2), returning the control to the run-unit (3) for invalid calls after setting the system communication locations. Once the validity is ensured, the DBCS scans through the tables in the object Subschema (2), object Schema and object Storage-schema (4), supplements the original arguments by the Storage-schema arguments, establishes correspondence between the Subschema and Storage-schema data items (unless binding takes place earlier, see section 3.4.3) and determines the relevant storage records required.

(3)   Using the Storage-schema information obtained, the DBCS searches for the required storage records in the system buffer (5) and, if one or more of the records are absent, it requests the operating system to deliver them (6).

(4)   The operating system scans through the data base directory (which can reside in the data base) to extract the necessary information to locate a wanted record in the data base (7), and delivers the record in the system buffer (8) if the call is successful.

(5)   The DBCS supplies status information to the system communication locations (3) for both successful and unsuccessful outcome of a call, returning the control to the application program if the call fails.

(6)   If the call is successful, steps (4) and (5) are repeated under the DBCS control if more records are required to satisfy the DML command.

(7)   If the relevant storage records are found, the DBCS constructs the Subschema record and transfers it to the UWA (9).

(8)   The record in the UWA is then manipulated by the run-unit as necessary by using the host language (10).

(9)   The DBCS administers the I-O system buffer and instructs the operating system to take specific action in case of buffer overflow.

To write a record back to the data base or to update a record, the sequence of operations is reversed. Additional checks for update consistency would also be made.

From this sequence of operations it is quite evident that data transfer between a data base and a run-unit is rather inefficient. The extent of inefficiency obviously depends on the DBS, some being more efficient than others, but generally, unless this inefficiency is acceptable, it is best not to contemplate the use of a data base.

EXERCISES

1. Assume that in a concurrent usage mode of a data base, three types of locks as described in the text are employed. The run-units use the preclaim strategy and,

if a request to lock fails, the run-unit is queued. Design the logic for a queueing system by means of a flowchart.

2. Discuss the role of a data dictionary in a data-base environment. (For further reference see the *Report of the BCS Data Dictionary Systems Working Party to the Codasyl DDLC, July 1976*—to be published by the BCS, 1977)

3. What would happen if the routines for the DML commands were not written in re-entrant code in a concurrent usage environment? (See Section 7.1.2 for answer.)

4. Discuss the facilities your organisation would like to see in a DBS for privacy and integrity protection.

5. Compare the relative merits of the host language and query language facilities. If you were forced to choose one for your organisation, which one would you choose and why?

6. In the future it may be possible to have a DBCS integrated with the operating system. Discuss the advantages and disadvantages of such an integration.

REFERENCES

[1] E. G. Coffman, M. J. Elphick and A. Shoshani, *ACM Computing Surveys*, 3 (1971) p. 67.
[2] G. G. Everest, *Data Base Management* (IFIP) (North Holland, Amsterdam, 1974) p. 241.
[3] D. Hawley, J. Knowles and E. Tozer, *Comput. J.* 18 (1975) p. 206.
[4] M. V. Wilkes, *Comput. J.* 15 (1972) p. 191.
[5] *CODASYL Cobol—Data Base Facility Proposal*, March 1973.
[6] A. Evans and E. Weiss, *Communs Ass. Comput. Mach.*, 17 (1974) p. 437.
[7] B. Plagman and G. Altshuler, *AFIPS, Fall Joint Computer Conference 1972*, p. 1133.
[8] CODASYL System Committee, *Comput. J.* 15 (1971) p. 154.
[9] *CODASYL Data Base Task Group Report*, April 1971.

5 *The Codasyl Model*

The Codasyl model is a proposed specification for a Data Base System resulting from international collaboration among all interested parties, including users and manufacturers. The specification is designed to fulfil user needs, and as such it incorporates many of the user facilities discussed in the previous two chapters. As mentioned in chapter 1, the model enjoys the active support of most manufacturers, software houses, user organisations and professional organisations such as BCS, ACM and IFIP. A number of data base packages founded on the Codasyl model are already available on the market.

Codasyl has taken an evolutionary approach in the development of the model. To date only the Schema DDL and the Cobol data base facilities have been formally specified, and work is continuing on new facilities and on improvements of those already specified. We shall discuss all these aspects of the model in this chapter. In section 5.1 we review the history of Codasyl's involvement with data bases, followed by the basic features of the model in section 5.2. The Schema DDL is presented in section 5.3, and Subschema DDL and DML in section 5.4, leaving the other characteristics of the model to section 5.5. The chapter is concluded in section 5.6 with a critical evaluation of the model.

5.1 CODASYL

On 8 April 1959 a small group of computer users and manufacturers met in the University of Pennsylvania, to review computer language developments for business applications. At their request, the U.S. Defense Department, the then major computer user, convened a meeting, at the Pentagon on 28 May 1959, of over 40 representatives from users, manufacturers and other interested parties to discuss the feasibility of a Common Business Oriented Language (COBOL). The meeting decided to press ahead with the development of Cobol and it agreed on the concept of the Conference On Data Systems Languages (CODASYL)—referred to here as Codasyl—as an informal and voluntary organisation of interested individuals supported by their institutions with the objective of designing and developing techniques and languages to assist in data systems analysis, design and implementation.

5.1.1 Involvement with Data Bases

After its great success with Cobol, Codasyl decided to extend its activities to all
developments that could be useful to Cobol. Accordingly in June 1965 the Cobol
Language Subcommittee of Codasyl created a List Processing Task Force to
develop list processing capabilities for Cobol. Two years later this was renamed
Data Base Task Group (DBTG), and activities were greatly inspired by three
individuals—W. G. Simmons of the U.S. Steel Corporation, C. W. Bachman, the
pioneer of the IDS (then General Electric, now Honeywell) and his co-worker
G. G. Dodd of General Motors.

In August 1968 Codasyl was reorganised to produce the following three
Standing Committees.

(1)   Systems Committee: to develop advanced languages and techniques for data
      processing, with the aim of automating the process of systems analysis,
      design and implementation.
(2)   Planning Committee: to assist in planning by collecting information from
      the users and implementors pertaining to the goal of Codasyl.
(3)   Programming Language Committee (PLC): to develop programming lan-
      guage specifications to facilitate compatible and uniform source programs
      and object results with reduction in changes necessary for conversion or
      interchange of source programs and data.

The PLC assumed all the functions of the former Cobol Language Subcommittee,
including the responsibility for all data base activities. In October 1969 the DBTG
submitted its first report to the PLC proposing a Data Description Language (DDL)
to describe a data base and a Data Manipulation Language (DML) to be used as an
extension to a host language to manipulate the data of the data base. The report
generated a great deal of excitement, discussion and criticism. A revised report[1]
was produced in April 1971, which suggested for the first time the use of two
data description languages, one for the Schema and the other for the Subschema.
This report, usually referred to as the 1971 DBTG report, was accepted by the
PLC despite objections from the IBM and RCA Corporation members.

Late in 1971 a new standing committee, called Data Description Language
Committee (DDLC), was formed to specify the Schema DDL based on the 1971
DBTG report. Two years later in April 1973, the DDLC published its proposal for
the Schema DDL in a *Journal of Development*[2] (to be referred to in this book as
the *1973 DDLC Journal*), recognising that the process of development in data base
languages should be evolutionary, as in Cobol. Since 1973 the DDLC has set up
two major task groups. One—based in the United States—is the Subschema Task
Group (SSTG) responsible for the development of Subschema facilities, and the
other—based in the United Kingdom—is Data Base Administration Working Group
(DBAWG) responsible for the development of tools for the use of the data base
administrator. The DBAWG is jointly sponsored by the British Computer Society
and its activities include, among others, the development of a Data Strategy

Description Language (DSDL) for reorganising the data base, and also the provision of concurrency and data protection facilities. Its preliminary report, known as the *DBAWG June 1975 Report*[3], has been published by BCS. Apart from providing support for the activities of these two groups, the DDLC is also engaged in improving the Schema facilities. The publication of the next DDLC Journal of Development is likely to be in 1977.

From the original DBTG of PLC, a Data Base Language Task Group (DBLTG) was later formed to develop Subschema DDL and DML. In May 1973 it produced a draft based on the 1971 DBTG report for the Cobol Subschema and DML,[4] the final specification being published in 1975 as the Cobol Data Base Facility in the *Codasyl Cobol Journal of Development*,[5] referred to in this book as the 1975 *Cobol Journal.*

5.1.2 The Scope of Codasyl Activities

From the aims and objectives of Codasyl in areas needing immediate attention, as reaffirmed at its 10th anniversary conference held in May 1969, we find[2]

(1)   The objective of Codasyl is to bring about design, development and specifica-tion of *common* user languages (*italics* by this author)
(2)   Codasyl accepts variations in implementation within the *common* features, but it recognises the need for uniformity and it feels that the responsibility for standardisation lies within the established services of the appropriate national bodies.

The first point defines the objectives and the second point qualifies its scope; Codasyl will produce all common user languages, but it cannot undertake their standardisation without intruding into the domain of the relevant national authorities for standardisation. As a result of this division of responsibility, many versions of Cobol emerged—all Codasyl compatible. The standardised version (ANSI Cobol) was imposed later by the American National Standards Institute and not by Codasyl. We should not therefore expect Codasyl to generate a stan-dardised Data Base System; its task should be, as it has already done, to provide the framework for systems with common features, leaving standardisation to be imposed later by such bodies as ANSI (section 9.3).

5.1.3 Current and Future Work on Data Bases

The various Codasyl subcommittees are pursuing developments and extensions of data base facilities. The areas of activity include[2,3]

(1)   The definition of the generic functional terms for DDL.
(2)   Development of Fortran Subschema and DML (see section 5.4.5).
(3)   Further development on the Subschema concept—for example, host lan-guage independent Subschema.

(4)   Development of self-contained capabilities.
(5)   Specification for a Storage-schema and its DSDL (which is the former Device Media Control Language or DMCL).
(6)   Provision of more storage independence in the Schema.
(7)   Improvement of concurrent usage facilities.
(8)   Guidelines for statistics generation for tuning.
(9)   Development of restructuring and reorganisation facilities required by the data base administrator.

5.2 BASIC FEATURES

The Codasyl proposal supports both the global and local views of data, which are described globally in the Schema by an independent Schema DDL and locally in the Subschema by a Subschema DDL based on a host language. Both the Schema and the Subschema are compiled independently of the host language. Storage-schema is not supported by the present model, but it is expected to be incorporated in the future. The operational concepts and the basic operations of the model are similar to those described in section 4.6 (figure 4.5).

In this section we shall present the basic concepts of the Codasyl model, including the characteristics of its data structures and access paths. We shall also show how these data structures are used to represent various data relationships. The concepts presented here are based on the *1973 DDLC Journal*. Some changes in them are expected (see section 5.3.6) in the next publication of the Journal.

5.2.1 Record and Area

The data units permitted in the Codasyl model are *data items, data-aggregates, records, areas* and *sets*. Data items, data-aggregates and records are defined as in chapter 2, except that the term *data item* is often used as synonymous with *data item value*. An entry for a record in the Schema constitutes a record type, which represents an arbitrary number of records. A record is the basic unit of access and may contain virtual data items.

Every record in a data base is given a unique logical pointer known as the *data base key*. The allocation of this key is permanent and may not be altered during the life of a record. It can be assigned to another record only when this record is deleted from the data base.

An *area* is a subdivision of the data base declared in the Schema and contains a collection of records belonging to one or more record types. The occurrences of a record type or a set type (see below) can be shared by a number of areas, but a particular record can belong to only one area, and may not migrate to another area.

5.2.2 Set

A dataset in the Codasyl model may consist of only a single A-set as defined in section 3.2.4, every A-set type being named and declared in the Schema. The Codasyl terms for them are *set* (not to be confused with the set of the 'set theory' of mathematics) and *set type*. More formally, a set type is defined as a named logical collection of one owner record type and one or more member record types, and a set or set occurence is characterised by an owner record from the owner record type of the set type and none, one or more member records from the member record types. The name given to a set type is its *set name*, which acts as the unique identifier for the set type, a set being identified by the set name plus the owner record indentifier.

Since a set is the basic building block of a Codasyl type data base, we shall elucidate the concept further with examples for clearer understanding. Consider in figure 5.1 three record types and their occurrences denoted by their respective keys.

Record Type	Record Occurrences
Doctor Records	D1, D2, D3, D4
Nurse Records	N1, N2, N3
Patient Records	P1, P2, P3, P4, P5, P6

Figure 5.1

Let us construct a set type named, say, DOCNP with record type Doctor as the owner and the other two record types as the members as shown in figure 5.2.

Set name   : DOCNP

Owner name   : DOCTOR

Member name : NURSE and PATIENT

Figure 5.2

We may represent set type DOCNP by what we shall call a *set diagram* (figure 5.3).

Set type DOCNP will represent as many sets as there are owner records, each set being owned by a specific owner record. Since the number of owner records can increase or decrease as a result of update, so too would the number of sets. Figure 5.3 could represent the four sets as shown in figure 5.4.

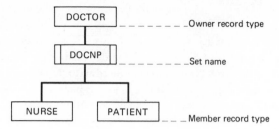

Figure 5.3 A set diagram

Sets	Owner	Members
Set 1	D1	
Set 2	D2	P5
Set 3	D3	N2, P2, P3
Set 4	D4	N1, N3, P1, P4, P6

Figure 5.4

Set 1 does not have any member and is therefore known as an *empty set.* As a result of subsequent update by an application program, the number of sets in the set type and also their memberships may change.

It can be observed in figure 5.4 that the same record does not appear in two sets. If the same patient is treated by two different doctors, we have a many-to-many relationship which cannot be directly represented in the Codasyl model owing to a *set restriction rule* (not a Codasyl term) built into the model. This rule may be stated as follows.

> A record may not appear more than once in the same set type and a record type may not provide both owner and member records to the same set type.

This restriction simplifies the pointer organisation for access paths, but disallows many-to-many relationships (see later).

Apart from this restriction, a record type can participate in many set types, in some as member and in others as owner, each set type being uniquely identified by its set name. Thus a record occurrence can own many sets (not belonging to the same set type) and can be a member in many other sets (not belonging to the same set type). A user may define as many set types as necessary and can construct a hierarchy of sets by using the owners of some set types as the members of some other set types. We present below some examples, assuming that, in addition to Doctor, Nurse and Patient records of figure 5.1 there are also some Drug records, each patient taking many drugs, and each drug being prescribed by many doctors. We can then construct the following set types as displayed by the set diagrams in figure 5.5.

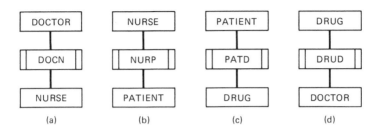

Figure 5.5 Set types

Both (a) and (b) represent $1:N$ relationships. In general a doctor and/or a nurse can have many patients. A particular doctor or nurse can likewise have zero patients, but as long as a patient does not belong to more than one doctor or more than one nurse, set types DOCN and NURP are valid. Similarly a patient has $1:N$ relationship to drugs and a drug has $1:N$ relationship to doctors. The set types DOCN and NURP together represent a three-level tree. The set type DOCNP of figure 5.1, together with set type NURP, constitutes a net, and the four set types of figure 5.5 form a cyclic net—or *cycle* to use the Codasyl term.

5.2.3 Access Paths

In the Codasyl model all access paths discussed in section 3.2.4 are permitted. The members of a set can be processed in a forward and optionally backward direction with an additional option for owner pointers from the member records. Facilities for direct access to the members of a set are also provided (see later). Access paths are transparent to the application programs.

Since the members can be processed both forwards and backwards, the logical order in which the members of a set appear is important. The Codasyl model supports several methods for the specification of this logical order as discussed later.

5.2.4 Data Representation

The Codasyl proposal supports sequential data structures, trees, nets and cyclic nets. A sequential data structure is a collection of records ordered according to a key as in a sequential file. The owner record is defined as a single dummy record called SYSTEM. The set type therefore contains only one set; hence such a set is known as a *singular set.*

1:N and M:N Relationships

As we have seen earlier, all three forms of one-to-many relationships, that is, trees, nets and cyclic nets, can be directly represented by set structures. However, with many-to-many relationships we have a problem because of the set restriction rule. In the absence of this restriction the $M{:}N$ relationship between 3 courses and 4 students of figure 3.9 could have been represented by a set type with 7 occurrences—one occurrence for each dataset—but such a representation clearly violates the set restriction rule as explained in section 3.2.3. Therefore we have to bypass this restriction by means of link records. This leads to the following set diagrams for the course and student relationships.

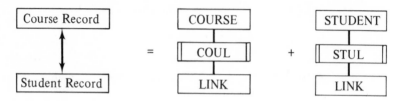

where the set type COUL is owned by COURSE record type and the set type STUL is owned by STUDENT record type, the LINK records being members in both the set types as in figure 3.12.

Representation of Loop

We mentioned in section 3.2.3 that loops showing $M{:}N$ relationships among the occurrences of the same record type can be represented by link records. Taking the example of cousins mentioned there, if a cousin is related to an arbitrary number of other cousins, then the corresponding link records will have variable length, which is inconvenient. This method of representation can cause other problems as well, for if A is the cousin of B and C but B and C are not cousins themselves, then a link record containing the keys of A, B, and C can only be owned by A and not by B or C. Furthermore, such link records are inconvenient for storing information on a relationship between two records. These problems are avoided by using a link record exclusively for the relationship between two records. We shall consider here a slightly more complex problem of part explosion and show how it can be resolved.

Suppose there are 4 part number records A, B, C and D, all belonging to the same record type, but A is made up of 2 Bs and 6 Ds, B being made up of 4 Cs and 3 Ds as shown in figure 5.6.

We may wish to find the components of a particular part number, or the superior part numbers, quantity required, and so on, of a given part number. To represent these relationships we need three record types as follows.

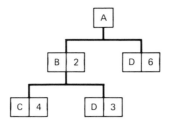

Figure 5.6

(1) Part number records (PART) each containing information such as part code, part description and suppliers. Assume that A, B, C and D are the keys of these records.

(2) Relationship records (REL) each containing a key R*i* as an identifier for the *i*th record, a pair of keys from the two related part numbers—one for the superior (SUP) and the other for the subordinate (SUB) part number—and QTY, the number of the subordinate part number used in that superior part number.

(3) Link records (LINK) each containing a pair of keys, one for a PART record and the other for the related REL record as shown in figure 5.7.

Key	Other Data
A	Other Information
B	Other information
C	Other information
D	Other information

PART records

Key	SUP	SUB	QTY
R1	A	B	2
R2	A	D	6
R3	B	C	4
R4	B	D	3

REL records

Key 1	Key 2
A	R1
A	R2
B	R1
B	R3
B	R4
C	R3
D	R2
D	R4

LINK record

Figure 5.7 Representation of part explosion data

We can now construct two set types, say, PARL and RELL as shown in figure 5.8.

The representation of this relationship without these LINK records will lead to the violation of the set restriction rule, as in the case of course and student records mentioned earlier (see also the two solutions for exercise 13 of this chapter).

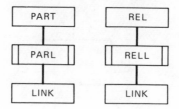

Figure 5.8

5.3 THE GLOBAL MODEL

In this section we shall describe the characteristics of the Schema in accordance with the *1973 DDLC Journal*. The changes so far agreed by the DDLC for the next Journal[6] are discussed at the end of this section. We begin here with the skeleton of the Schema.

5.3.1 Schema Skeleton

The Schema is the description of the whole data base, with entries being made using the Schema DDL. A skeleton of Schema entries is shown in figure 5.9.

```
        SCHEMA NAME IS . . . .
            [ON . . . . . . . . .]
            [PRIVACY LOCK . . ]

        AREA NAME IS . . . .
            [ON . . . . . . . . .]
            [PRIVACY LOCK . . . ]

        RECORD NAME IS . . . . .
            WITHIN . . . .
            LOCATION MODE . . . .
            [ON . . . . . .      . . . .]
            [PRIVACY LOCK    . . . .]

        Level number dataname
                [PICTURE IS . . . .]
                [TYPE IS . . . . . .]
```

[CHECK . . . .]

[{ENCODING / DECODING} . . . . .]

[{VIRTUAL / ACTUAL} {SOURCE . . . / RESULT OF . . .}]

[ON . . . . .]
[PRIVACY LOCK . . . . .]

SET NAME IS . . . .

    OWNER IS . . . . .

    [SET IS   ‖ DYNAMIC / PRIOR PROCESSIBLE ‖]

    ORDER IS . . . . .

    [ON . . . . .]
    [PRIVACY LOCK . . . .]

    MEMBER IS . . . .

{MANDATORY / OPTIONAL}   {AUTOMATIC / MANUAL}   [LINKED TO OWNER]

    [KEY IS . . . .   ]
    [SEARCH KEY IS . . . . .]
    SET SELECTION . . . . .
    [ON . . . . .]
    [PRIVACY LOCK . . . . .]
    END SCHEMA

Figure 5.9 The skeleton of Schema entries

The notations used are as follows.

(1)   Uppercase underlined: key words that must be present.
(2)   Uppercase but not underlined: optional words.
(3)   Lowercase: entries to be supplied by the user.
(4)   Clauses enclosed in [ ] : optional facilities.

(5)   Clauses enclosed in { } : only one of them must be present.

(6)   Clauses enclosed in ‖ ‖: at least one of them must be present.

There are four types of entry that make up a Schema

(1)   Schema name entry
(2)   area entry
(3)   record entry
(4)   set entry.

The last line of a Schema is END SCHEMA, which indicates the end of a Schema. We shall discuss below the other entries and the major clauses. A sample Schema is presented in section 5.3.5.

5.3.2 Schema Name and Area Entries

The Schema name entry is the first entry of a Schema and is used for assigning a name to the Schema and for specifying optional privacy locks and so on. There must be only one such entry for a data base.

An ON clause can be associated with all entries and subentries (see later) of the Schema; it allows a data base procedure to be called for special actions in case of errors or other specified conditions. PRIVACY LOCKs can also be applied with all entries and subentries. Some examples for both can be seen in the sample Schema.

One area entry is made for every area of the data base. Each entry includes an area name and optional PRIVACY and ON clauses.

5.3.3 Record Entry

There is one record entry per record type, each entry consisting of one record subentry and a number of data subentries. A WITHIN clause is used in the record subentry to specify the area where some (with conditions for selection) or all the records of this record type should belong. A LOCATION MODE clause in the record subentry is used to assign data base keys to the records of this record type. It can be used in four modes as follows.

(1)   DIRECT: the value of specified data items in the Schema is taken as the data base key.

(2)   CALC: the data base key is calculated by a named data base procedure using specified data item values from the record concerned.

(3)   VIA setname: the data base key is selected by the DBCS as though it were to become a member of a set in the named set type. To enable the DBCS to select the correct set of the named set type, a SET SELECTION criteria is specified in the set entry (see later).

(4)   SYSTEM: the data base key selected by the DBCS as convenient.

A data subentry is used for each data item of the record type, a data item being described in a manner similar to that of Cobol using level numbers and PICTURE clauses. The TYPE clause can be used instead of the PICTURE clause to describe the format of a data item, and also to declare a data item as the data base key (for LOCATION MODE DIRECT). Special encoding and decoding procedure for a data item can also be stipulated through a pair of ENCODING/ DECODING clauses. A CHECK clause is used for the validation of a data item value either by invoking a data base procedure for the purpose or by checking the value against a set of prescribed values.

Direct or indirect data redundancy can be avoided by qualifying the redundant data item with a SOURCE . . . or a RESULT OF . . . clause respectively. The first stipulates the source data item of which this redundant data item is a copy, and the second names a data base procedure to evaluate this redundant data item from other data items specified as parameters. Either clause can be VIRTUAL—in which case the value of the redundant data item is never stored, but is presented to the program when necessary—or ACTUAL—in which case the redundant data item value is physically stored, thus providing faster access but needing continuous update. The problem is particularly bad in the case of the ACTUAL RESULT option with many parameter data items, since the change in any one of them requires an update following what could be a lengthy calculation. A new option, POSTPONED RESULT, will be available (see section 5.3.6) in the future. It is the same as the ACTUAL RESULT, except that the value of the redundant data item will be updated only when it is accessed next rather than whenever the parameters are changed, thus reducing the number of updates.

5.3.4 Set Entry

There is one set entry per set type in the Schema. Each consists of one set subentry and a number of member subentries, one per member record type of the set type. The SET NAME and OWNER clauses in the set subentry are used to specify the set name and the owner record name respectively. All members of a set, irrespective of their record types, can be processed in the forward direction, and optionally in the backward direction if a PRIOR PROCESSIBLE clause is specified. The function of the DYNAMIC clause is explained later.

Order Clause

An ORDER clause is used to specify the logical position (see section 5.2.3) of a member in a set in relation to the other members of the same set in any one of the following ways.

(1)   SORTED: all member records of the set type are placed in ascending or descending order of a user defined sort key, which can be constructed from

the data base key (DATA-BASE-KEY option) or a *sort control key*. A sort control key is defined for each member record type in its member subentry by a KEY clause using one or more of its data items; the members can be sorted (for each set), either within each record type separately (RECORD-NAME option) or irrespective of record types (DEFINED KEYS option), depending on the option specified. In each case index tables for each set separately can be built for direct access to members through the sort control key.

(2)   Positional: a member record can be stored as the FIRST (starting from the owner) or the LAST member of the set, or PRIOR or NEXT to another member of the set.

(3)   IMMATERIAL: the DBCS specifies an order as convenient.

The ORDER specified can be PERMANENT or TEMPORARY, and if TEMPORARY the logical positions of the members can be changed by an application program using a DML command ORDER. The ORDER must be PERMANENT for the SORTED option.

Summarising, all member records of a set can be processed in the forward and optionally in the backward direction, the members being sequenced by an ORDER clause either independently of their record types or within each record type depending on the specification. Direct access facilities can be provided by index table for the sort control keys.

Member Subentry and Membership Class

In the member subentry the member record name is specified in the MEMBER clause. A record type may have different kinds of membership in different set types. A record can be inserted into a set either automatically or manually. If a record type is declared AUTOMATIC in the member subentry, then as soon as a record of this type is stored in the data base, the DBCS will automatically make it a member of the appropriate set occurrence of the set type concerned, the set being selected on the basis of the specified SET SELECTION criteria.

If a membership is MANUAL, then a record will be made a member of a set in accordance with a DML command issued from an application program. This facility is very useful for conditional membership. Consider for instance an organisation having Department records and Employee records, each department having a number of employees, some of whom are entitled to commission. We may construct a set type COMMISSION owned by the Department records with the employees on commission as the members. Here the membership class of the record type Employee should be MANUAL, so that the application programmer can choose only the employees on commission for membership.

Once a record is made a member of a set its membership may or may not be cancelled depending on the option specified. If the membership is OPTIONAL, the record concerned can be terminated from the membership without any restrictions. On the other hand, if it is MANDATORY, the record must remain a member of the set type, although its membership may be switched from one set to another of the same set type. Finally a new option, FIXED, will be available in the future (see section 5.3.6) and if this option is specified, the record cannot be removed from the membership of a particular set—it will remain a member until the record is deleted.

Combining these options, a member can become MANDATORY AUTO-MATIC, OPTIONAL AUTOMATIC, MANDATORY MANUAL, OPTIONAL MANUAL, FIXED AUTOMATIC or FIXED MANUAL. If a set type is declared DYNAMIC in the set subentry, the application program can insert any record of any type as a member and remove any record from membership. All members of dynamic sets are in effect OPTIONAL MANUAL, but no membership entries are required for them in the member subentry.

Auxiliary Access Facilities

In addition to the general access facilities provided in the set subentry, exclusive optional facilities can be built for the member records of a given type per set of a set type by specifying appropriate clauses in the member subentry of the set type. The first of these is the LINKED TO OWNER clause, which is specified in a member subentry. It creates owner pointers for the member records of this record type per set of the set type to which this member record type belongs. This provides faster access to other set types where this owner is either a member or an owner.

The second facility is the SEARCH KEY option, defined in a member subentry as a function of specified data items of the member record type. If this clause is specified, the DBCS will create index tables for the SEARCH KEY—one such table for every set of the set type, to provide direct access to the member records of this record type through this SEARCH KEY. If the data items of the SEARCH KEY are subsequently used in a SET SELECTION clause or a FIND command of the DML, the member record concerned can be accessed speedily. More than one SEARCH KEY can be declared in each member subentry.

The function of the KEY clause has been explained earlier in connection with the ORDER clause. There can be only one KEY clause in a member subentry.

Set Selection Clause

The SET SELECTION clause provides the DBCS with the capability to select the correct occurrence of a set type for a given member record. Such automatic selections are required for the LOCATION MODE VIA clause and AUTOMATIC membership clause as mentioned earlier. There are also other cases, as we shall see in section 5.4.3, where such automatic set selection by the DBCS is necessary. A set can be selected by using any one of the following options.

(1)   From SYSTEM for singular sets (SYSTEM option).
(2)   From the current record (see section 5.4.2) of the set type if the record is a member or the owner of the required set (CURRENT option).
(3)   From the data base key of the owner record either supplied directly (DATA-BASE-KEY option) or obtained through LOCATION MODE CALC (CALC-KEY option).
(4)   From SET SELECTION clause of another member record type (MEMBER option).
(5)   From a data base procedure (SELECTION IS BY PROCEDURE format).
(6)   From a hierarchical search of a tree down the successive lower levels of the hierarchy—assuming the root record as the highest level of a hierarchy.

In the hierarchical search, the owner at a level is first identified using one of the first four methods. Then a member of this owner is selected, as the owner of the next level down the hierarchy, using the specified data item values of the first owner. The process is repeated until the wanted set at the lower level of the hierarchy is reached. When a set is selected hierarchically, the application programmer must initialise the appropriate variables for the first set; if this is not done, the wrong set will be selected. The fifth option is self-contained—the user writes his own data base procedure to find the wanted set, by searching hierarchies if necessary.

Note that, for a given set type, one member subentry is made per member record type, each with its exclusive specification of the membership class, auxiliary access facilities and SET SELECTION clause. If a record type is a member of two or more set types, member subentries for this record type must be provided in each set type separately, each entry with its exclusive specifications.

5.3.5 A Sample Schema

In this subsection we shall present an example of Schema written according to the Codasyl specification. Note that this is a hypothetical situation and no deeper meaning should be sought on the reasons for using the specific data structures, privacy clauses and other details.

In our example we have represented the data of a college in six record types belonging to seven set types distributed over five areas in the Schema. The Schema can be entered either through a privacy lock or a data base procedure as shown. No privacy locks are used for areas. The data subentries in the record types are self-explanatory, except that the CHECK clause as used here calls a procedure to validate the data items. The DUPLICATES ARE NOT ALLOWED clause in record subentries means that more than one record is not permitted to have the same value for the data items associated with LOCATION MODE CALC; if a second record has the same value, the DBCS will flag an error. For the record EMPLOYEE, the records are distributed to EMP-AREA1 or EMP-AREA2 depending on the value of EMP-AREA supplied by the application program. If the employee is a teacher, his record goes to EMP-AREA2. The *M:N* relationships between the COURSE and STUDENT records are represented by using link record type PERFORMANCE.

The set types defined represent a variety of data structures, including sequential and network structures with facilities for backward processing with or without owner pointers. The SEARCH KEY facility is provided in set type JOBE for direct access to the EMPLOYEE records. The placement of records in sets is also varied. In the set type TEACHER, the member record types are SORTED within each record type in order of KEY, KEY being COURSE-CODE for the record type COURSE and ST-NUM for the record type STUDENT as defined in their respective subentries. A STUDENT record is made a member of the set type TEACHER only when the student is accepted by a teacher, but it can be stored in the data base prior to this acceptance, and therefore its membership class is MANUAL. The value of the data item ST-STATUS in STUDENT record is set to M if the record is made a member, otherwise it is a space. In the set type COUP and STUP the member records are SORTED according to KEY, which in both cases is defined as ST-NUM1 and holds the duplicate values of the data base keys (student numbers) of the STUDENT records.

```
SCHEMA NAME IS COLLEGE-DATA
       PRIVACY LOCK SCHEM-LOCK
              OR PROCEDURE SECURITY.
AREA NAME IS DEPT-AREA
AREA NAME IS EMP-AREA1.
AREA NAME IS EMP-AREA2.
AREA NAME IS COURSE-AREA.
AREA NAME IS ST-AREA.


RECORD NAME IS DEPARTMENT
       LOCATION MODE CALC PROCEDURE-DEPT USING DEPT-CODE
              DUPLICATES ARE NOT ALLOWED
       WITHIN DEPT-AREA
       ON DELETE CALL DEPT-PROC.

   03    DEPT-CODE              PIC X(4)
                CHECK IS DCODE-CHECK.
   03    DEPT-NAME              PIC X(20).
   03    JOB-TYPE               PIC 9.
   03    JOBS-IN-TYPE           PIC 99 OCCURS JOB-TYPE TIMES.


RECORD NAME IS JOB-TITLE
       LOCATION MODE CALC PROCEDURE-JOB USING JOB-CODE
              DUPLICATES ARE NOT ALLOWED
       WITHIN DEPT-AREA
       ON DELETE CALL JOB-PROC.
```

```
    03   JOB-CODE                    PIC X(4)
              CHECK IS JCODE-CHECK.
    03   JOB-NAME                    PIC X(20).
    03   SALARY-RANGE OCCURS 15 TIMES
              ON MODIFY CALL SAL-PROC.
       05   SALARY-POINT             PIC 99.
       05   SALARY                   PIC 9(5)V99.
    03   HOLIDAYS                    PIC 99.


RECORD NAME IS EMPLOYEE
       LOCATION MODE CALC PROCEDURE-EMP USING EMP-NUM
              DUPLICATES ARE NOT ALLOWED
       WITHIN EMP-AREA1, EMP-AREA2
              AREA-ID IS EMP-AREA
       ON DELETE CALL EMP-PROC.

    03   EMP-NUM                     PIC 9(4)
              CHECK IS EMP-CHECK.
    03   EMP-NAME                    PIC X(25).
    03   SALARY-POINT                PIC 99.
    03   TAX-CODE                    PIC X(5).
    03   DATE-OF-BIRTH               PIC 9(6).
    03   AGE                         PIC 99
              IS VIRTUAL RESULT OF PROC-CALC ON THIS PERIOD
                 USING DATE-OF-BIRTH.


RECORD NAME IS COURSE
       LOCATION MODE SYSTEM
       WITHIN COURSE-AREA.
    03   COURSE-CODE                 PIC X(5)
              ON MODIFY CALL C-PROC1
              ON STORE CALL C-PROC2.
    03   COURSE-NAME                 PIC X(20).
    03   YEAR                        PIC 9.
    03   LIMIT-ON-INTAKE             PIC 99.


RECORD NAME IS STUDENT
       LOCATION MODE DIRECT ST-NUM
       WITHIN ST-AREA.
    03   ST-NUM                      TYPE IS DATA-BASE-KEY
              CHECK IS ST-PROC.
    03   ST-NAME                     PIC X(20).
    03   ST-ADDRESS                  PIC X(40).
    03   ST-STATUS                   PIC X.
```

RECORD NAME IS PERFORMANCE
    LOCATION MODE VIA COUP
    WITHIN COURSE-AREA
    PRIVACY LOCK FOR MODIFY PLOCK.

03	ST-NUM1	TYPE IS DATA-BASE-KEY.
03	COURSE-CODE1	PIC X(5).
03	EXAM1	PIC 99.
03	EXAM2	PIC 99.
03	EXAM3	PIC 99.

SET NAME IS DEP-SET
    OWNER IS SYSTEM
        ORDER IS PERMANENT
        SORTED BY DATA-BASE-KEY.
    MEMBER IS DEPARTMENT
        MANDATORY AUTOMATIC
        SET SELECTION THRU DEP-SET OWNER IDENTIFIED BY
            SYSTEM.

SET NAME IS JOB-SET
    OWNER IS SYSTEM
        ORDER IS PERMANENT
        SORTED BY DATA-BASE-KEY.
    MEMBER IS JOB-TITLE
        MANDATORY AUTOMATIC
        SET SELECTION THRU JOB-SET OWNER IDENTIFIED BY
            SYSTEM.

SET NAME IS DEPE
    OWNER IS DEPARTMENT
        ORDER IS PERMANENT LAST.
    MEMBER IS EMPLOYEE
        MANDATORY AUTOMATIC
        LINKED OWNER
        SET SELECTION THRU DEPE OWNER IDENTIFIED BY CURRENT
            OF SET.

SET NAME IS JOBE
    OWNER IS JOB-TITLE
        ORDER IS PERMANENT IMMATERIAL.
    MEMBER IS EMPLOYEE
        MANDATORY AUTOMATIC
        LINKED TO OWNER
        SEARCH KEY IS ASCENDING EMP-NUM

SET SELECTION THRU JOBE OWNER IDENTIFIED BY CURRENT
OF SET
PRIVACY LOCK FOR FIND ELOCK.

SET NAME IS TEACHER
    OWNER IS EMPLOYEE
        ORDER IS PERMANENT
        SORTED WITHIN RECORD-NAME.
    MEMBER IS COURSE
        MANDATORY AUTOMATIC
        KEY IS ASCENDING COURSE-CODE
        SET SELECTION THRU TEACHER OWNER IDENTIFIED BY
           CURRENT OF SET.
    MEMBER IS STUDENT
        MANDATORY MANUAL
        KEY IS ASCENDING ST-NUM
        SET SELECTION THRU TEACHER OWNER IDENTIFIED BY
           CURRENT OF SET.

SET NAME IS COUP
    OWNER IS COURSE
        SET IS PRIOR
        ORDER IS PERMANENT
        SORTED BY DEFINED KEYS.
    MEMBER IS PERFORMANCE
        MANDATORY AUTOMATIC
        LINKED TO OWNER
        KEY IS ASCENDING ST-NUM1
        SET SELECTION THRU COUP OWNER IDENTIFIED BY
           CURRENT OF SET.

SET NAME IS STUP
    OWNER IS STUDENT
        SET IS PRIOR
        ORDER IS PERMANENT
        SORTED BY DEFINED KEYS.
    MEMBER IS PERFORMANCE
        MANDATORY AUTOMATIC
        LINKED TO OWNER
        KEY IS ASCENDING ST-NUM1
        SET SELECTION THRU STUP OWNER IDENTIFIED BY
           DATA-BASE-KEY.

END SCHEMA.

5.3.6 Future Changes

One of the most important changes agreed by the DDLC is the removal of the concept of the data base key. Instead an optional IDENTIFIER clause for each record type will be provided to define one or more keys to access the records. This clearly will provide additional access facilities. However, IDENTIFIERS are not unique, since two records can have the same value in an IDENTIFIER. In the future, facilities for implementor-defined unique record identifiers are likely to be provided[7] that is, data base keys through the back door.

The DIRECT option of the LOCATION MODE clause will be withdrawn, the concept of data base key being dropped. Eventually the whole LOCATION MODE clause, along with the concept of area, will probably be removed from the Schema[7] to the Storage-Schema where a LOCATION MODE clause can be used for the strategic placement of storage records into storage areas to improve data base performance (see section 5.6).

In set selection both the DATA-BASE-KEY and CALC-KEY options will be removed and an IDENTIFIER option will be inserted instead to identify the owner record through keys declared in its record entry by the IDENTIFIER clause mentioned above. A new set selection option called STRUCTURAL CONSTRAINTS will be available for the identification of a set through the identical data item values of a member record, provided that these data items are declared in a STRUCTURAL CONSTRAINT IS . . . clause in the appropriate member subentry. Consider the set type COUP in our sample Schema of section 5.3.5, where owner record type COURSE and member record type PERFORM-ANCE hold the values of course number in COURSE-CODE and COURSE-CODE1 respectively. There in the member subentry of record type PERFORMANCE we would be able to write

STRUCTURAL CONSTRAINT IS COURSE-CODE1 EQUAL TO COURSE-CODE.
SET SELECTION IS STRUCTURAL CONSTRAINT.

The other changes are relatively minor, some of them being as follows.

(1) Throughout the Schema the term PRIVACY LOCK will be replaced by the term ACCESS-CONTROL LOCK.

(2) Throughout the Schema the ON clause will be replaced by a CALL data base procedure on specified condition clause.

(3) There would be an option to place a record type in any area rather than a named area.

(4) At present it is possible to create a workspace in the data base by declaring a TEMPORARY AREA; this facility will be withdrawn.

(5) A new membership option, FIXED, in addition to MANDATORY and OPTIONAL, will be available as explained in section 5.3.4.

(6) ENCODING/DECODING clauses will be withdrawn; they would probably appear in the Storage-schema as an ENCRYPTING clause.

The changes discussed in this subsection are taken from reference 6 except where reference 7 is indicated.

5.4 THE LOCAL MODEL

In this section we shall discuss the Cobol data base facilities of the Codasyl model, Cobol being the only language for which the Subschema DDL and DML have so far been approved. The material presented here is drawn from the *1975 Cobol Journal*—some changes there are expected in the future in accordance with the alterations in the Schema DDL mentioned earlier. A draft for the Fortran data base facility has been prepared and is awaiting final approval. It will be briefly discussed in section 5.4.5 along with the likely future changes in the Cobol facility.

5.4.1 Subschema Characteristics

The Cobol Subschema proposed consists of entries in a DDL and is divided into three Divisions: Title, Mapping and Structure. The Subschema is named in the Title Division. The Mapping Division provides the ability to define logical relationships between the Schema and the Subschema definitions, and contains an Alias Section where the Schema data names can be renamed for the Subschema. Such renaming is essential if the Schema data names are illegal in the host language. The Structure Division has three sections: Realm, Set and Record Sections, Realm being the Subschema term for area of the Schema. The Realm, Set and Record Sections contain entries similar to those in the area, set and record entries of the Schema, except that the AREA NAME IS, SET NAME IS and RECORD NAME IS clauses are replaced in the Subschema by RD, SD and 01 respectively. Since 01 is reserved for the record name, the data subentries in the Subschema must use higher level numbers, but the data names themselves must remain unchanged, unless they are renamed in the Alias Section. Any of the Sections mentioned here can be omitted from the Subschema if they are not needed.

The data items of a record are described in data subentries, using Cobol clauses and conventions such as level numbers, PIC clauses, COMP clauses and condition names. One variation from Cobol is the CHECK clause, which is used in the Subschema for data item validations.

Certain clauses such as the CHECK clause, SET SELECTION clause and PRIVACY clause, can be specified both in the Schema and in the Subschema. If they are specified in both, the Schema specifications are ignored. Note that in the Subschema the SET SELECTION clause is specified in the set subentry for each member record. A Subschema skeleton is given in figure 5.10.

TITLE DIVISION.

SS   Subschemaname WITHIN Schemaname

  [PRIVACY LOCK . . . .]

  [PRIVACY KEY   . . . .] to enter the Schema

MAPPING DIVISION.

ALIAS SECTION.

$$
AD \begin{Bmatrix} \text{Realmname-1} \\ \text{Setname-1} \\ \text{Recordname-1} \\ \text{Identifier-1} \\ \text{Implementorname-1} \end{Bmatrix} \quad \text{BECOMES} \quad \begin{Bmatrix} \text{Realmname-2} \\ \text{Setname-2} \\ \text{Recordname-2} \\ \text{Identifier-2} \\ \text{Implementorname-2} \end{Bmatrix}
$$

STRUCTURE DIVISION.

REALM SECTION.

RD   Realmname

  [PRIVACY LOCK . . . . .]

SET SECTION.

SD   Setname

  [SET SELECTION FOR recordname IS . . . .]

  [PRIVACY LOCK . . . .]

RECORD SECTION.

O1   recordname [WITHIN realmname . . . . .]

  [PRIVACY LOCK . . . . .]

    Data subentries
      .
      .
      .

Figure 5.10 A skeleton of Subschema entries

Subschema Independence

The Codasyl model allows the following major variations between the Schema and the Subschema.

(1) Data items: the format of a data item in the Subschema can be different from that in the Schema. A group of data items can be selected from the Schema and given a new group name in the Subschema. New validation procedure for the data item can be specified in the Subschema, suppressing those in the Schema.

(2) Record: a Subschema record can be constructed from a subset of the data items of a given Schema record, and the data items can be reordered. The unnecessary record types can also be omitted, but the facility to create new record types from data items belonging to several Schema records is not supported, although this facility is recommended in the *DDLC Journal.*

(3) Set: unnecessary set types and member record types can be excluded from the Subschema, and new set selection criteria can be specified in lieu of those in the Schema.

(4) Privacy locks: privacy locks can be declared in the Subschema for the realms, set types and record types in preference to those in the Schema.

All access paths are transparent to the application programmer who accesses the data base following the standard DML commands. A Subschema is independently compiled and stored, to be invoked by an application program subsequently. Although a Schema can support an unlimited number of Subschemas with two Subschemas sharing the same part of the data base if necessary, an application program can use only one Subschema. The binding between the Subschema and the data base is implementor dependent.

A Sample Subschema

We present here a sample Subschema drawn from the Schema of section 5.3.5. Note that data item ST-NUM of STUDENT record is declared in the Subschema as a data base key (DB-KEY); its format is implementor defined, but we have here assumed it to be a five-digit number. This facility for declaring a data item as a data base key is also extended to the Cobol host language (see the sample program in section 5.4.4).

TITLE DIVISION.
SS   STUDENT-PERFORMANCE WITHIN COLLEGE-DATA.

MAPPING DIVISION.
ALIAS SECTION.
AD   PERFORMANCE BECOMES LINK-REC.

STRUCTURE DIVISION.
REALM SECTION.
RD   EMP-AREA2.
RD   COURSE-AREA.
RD   ST-AREA.

SET SECTION.
SD   TEACHER.
SD   COUP.
SD   STUP
     SET SELECTION FOR LINK-REC IS VIA STUP OWNER CURRENT.

RECORD SECTION.
01	EMPLOYEE.	
03	EMP-NUM	PIC 9(4).
03	EMP-NAME	PIC X(25).
01	COURSE.	
03	COURSE-CODE	PIC X(5).
03	COURSE-NAME	PIC X(20).
01	STUDENT.	
03	ST-NUM	PIC 9(5) DB-KEY.
03	ST-NAME	PIC X(20).
03	ST-ADDRESS	PIC X(40).
03	ST-STATUS	PIC X.
01	LINK-REC.	
03	ST-NUM1	PIC 9(5).
03	COURSE-CODE1	PIC X(5).
03	EXAM1	PIC 99.
03	EXAM2	PIC 99.
03	EXAM3	PIC 99.

5.4.2 Currency Indicators

The retrieval facilities of the Codasyl model are centred on a concept of what are called *currency indicators*. In conventional file processing, the current record of a program may be defined as the last record read by the program. This concept is extended in the Codasyl model as follows (for more accurate definitions see next subsection).

(1)   Current of each record type: the last record read or inserted in each record type used by the run-unit.

(2)   Current of each set type: the last record read or inserted in each set type used by the run-unit. The record can be the owner or a member of a set in the set type.

(3)   Current of each realm: the last record read or inserted in each realm used by the run-unit

(4)   Current of the run-unit: the last record read or inserted by the run-unit

Special indicators, known as the currency indicators, are maintained by the DBCS to hold the unique identifiers (implementor defined) of the current records. Note that many of these indicators will point to the same record, for instance, the current of the run-unit would generally be the same as the current of the record type, set type and realm to which it belongs (see below). At the start, all indicators are set to null values. They are updated automatically unless suppressed by the user.

There are some problems in using the currency indicators. These are documented in an IBM position paper by Heywood[8] and subsequently in another paper by Engles[9] of IBM. When a record is deleted the current of the run-unit is null, but other currency indicators containing this deleted record as the current of record type, set type and realm remain unchanged, and therefore these other current records can be referring to a non-existing record. If a record is removed from the membership of a set type, this record still remains the current record of the set type to which it no longer belongs. There are other occasions where the programmer must selectively suppress the updating of the currency indicators to avoid errors (see later). If a record that has been read happens to be a member of several set types currently being used by the application program, then this record will become the current of all these set types. If the former currency indicators of these other set types were used in set selection, then unless the currency update is suppressed, wrong sets will be selected, since this present record may belong to a different set. The currency indicators thus put the heavy burden of maintaining data integrity on to the programmer. On the other hand, they provide great flexibility in data retrieval by facilitating the selection of records from a given record type, or set type or realm with ease, and also by permitting set selection through the current of set.

5.4.3 Data Manipulation Language

The DML serves as the interface language between the host language program and the data base. A Cobol program wishing to use the data base must invoke the required Subschema in a Subschema Section of its Data Division as shown below.

DATA DIVISION.

SUBSCHEMA SECTION.

DB Subschemaname   WITHIN   Schemaname.

FILE SECTION.

. . . . . .

. . . . . .

WORKING-STORAGE SECTION.

. . . . . .

. . . . . .

PROCEDURE DIVISION.

. . . . . .

. . . . . .

Every Cobol application program is given (1) an exclusive User Working Area (UWA) for the Subschema data and (2) system communication locations for the status indicators as explained in section 4.6. By using a DML command, the application program can transfer data between the data base and the UWA, which can then be accessed by a host language command.

DML Commands

The following DML commands have been proposed.

(1) READY: to open one or more realms for exclusive retrieval, protected retrieval, exclusive update or protected update. In the exclusive mode, no other run-unit can open the same realm, while in the protected mode other run-units can open the realm concerned for retrieval but not for update.
(2) FINISH: to release one or more realms from a run-unit.
(3) ACCEPT: to extract a data base key from a currency indicator, or to find the realm name from a current record or from a data base key.
(4) FIND: to select a record either for retrieval by a subsequent GET command, or to extract the data base key of the selected record for subsequent use. The object record of a successful FIND command becomes the current record unless the updating of the relevant currency indicators is suppressed by using a RETAINING CURRENCY clause. A number of different record selection formats can be used in conjunction with the FIND command (see later).
(5) GET: to retrieve specified data items or all the data items of a record selected previously by a FIND command.
(6) MODIFY: to modify one or more data items of a record or to change the set membership of a record. In the latter case the DBCS will select the appropriate set on the basis of the SET SELECTION criteria specified. The application programmer must initialise the necessary parameters for the SET SELECTION clause, otherwise a wrong set will be selected.
(7) STORE: to insert a new record into the data base. The stored record becomes the current record unless the updating of the relevant currency indicators is suppressed by using a RETAINING CURRENCY clause.

(8) ERASE: to delete a record from the data base. The current of the run-unit becomes null after deletion, but all other indicators remain unaltered.

(9) ORDER: to reorder the logical positions of the members of a set in accordance with a specified key. Its effect is local to the run-unit if the ORDER in the Schema is specified as PERMANENT (see section 5.3.4).

(10) CONNECT: to make a record a member of one or more sets.

(11) DISCONNECT: to remove a record from the membership of one or more sets. However, the disconnected record remains the current of the original set, that is, the currency indicators do not change.

(12) KEEP: to keep a record in extended monitored mode for concurrent usage (see section 5.5.2).

(13) REMONITOR: to rejuvenate a KEEP command (see section 5.5.2).

(14) FREE: to nullify a KEEP.

(15) USE: to specify data base procedures to be invoked on specified execution conditions.

In addition to these DML commands, two data base conditions are provided.

(i)   *Tenancy condition* to determine whether a record is an owner, or a member or either of a set. A record is a tenant if it is the owner or a member of a set.

(ii) *Member condition* to find whether a set is empty, that is, has no members.

The object record of a FIND and STORE command becomes the current record of the run-unit, record type, set type and the realm concerned. If there are more than one set types used by the run-unit in which this record is a tenant, then this record becomes the current record of all these set types. The updating of currency indicators can be prevented by specifying the RETAINING CURRENCY clause, either individually for the run-unit, record type, realm, set type (or set types) as necessary, or collectively for all of them. The ERASE command acts only on the current of the run-unit, but after the command is successfully executed, the value of the currency indicator for the current of the run-unit is set to null. This cannot be suppressed. No other currency indicators are affected; thus the deleted record remains the current of the record type, realm and set types concerned. All other DML commands act on the current of the run-unit and they do not alter any currency indicator, except in the case of the MODIFY command where, if a record is changed to a new set type, it becomes the current of this set type.

If the execution of a DML command fails owing to data base exception conditions (that is, errors), then the error messages in the form of preassigned codes—known as the status indicators—are held in the system communication locations of the relevant application program. If a status indicator is zero, then the command is successfully executed. Application programmers are strongly advised to check status indicators after every DML command and to take appropriate action in the event of errors.

Recorded Selection Expressions

A record can be selected by a FIND command using any one of the seven different selection formats supported by the DBCS as follows.

Format 1:   Access by data base key directly

[Recordname] DB-KEY IS identifier

is used to find any record of the data base directly by data base key (DB-KEY) held in the identifier. Recordname is unnecessary, but if specified, it must be the one for the record to which this data base key is associated.

Format 2:   Access by data base key with Calc.

ANY recordname

can be used to access a record that was placed with LOCATION MODE CALC. The DBCS calculates the data base key using the data base procedure specified in the LOCATION MODE clause in the Schema. The programmer must initialise the data items used by the data base procedure correctly.

Format 3:   Access by searching set with a user-defined key

DUPLICATE WITHIN setname USING key

is used to find a member record through the current record of the set type, if both records belong to the same record type and have identical value of the key which may consist of one or more data items of the record type. The DBCS searches for the wanted record from the current record in the order specified by the set ordering criteria.

Format 4:   Access by position

{ FIRST, LAST, etc.} [recordname] WITHIN {setname or realmname}

is used to access the FIRST, LAST or nth record in a set (selected by the current record of the set type) or a realm. The PRIOR or NEXT record in a set or realm in relation to their current records can also be selected. If recordname is specified, all other record types are ignored in evaluating the position. In a realm the sequential order of the records is defined in relation to the data base keys, while in a set it is specified by the set ordering criteria.

Format 5:   Access by currency indicators

CURRENT recordname or CURRENT WITHIN {setname or realmname}

is used to select the current record of the named record type, or set type or realm from their respective currency indicators.

Format 6:   Access to owner record

OWNER WITHIN setname

is used to find the owner record of a set from a member record, if the member record is the current record of the set type.

Format 7:   Access by set selection criteria and with a user-defined key

Recordname WITHIN setname [CURRENT] [USING key]

is used to find a member of the named record type in a set type. If CURRENT is specified, the set is selected from the current record of the set type, otherwise the DBCS uses the specified set selection clause to find the set. The key in the USING option may consist of one or more data items of the record type, and its value is used to identify the wanted record in the selected set uniquely. The search will be particularly fast if a SEARCH KEY containing the data items of the key is specified in the Schema. If the USING option is not specified, the first record of the named record type in the selected set will be identified.

There are some additional options in these seven formats which we have not described here.

5.4.4 A Sample Program

We present here some examples of the uses of DML commands in a Cobol program based on the Subschema of section 5.4.1. The program only shows a PROCEDURE DIVISION and parts of the DATA DIVISION. Strictly speaking the status indicators (ERROR-STATUS) should be checked after every DML command, but for the sake of simplicity we have refrained from doing so. The logic is deliberately kept simple for ease of understanding.

In the first part of the program we list (using the Cobol DISPLAY verb) the name of every student in student number order, each name being followed by the list of courses the student has taken. In the second part of the program student records are updated from input supplied on punched cards. There are two types of input record, (1) record type RT = A (INREC1) for the amendments of student addresses, each record containing, besides RT, student number SN and student address SADD; and (2) record type RT = I (INREC2) for insertion of new records, each record containing, besides RT, the student record SREC to be inserted and the employee number ENUM for the owner of the student record in set type TEACHER. When a new student record is stored, it is also made a member of the appropriate set, unless ENUM is less than 1 for this student. Note that SN in INREC1 is declared as a data base key.

```
DATA DIVISION.
SUB-SCHEMA SECTION.
DB STUDENT-PERFORMANCE WITHIN COLLEGE-DATA.
FILE SECTION.
FD CARDFILE
      LABEL RECORDS OMITTED.
01    INREC1.
      02    RT                    PIC X.
      02    SN                    PIC 9(5) DB-KEY.
      02    SADD                  PIC X(40).
01    INREC2.
      02    RT                    PIC X.
      02    SREC                  PIC X(65).
      02    ENUM                  PIC 9(4).


PROCEDURE DIVISION.

PARA-10.
      READY COURSE-AREA
          USAGE-MODE IS PROTECTED RETRIEVAL.
      READY ST-AREA EMP-AREA2
          USAGE-MODE IS EXCLUSIVE UPDATE.

PARA-20.
      FIND FIRST STUDENT WITHIN ST-AREA.

PARA-30.
      GET ST-NAME.
      DISPLAY ST-NAME.
      FIND FIRST LINK-REC WITHIN STUP.

PARA-40.
      FIND OWNER WITHIN COUP.
      GET COURSE-NAME.
      DISPLAY COURSE-NAME.
      FIND NEXT LINK-REC WITHIN STUP.
      IF ERROR-STATUS = 0, GO TO PARA-40.
      FIND NEXT STUDENT WITHIN ST-AREA.
      IF ERROR-STATUS = 0, GO TO PARA-30.

PARA-50.
      OPEN INPUT CARDFILE.

PARA-60.
      READ CARDFILE AT END GO TO PARA-80.
      IF RT NOT= "A" GO TO PARA-70.
      FIND STUDENT DB-KEY IS SN.
      IF ERROR-STATUS NOT = 0,
```

```
            DISPLAY "ERROR ON UPDATE", INREC1,
            GO TO PARA-60.

MOVE SADD TO ST-ADDRESS.
    MODIFY ST-ADDRESS.
    GO TO PARA-60.
PARA-70.
    IF RT NOT = "I",
            DISPLAY "ERROR ON UPDATE", INREC2,
            GO TO PARA-60.
    MOVE SREC TO STUDENT.
    IF ENUM < 1,
            MOVE SPACE TO ST-STATUS,
            STORE STUDENT,
            GO TO PARA-60.
    MOVE "M" TO ST-STATUS.
    MOVE ENUM TO EMP-NUM.
    FIND ANY EMPLOYEE.
    STORE STUDENT.
    CONNECT STUDENT TO TEACHER.
    GO TO PARA-60.
PARA-80.
    FINISH COURSE-AREA, ST-AREA, EMP-AREA2.
    CLOSE CARDFILE.
    STOP RUN.
```

In PARA-10 the relevant realms are opened in appropriate modes. In PARA-20 the first student record (stored in student number order as specified in the Schema) in the data base is selected, and the student name extracted and displayed. In PARA-30 the first link record of the set type STUP is selected by locating the owner (Student record) from the current of the set type as specified in the SET SELECTION clause of the Subschema. In PARA-40 the owner (Course record) of the current link record in set type COUP is selected by record selection format 6. Course name is then retrieved and displayed. We have used ERROR-STATUS $\neq 0$ as the indicator for the end of a set or a realm. Alternatively we could have checked for the appropriate code signifying the end of a set or a realm. In PARA-60 student records are retrieved directly by data base key (record selection format 1) supplied by SN. In PARA-70, if ENUM < 1, the student record concerned is not made a member of the set type and ST-STATUS is filled with space, and if ENUM $\geqslant 1$, the student record is made a member and M is moved to ST-STATUS. The relevant owner records (Employee records) for the set type TEACHER are obtained by record selection format 2, which derives the data base key from the relevant data base procedure as specified in its LOCA-TION MODE CALC clause in the Schema using data item EMP-NUM (employee number). Note that the connection of a new student record to a set must follow its storage in the data base so that the record becomes the current record of the run-unit before it is connected, since the CONNECT command operates only on the current of the run-unit.

5.4.5 Future Changes and Extension

Future Changes to Cobol Data Base Facilities

In view of the proposed changes in the Schema as discussed in section 5.3.6, the Subschema facilities will also change. Format 1 will probably give way to another one for direct access to records by the IDENTIFIERs defined in the record sub-entry of the Schema. Format 2 is likely to disappear when the LOCATION MODE CALC is withdrawn from the Schema.

Extension of Data Base Facilities to Fortran

The next language to have a Subschema interface to the Codasyl model is Fortran. A draft[10] for Fortran data base facility was finalised in February 1976 and is expected to be published as a Journal of Development soon. This draft is based on the Cobol data base specification of the *1975 Cobol Journal* and provides similar facilities. The syntax used in the Fortran draft resembles Backus Normal Form; except for this deviation, the semantics and even the major terms used (SUBSCHEMA, ALIAS, PRIVACY LOCKS, EXCLUSIVE, PROTECTED, DUPLICATE, CURRENT, RETAINING, and so on) in the two cases are essentially identical.

The data items of a record are declared in TYPE statements, each statement specifying the name and format of a data item. The permitted formats are INTEGER, REAL, DOUBLE PRECISION, COMPLEX, LOGICAL and CHARACTER, with facility to specify the size of a data item if used for CHARACTER. The CHECK clause appears to be missing, but all other Cobol Subschema facilities such as the privacy clauses, realms, sets and set selection criteria are provided. Data items can be renamed by ALIAS statements. The Sub-schema independence allowed is the same in both cases.

All the DML commands (called DML statements), with the exception of KEEP, FREE and REMONITOR, are retained. Three new commands are intro-duced: FETCH, INVOKE and PRIVACY. FETCH has the combined effect of a FIND followed by a GET command. The INVOKE command is used to invoke a Subschema for a Fortran host language program, and as such acts as the DB Sub-schemaname paragraph of Cobol. A PRIVACY command is used to provide keys for the locks in the Schema and the Subschema. This command is executed prior to the DML command that needs the privacy key. All the seven record selection formats are allowed. The currency suppression clauses are also available with the appropriate DML commands. In the absence of KEEP and other commands, the concurrent usage is permitted through locks on realms, which can be opened in an exclusive or a protected mode by the READY command as in Cobol DML.

5.5 OTHER CHARACTERISTICS

In this section we shall discuss data independence, concurrent usage and data protection aspects of the Codasyl model. The remaining issues will be covered in the next section when we evaluate the model critically. Here we begin with data independence.

5.5.1 Data Independence

The Subschema independence available in the Codasyl model has already been discussed in section 5.4.1. As regards storage independence, the present model offers very little except the freedom in record placement provided by the data base keys, which, being unique record identifiers independent of the physical devices, permit records to be moved from one physical device to another with minimum difficulty. In such a change-over, it is necessary to modify only the index table relating the data base keys to the physical addresses, all records being referenced internally in the Schema by the data base keys. No other facilities for storage independence are available at the moment.

5.5.2 Concurrent Usage

The Codasyl model at present provides two methods to resolve the concurrency problem. The first method, known as the notification scheme, relies on the issuance of a KEEP command by the updating run-unit on the records of interest.

The current record of a run-unit is said to exist in a *monitored mode,* because if a run-unit tries to update its current record, the attempt will fail, resulting in a data base exception condition if this record has been modified by a second run-unit after it became the current of the first run-unit. This is the essence of the notification scheme. It is up to the first run-unit to take any action it sees fit. In the absence of any detailed information concerning the actual changes in the record, the updating run-unit can only reread the record and try again.

The monitored mode expires when a record ceases to be the current of the run-unit. The KEEP command is used on the current of a run-unit to extend its monitored mode; so the record behaves as if it were in a monitored mode, even when it ceases to be the current of the run-unit. This *extended monitored mode* is terminated by a FREE command. A run-unit can keep a number of records in the extended monitored mode at the same time, provided the KEEP command was applied on each record when it was the current of the run-unit. Any attempt to update any of these records would fail if a second run-unit modifies the record after it became the current (monitored mode) of the first. If a run-unit requires a number of records for a consistent set of updates, it may wish the monitored mode to be effective on all the records simultaneously only after the last record for update is read. This is required to avoid the error messages and failure due to concurrent modification that took place prior to the reading of the last record. This is facilitated by a REMONITOR command, which can be applied to any number of records in the monitored or extended monitored mode—it cancels all the previous monitored or extended monitored modes, and begins a new monitored or extended monitored mode for the specified records.

The second method is based on locking data resources. The model does not support locking at record level owing to heavy overheads involved in such low level locking. Instead it suggests realms (areas) to be locked on the basis of the preclaim strategy (section 4.2.3). In other words, for a consistent series of updates, all realms necessary must be locked before any of them are read. A lock can be applied selectively, for update or retrieval, and in each case it can be exclusive or protected. If an exclusive lock is applied, no other run-unit can open that realm. A protected lock prevents concurrent update, but permits concurrent retrieval.

Locks are applied when realms are opened, and released when they are closed.

5.5.3 Data Protection

As mentioned earlier, a certain amount of data validation can be carried out by specifying the CHECK clause for a data item in the Schema or in the Subschema. This allows the value of the data item to be vetted against individual values or ranges of values. The CHECK clause can also invoke a user-written data base procedure if specified. No other validation check is available at present. However, the DDLC is considering a new clause, VALIDATE, for consistency checking in data items and records.[7] The present model has not stipulated any backup files or recovery procedure in the event of failure—it is left to the implementor—but the DBAWG is looking into this area.

The privacy of data in the data base is controlled through a system of privacy locks and privacy keys. Locks can be specified in the Schema for the Schema itself, and for each area, record type, data item and set type. In the Subschema separate locks can be imposed for the Subschema, and for each area, record type and set type. If both the Schema and Subschema locks are provided for a data unit, the Subschema locks take precedence. The run unit supplies the keys, which, if identical with the value of a lock, permits access. Locks can be applied selectively for exclusive update, protected update, exclusive retrieval or protected retrieval. Provision also exists to generate adequate warning messages in case of wrong keys.

5.6 CRITICAL EVALUATION

The model supports a wide variety of data structures from simple to complex providing the flexibility needed for a large data base. The set concept permits the
representation of sequential tree, net and cyclic net structures, the members being
processible in both backward and forward direction in accordance with a predefined order. Direct access to members of a given record type, or to all members
irrespective of record types, are also supported with additional facilities for
owner pointers. Any record of the data base can also be accessed directly. The
replacement of the data base keys by identifiers will in the future permit direct
access to a record independently of set types by multiple keys in line with the
facility of inverted files. However, it would in a sense curtail data independence,
since these identifiers of the Schema records and the data items involved cannot
be changed without affecting application programs. The direct representation of
M:N relationships is not permitted by the model, but in view of high processing
cost of such representation, this is perhaps a sensible decision. Data redundancy
can be avoided by using the options for virtual data.

DML commands and currency indicators are often criticised as complex,[5] but
flexibility in data manipulation cannot be gained without introducing complexity.

The model does not specify any binding procedure; it is entirely left to the
implementor. As regards logical data independence, it is quite satisfactory at data
item level. At the record level, the proposed Cobol Subschema does not support
the definition of new local record types, although the *DDLC Journal* recommends
it. The absence of any facility to define a new logical record relationship, that is,
a new set type, in the Subschema should be viewed as a shortcoming, but it must
be pointed out that the other currently available products are not any better in
this respect. The use of the LOCATION MODE clause curtails application program
independence to the extent that the programmer has to know how they are
assigned to the Schema records. However, this clause is expected to be removed
from the Schema, direct access to the records being provided through Schema-
defined identifiers, thus eliminating the problem of the LOCATION MODE clause.
A DSDL is currently being specified to provide the facilities discussed in section
3.4.1. It will permit the fragmentation of a Schema record to several storage
records and their strategic placement into specified subdivision (storage-area) of
the physical storage to improve data base performance. Access path clauses will
also be declared there. The present concept of area in the Schema will then be
largely redundant. The compiled Storage-schema will include its mapping to the
Schema to enchance data independence.

The present facilities for concurrent usage are poor and inadequate. The notification scheme is a real non-starter. This scheme relies entirely on the application
programmer to preserve data integrity, thus inviting data corruption. Having used
the complex series of KEEP and REMONITOR commands, the programmer
would hardly be in a safe position to secure data integrity, since it is impossible
to guarantee that the records placed in extended monitored mode are the latest

versions, or that they will remain so during modification. Problems can also be expected when a consistent series of records is written back to the data base. For instance, consider the situation encountered when two records forming a consistent series for update are modified and record 1 is successfully written back to the data base, but attempts to write record 2 back fail owing to its being modified in the meantime by another run-unit. The original record 1 would be lost and hence cannot be reread. Under such a condition, we might try to resolve it by keeping a copy of the original record 1, but in the meantime another run-unit might have changed the record 1 in the data base. We can construct many other examples to show that the scheme is unworkable. In fact the uselessness of this scheme is now generally recognised and it is certain to be changed in the future.

The second method, providing locks at area level for concurrent usage, can work, but areas are too large as units of data resources. As mentioned earlier, the DBAWG is currently considering ways and means to improve this.

Adequate data validation is provided at the data item level. Additional facilities required for consistency checking will be available in the future. The set selection procedure can lead to selection of a wrong set if the required parameters are not initialised correctly in the application program. There is no way the system can check the validity of the selection path, and therefore this poses a threat to data integrity. Backup facilities, error recovery and restart procedures are left to the implementors. However, several levels of privacy protection are provided through privacy locks.

In the Codasyl proposal, no recommendation has been made for data dictionary or communication facilities. Data base procedures are supported, but they reduce data independence, since, in the event of Schema restructuring, the parameters used in a procedure could change, and this would require alterations in the application programs initialising these parameters.

The proposal recognises the need for a query language and has suggested a number of support facilities for the DBA. In fact work is in progress for the specification of the facilities required for performance evaluation and tuning, including guidelines for statistics generation. Most of the utilities discussed in section 4.5.2 are accepted in the Codasyl proposal as necessary, but no specifications for them have been provided.

In spite of the shortcomings described above, the Codasyl model provides facilities unmatched by any other existing formatted system. The model is evolutionary, adding new facilities as time goes on. Perhaps in a few years the model will stabilise, and subsequent changes become less drastic for the existing users. However, it is a large and complex model suitable for large users; for small users, a subset of these facilities with less complexity would be more appropriate.

EXERCISES

The reader's attention is drawn to the three case-study problems presented in exercises 11, 12 and 13, which he should try to solve for a deeper appreciation of the facilities offered by the model.

1. In the Codasyl model, link records are used to represent network relationships. Do they have to include the keys of the relevant owner records?

2. Describe the situation where set selection criteria are used by the DBCS. (Read sections 5.3.4 and 5.4.3.)

3. Produce an example when the membership option FIXED is useful.

4. Membership class DYNAMIC has not been provided in a number of Codasyl implementations (including DMS 110 and IDMS). Can you think why?

5. A problem similar to that of dynamic set types, but more difficult, appears if *M:N* relationships are allowed. Explain how the link records solve this.

6. The conditional membership of a set is facilitated by membership class MANUAL. Suggest a new facility to be introduced in the Schema to declare conditional memberships, and discuss its advantages over MANUAL memberships, if any.

7. The Subschema does not permit the definition of a new set type. Give an example where such facilities can be provided with minimal mapping overheads.

8. Discuss the importance of the currency suppression clause, and explain, with examples, the problems a programmer would face in the absence of this clause, and show how he can circumvent them.

9. Discuss the additional facilities you would like to see in the Codasyl model.

10. Evaluate the Codasyl model in accordance with the requirements of your organisation.

11. A food-distribution company accepts daily orders from its regular customers for a month at a time, up to a month in advance with a minimum of a fortnight's notice. Each order contains a customer number, item codes, and quantities for each item type for up to 31 days. The customers are divided into 28 invoicing groups, each group being invoiced monthly on different days, 1 to 28, of a month for the previous 28 to 31 days as the case may be. Each invoice contains an invoice number, date, the customer number, quantity in each item type in the invoicing period, cost per item and the total value.

The company has a fleet of vans to deliver the goods to the customer, but not all customers use this service; however, a route number (depending on the delivery point) is allocated to each customer in case any of them use the service. Delivery is free only for goods exceeding a certain total value in the invoicing period, which can be checked when the invoices are produced. A small charge per delivery is made for the customer whose total invoice value falls short of the minimum required. Information on the total number of times the delivery service was used in the invoicing period is maintained for each customer, but the actual dates are not recorded. A van-loading schedule is prepared daily, one or more vans being allocated to a route, depending on the sizes of the vans and the demand of a route on that particular day.

The company also keeps monthly sales data on each item type for the past 24 months for sales analysis.

(a) Sketch a Schema for a data base to be used for the following purposes: (1) to accept customer's orders and invoice them as described; (2) to produce van-loading schedules; (3) to generate sales reports as indicated.

Design Guidelines

In describing record types ignore the Picture clauses. Just give the record name, followed by a list of contents for each. However, indicate Location mode, if intended to be used for access. In each set type indicate the set names, owner name, member names, access paths and set ordering criteria (only if relevant). Do not bother about the actual syntaxes and other Schema requirements such as areas, privacy clauses and so on. A Schema should be reasonably flexible so that it can cater for all the likely processing requirements of an organisation. Therefore, when specifying a record type, think carefully whether direct or sequential access or both are likely to be needed.

(b) Assuming that the Schema you have designed also represents a Subschema, show, by writing down the DML commands, how it is possible to produce invoices from this data base for a particular day number of a month.

12. A car-rental firm owns fleets of cars, each fleet using a different model, each having a fixed hiring charge per day plus an additional charge per mile. Cars may be booked for whole days, from one day to 28 days, 3 months in advance. If no car of the requested model is available, the firm quotes the next more expensive (based on the fixed daily charge) model. If subsequently a car of the booked model is not available owing to breakdown or other reasons, the customer is given a car of the next more expensive model at the price of the originally booked model—or alternatively, if the customer prefers, a car of the next cheaper model at its usual cheaper price.

Every car is serviced regularly, but servicing does not take more than one day at a time. The firm prefers the service intervals not to be exceeded by more than 15 per cent. Occasionally a car needs repair lasting up to a week. All cars are sold off after one year, all information on the sold cars being subsequently destroyed.

(a) Design a Schema, in accordance with the design guidelines given in the previous question, for a data base to be used for the following activities.

(1)   To respond to booking requests quickly.

(2)   To provide the after-booking service (such as a car of a different model if a car of the original model is not available) as described earlier.
(3)   To invoice the customers monthly for the bookings which end in the month, each invoice containing the customer number the order number the start and finish dates, the model and cost of each booking, the cumulative year to date (YTD) sales, the amount paid and the amount outstanding. (Assume that the order numbers are unique only within a given customer number, and that there is a separate order number for every car booked).
(4)   To produce quarterly reports on the age, and the mileage of every car, model by model.

(b) Assuming that the Schema you have designed also represents a Subschema, answer the following questions.

(1)   Write the DML commands to update the total mileage of a car after it is returned by the customer. Assume that the customer number and the order number are given to you to identify the car.
(2)   Suppose that a booked car is broken down, and has to be replaced. Write down the DML commands necessary to search for a car of the same model, failing that a car of the next more expensive model and failing that a car of the next cheaper model. Assume you have read the registration number of the broken car into a data name OLDRN.

13. An electronic component manufacturing company produces 2000 types of component, each component containing up to 10 levels of hierarchy and 50 subordinate components, and it maintains 100 000 items of components and 3000 items of raw materials in stock. When an order is received, the company searches through its stock of components, first for the ordered items themselves (the top level components), failing that, their successive lower level components. All the available components are then withdrawn from stock, and the top level components are assembled from the lower level components if necessary. If some of the lowest level components are out of stock, they are fabricated from raw materials, and if raw materials in stock are insufficient, they are quickly ordered from the suppliers. (Note that a basic component may use more than one item of raw material, and that the same raw material may be needed in more than one basic component.) The company does not employ two suppliers for the same raw material but a supplier usually supplies more than one raw material.

Owing to rapidly advancing technology, components quickly become obsolete and are replaced by new products. Since the same component may appear as a subordinate component of some components, and as a superior component of some others, the change of one component usually affects many others. To respond effectively to such changes, the company needs to know quickly about all the affected superior and subordinate components.

(a) Design a Schema, in accordance with the guidelines given in exercise 11, for a data base to hold information on components, raw materials, and suppliers, so that the need of the company, as described above, can be efficiently met.

(b) Assuming that the Schema you have designed also represents a Subschema, answer the following questions for a component code held in a data item COMPC.

(1) Find, by DML commands, the detailed information (component code, description, reorder level, quantity in stock, standard manufacturing time and price) on all its subordinate and superior components.

(2) Find, by DML commands, its successive first subordinate components (that is, take only one component, ignoring others if there are more, from each subordinate level).

REFERENCES

[1] *CODASYL Data Base Task Group Report*, April 1971.

[2] *CODASYL DDL Journal of Development*, June 1973.

[3] *DBAWG Report*, June 1975 (BCS).

[4] *CODASYL Cobol Data Base Facility Proposal*, March 1973.

[5] *CODASYL Cobol Journal of Development*, May 1975.

[6] *CODASYL DDLC Journal of Development*, February 1976 (unpublished).

[7] *CODASYL DDLC Meeting*, July 1976.

[8] T. R. Heywood, *BCS October 1971 Conference on DBTG April 1971,* Report page 81.

[9] R. W. Engels, Currency and Concurrency in the Cobol Data Base Facility (to be published in IFIP TC-2 Working Conference on Modelling in DBMS, 1975.)

[10] CODASYL Fortran Data Base Facility, February 1976 (Working document for a Journal of Development).

6 *The Relational Model*

A *relation* is a mathematical term for a two-dimensional table such as the one shown in figure 3.15. It is characterised by rows and columns, each entry there being a data item value. The reason for calling this a relation rather than a matrix lies in the lack of homogeneity in its entries – the entries are homogeneous in the columns but not in the rows. A relational data base consists of such relations, which can be stored on a physical device in a variety of ways.

From the late 1960s a number of people[1] toyed with the idea of constructing data bases with relations as the basic building blocks. Most of these early systems[2] were restricted to relations with only two columns, and all of them were special-purpose models incapable of meeting general data-processing requirements. In 1970 E. F. Codd[3] of IBM proposed a model for a generalised relational Data Base System chiefly to provide data independence and data consistency, which are difficult to achieve in the formatted Data Base Systems. The model was subsequently improved and expanded by Codd and is now regarded by many as the future of all Data Base Systems. Needless to say, the term *relational data base* or *relational model* is nowadays generally identified with Codd's model alone. In this chapter we shall describe this model.

In section 6.1 we shall discuss the general characteristics of the relational model followed by the basic concepts in section 6.2. The third section will be devoted to the concept of normalisation and, in particular, the third normal form for logical data representation. Data retrieval languages – relational algebra, calculus and DSL Alpha – will be discussed in the fourth section, leaving the expected facilities and the implementation prospects to the last section. We should mention here that the model deals only with logical data structures and their access needs, leaving the problems of storage representation to the implementor. However, we shall discuss some implementation problems in the last section.

6.1 GENERAL CHARACTERISTICS

Data structures in a formatted data base are designed to meet the access requirements and if the access requirements change, the data structures need to be changed as well. However, Codd's relational model is free from such considerations, since the access paths there are universal – that is, any data item value, or any set of data item values, can be retrieved from one or more relations with equal ease. This freedom of access path is achieved firstly by expressing relations in what Codd defines as third normal form and secondly by using a powerful data retrieval language known as relational algebra. The basic operations on relations, such as those required to extract a data item value or to combine parts of two relations to form a third relation, are carried out by relational algebra. From this relational algebra, Codd developed a predicate calculus known as relational calculus, which he subsequently used to construct a data manipulation language named Data Sub-language (DSL) Alpha.

A basic feature of the relational model is its simplicity. A relation is a table of data and it may consist of only one row and one column, thus providing the simplest possible data structure which can be used as the common denominator of all data structures. It simplifies the design of the Schema since there is only one logical data structure – the relation – to consider, without having to worry about the construction of the right data structures to represent complex data relationships. Furthermore the relational model provides an unparalleled freedom to the application programmer by enabling him to access any data item value in the data base directly, the access mechanism being associative or content addressable since a data item is accessed directly by its value rather than by its relative position or by a pointer.

The concepts of the relational model are founded on mathematics, and all the terms used are mathematical. This has the effect of scaring off most people who would normally be interested in a data base.

In this chapter we shall keep the involvement with mathematics to a minimum. All concepts will be defined in non-mathematical terms in a simplified manner, sacrificing in the process some of the mathematical rigour which is really unnecessary for the understanding of the model. We shall also give the data-processing equivalent of the commonly used relational concepts.

6.2 BASIC CONCEPTS

As mentioned earlier, a relation is a mathematical term used to define a special kind of table. Each column is called a *domain* containing all the values of an attribute, and each row a *tuple*. The word tuple is taken from the description of groups, such as quin*tuple* and sex*tuple*. Thus a group of n elements is an *n-tuple*. In a relation of n domains, each tuple, that is, each row, is an n-tuple. The number of rows or tuples in a relation is its *cardinality*, and the number of columns is its *degree*. The individual elements in a relation are attribute values. If we consider an $m \times n$ relation (m rows and n columns), we have

> a relation of degree n and cardinality m, that is, a relation containing n domains and m tuples, each tuple being an n-tuple. There are $m \times n$ attribute values, each tuple having n columns or n attribute values.

A relation of degree 1 is called *unary,* degree 2 *binary,* degree 3 *ternary* and degree *n n-ary* relation. The characteristics of a relation are as follows.

(1) All entries in a domain are of the same kind.
(2) Domains are assigned distinct names called *attribute-names.*
(3) The ordering of the domains is immaterial.
(4) Each tuple is distinct, that is, duplicate tuples are not allowed.
(5) The ordering of the tuples is immaterial.

Attribute and Domain Names

A domain, unlike a tuple, can be duplicate. A domain name is the same for identical domains whereas attribute names can be distinct, one for each individual domain. Attribute names for identical domains are constructed from the common domain name by attaching suitable prefixes to it. Consider, for instance, a relation called COMPONENT containing two identical domains — one for the superior part number and the other for subordinate part number — both holding the same type of information, that is, part number codes. If we assume a common domain name, PART, then we can construct two attribute names, SUP-PART for the superior part numbers, and SUB-PART for the subordinate part numbers. Using QUANTITY as the attribute name for the third domain which contains the numbers of a subordinate part numbers present in its superior part number, we can represent the triplet as shown in figure 6.1.

COMPONENT	(SUP-PART	SUB-PART	QUANTITY)
	A180	C240	7
	C240	H100	3
	D450	C120	7
	E110	B153	10
	E120	E110	2

Figure 6.1 A relation of degree 3

From the mathematical point of view, a domain can be simple or nonsimple, a simple domain containing a single attribute and a nonsimple domain containing a repeating group or a multiple of attributes. Therefore the name of a simple domain can be identical with that of its attribute. A nonsimple domain can be broken down into simple domains, giving each a unique attribute name as we have done in the example above. However, in this book we shall assume all domains to be simple, and, wherever necessary, represent a nonsimple domain as a series of simple domains. Therefore no distinction will be made between domain name and attribute name except where otherwise indicated.

Keys and Attributes

A tuple is identified by its *key*, constructed from a combination of one or more attributes so that no attribute there is redundant (cf. a record key). A tuple can have more than one possible key, each of which can uniquely identify the tuple. All these possible keys are known as the *candidate keys*. One of these keys is arbitrarily selected to identify the tuple and this key is known as the *primary key*. For example, consider a tuple with the following attributes

Division Code, Dept Code, Dept Manager No.,
No. of employees

If we assume that every department has its own separate manager, then this tuple can be uniquely identified either by

Division Code + Dept Code,

or

Division Code + Dept Manager No.

These then are two candidate keys, one of which can be selected as the primary key. Since a key must not contain redundant attributes, the Dept Code and Dept Manager No. cannot appear in the same key, because the Dept Manager No. implicitly defines Dept Code.

If a tuple has attributes whose combination is the primary key in another relation, then this combination is called a *foreign key*. For instance Division Code can be a foreign key. An attribute that forms a part of a candidate key is a *prime attribute* of the tuple. The other attributes are *nonprime*. In the example given above, the Division Code, Dept Code and Dept Manager No. are prime attributes, and the No. of employees is a nonprime attribute.

Comparison with Standard Data-processing Concepts

In data-processing terms we may approximate a relation to the occurrences of a record type, a tuple to a record occurrence, and an attribute to a data item, a domain being the collection of all values for a single data item. Degree is the number of data items in the record and cardinality is the total number of records in the record type. A unary relation is a record type consisting of a single data item; a binary relation is a record type of two data items; and so on.

However, there are some differences between record types and relations in third normal form, a record type being equivalent to an unnormalised relation where repeating groups are permitted (see the next section). The ordering of the data items—that is, their relative positions—is fixed in a record type and cannot be altered, but the domains of a relation are independent of their relative positions since they are addressed individually by their attribute names. In a relation, the ordering of tuples is also unimportant because each of them is accessed directly, but this is not generally true for the records of a record type, unless they are specifically stored for direct retrieval. These access advantages follow directly from the content-addressable accessing concept used in relations as mentioned earlier. Finally by definition a relation cannot have a duplicate tuple, but there is no such conceptual restriction on the existence of a duplicate record in a record type. These discussions are summarised in figures 6.2a and b.

Relational Terms	Data-processing Terms
Relation	All the occurrences of a record type
Tuple	Record
Attribute	Data item
Domain	All the values of a data item
Degree	Number of data items in the record type
Cardinality	Total number of records in the record type

Figure 6.2 (a)
Equivalence of relational terms with data-processing concepts;

Item	Relation	Record Type
Repeating group	Not allowed in normalised relations	Allowed
Ordering of domains or data items	Immaterial	Important
Ordering of tuples or records	Immaterial	Important
Duplicate tuple or record	Not allowed	Immaterial

Figure 6.2 (b)
difference between relation and data-processing concepts

6.3 NORMALISATION

The real world with entities and their properties displays a multitude of entity relationships which can be expressed in the form of two-dimensional tables or relations. These relations will in general be unnormalised, that is, they may contain repeating groups whose presence creates serious access problems leading to reduction in data independence. A relation may also contain nonprime attributes with partial and indirect dependence on the candidate keys. If a candidate key consists of several attributes, a nonprime attribute can be dependent only on some of them, being independent of the others, thus showing partial dependence. Indirect or transitive dependence would occur if a nonprime attribute is not directly dependent on the candidate keys, but instead it is dependent on another nonprime attribute which is dependent on the candidate keys (see section 3.2.1.). Both partial and indirect dependence cause serious update problems, as we shall see later.

These undesirable associations are removed from a relation by *normalisation*[4] which can be defined as a step-by-step reversible process for transforming an unnormalised relation into relations of progressively simpler structures. Since the process is reversible, no information is lost during the transformation.

Codd has defined three stages of normalisation, known as the *first* (1NF), *second* (2NF) and *third* (3NF) *normal forms* corresponding to the three types of undesirable association discussed above, namely, the elimination of the repeating groups, partial dependence and indirect dependence. The levels of normalisation are shown in figure 6.3.

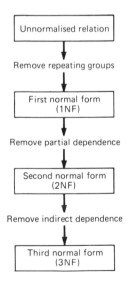

Figure 6.3 Three levels of normalisation

A relation in the first normal form is known as a *normalised relation*. We shall use the adjective 'fully normalised' for a relation in third normal form where, by definition, no repeating groups exist and every nonprime attribute shows full and direct dependence on the candidate keys. In a formatted data base the DBA has to use a number of different data structures, each being chosen to represent a specific type of entity relationships with necessary access paths. In the relational model, a relation in 3NF is always used, irrespective of the nature of the relationship and its access requirements.

6.3.1 First Normal Form

An unnormalised relation is transformed into 1NF by splitting the relation into two, one for the repeating groups and the other for the rest. Consider a relation CORD for customer orders containing attributes for Order number (O#), Customer number (C#), Customer name (CN), Item code (IC) for the items ordered by the customer, their Unit price (UP) and Quantity ordered (QO) as shown in figure 6.4. This is clearly an unnormalised relation, since it includes

CORD (O#	C#	CN	IC	UP	QO)
1	241	H. PRATT	A10	5	10
			C13	3	20
			P15	7	18
2	250	M. HALL	A10	5	15
			B16	12	2
			B20	8	1
			C13	3	5
3	241	H. PRATT	B16	12	11
			B21	2	15

Figure 6.4 An unnormalised relation with repeating group

the repeating groups of Item code, Unit price and Quantity ordered. This relation is transformed into first normal form by splitting it into two relations CUST (O# C# CN) and C2 (O# IC UP QO) as shown in figure 6.5.

In first normal form, the repeating group is separated to form relation C2 whose sole candidate key is (O# + IC). Relation CUST has also a single candidate key, namely O#. Note that the relation CUST can be broken down into two

CUST (O#	C#	CN)
1	241	H. PRATT
2	250	M. HALL
3	241	H. PRATT

C2 (O#	IC	UP	QO)
1	A10	5	10
1	C13	3	20
1	P15	7	18
2	A10	5	15
2	B16	12	2
2	B20	8	1
2	C13	3	5
3	B16	12	11
3	B21	2	15

Figure 6.5 Relations in 1NF; the unnormalised relation of figure 6.4 is split into two relations

other relations to remove the redundancy generated by the presence of both customer name and customer number. The process of normalisation does not deal with such redundancies; these are dealt with separately (see section 6.5.1).

The problem created by the presence of a repeating group in a relation can be demonstrated by writing down relation CORD (O# C# CN IC UP QO) in its expanded form, including the repeating group as CORD (O# C# CN IC UP QO) IC UP QO IC UP QO . . .). Its tuples have variable length, and the ordering of the domains is no longer independent, since the domains of a group are associated with one another more closely than with those of the other groups. Access can only be made by searching the tuple and identifying the repeating group needed by some means. This destroys the whole basis of relational algebra, which is designed to access an individual domain directly (see later) to provide data independence. Furthermore the subsequent evolution of the data base may force the separation of the repeating group into a separate relation. This will require changes in the old application program specifically designed to handle repeating groups. All these problems are avoided by a surgical operation on relations at birth, that is, by converting them into first normal form.

6.3.2 Second Normal Form

The second normal form is formally defined in terms of what is called *functional dependence*. Given a relation R, domain B of R is functionally dependent on domain A of R if and only if each value of B has associated with it *at least* one value in A. For instance, consider a relation R with three domains, Employee number, Employee name, and Department as follows.

R(E#	EN	DT)
12	W. COX	A17
14	A. BAKER	A17
15	D. EDAM	B20
16	J. YUKAWA	C20
18	K. FORD	C20

A17 is a value in domain Department (DT), which is associated with two values in domain Employee name (EN), namely W. Cox and A. Baker. The value C20 of domain DT also has two associated values in domain EN, while the value B20 has only one associated value in domain EN. Similarly to each value of domain DT there is at least one value in domain Employee number (E#) (assuming that we would not introduce a department into this relation unless it has at least one employee in it). Therefore domain DT is functionally dependent on both EN and E separately, but they are not functionally dependent on domain DT. Note that there is a one-to-one correspondence between the values of domains E# and EN, or in other words to each value of domain E# there is at least one value in domain EN and vice versa, and therefore these two domains are functionally dependent on each other. The statement that B is functionally dependent on A means that A identifies B, that is, if a value of A is known, the value of B can be found, or in other words A can act as the key for B.

A domain or a collection of domains B of relation R is fully functionally dependent on a domain or a collection of domains A of R, if B is functionally dependent on *all* the domains of A, but not on any subset of A. Domain DT in our example above is not fully functionally dependent on the collection of domain (E# + EN) as DT is functionally dependent on either individually, but domain QO of relation C2 in figure 6.5 is fully functionally dependent on the collection of domains (O# + IC). Domain UP of relation C2 is functionally dependent on domain IC (two items can have the same unit price, but one item cannot have two unit prices), but not on the candidate key (O# + IC). The unit price is independent of the order number and is therefore only partially dependent on the key (O# + IC).

A normalised relation is said to be in the second normal form if all its non-prime attributes are fully functionally dependent on each candidate key, in other words, if the nonprime attributes do not show any partial dependence on the candidate keys. It follows from this definition that relation C2 of figure 6.5 is not in 2NF as one of its nonprime attribute UP is not fully functionally dependent on the candidate key (O# + IC). Note that relation CUST of figure

6.5 is in 2NF since its nonprime attributes are fully dependent on the candidate key O#; in fact it is in 3NF, as we shall see later.

The partial dependence of nonprime attributes on candidate keys causes the following update anomalies.

(1) Insertion: if we wish to introduce a new item in relation C2 with specific unit price, we cannot do so unless a customer places an order, since we need an order number; we are thus prevented from storing data about a new item.

(2) Deletion: if the data about a customer order are deleted, the information (price in this case) about the item is also deleted. If this happens to the last order for that item, the information about that item will be lost from the data base.

(3) Amendment: since the information about an item appears as many times as there are orders for it, amendment on the data of the item would be very difficult, since it will be necessary to search through every tuple of the relation.

These problems are avoided by eliminating the partial dependence in favour of full dependence by splitting a normalised relation into two others as shown in figure 6.6.

CUST (O#	C#	CN)
1	241	H. PRATT
2	250	M. HALL
3	241	H. PRATT

ORD (O#	IC	QO)	PRICE (IC	UP)
1	A10	10	A10	5
1	C13	20	C13	3
1	P15	18	P15	7
2	A10	15	B16	12
2	B16	2	B20	8
2	B20	1	B21	2
2	C13	5		
3	B16	11		
3	B21	15		

Figure 6.6 The normalised relations of figure 6.5 in 2NF:
the partial dependence of unit price (UP) on the key
(O# + IC) is now removed

6.3.3 Third Normal Form

A normalised relation is said to be in third normal form if all its nonprime attributes are fully functionally and directly dependent on each candidate key. In other words, if a relation is in 2NF and if, in addition, all its nonprime attributes are directly dependent (see section 3.2.1) on each candidate key, then this relation is in 3NF. The three relations of figure 6.6 do not show any transitive dependence on the candidate keys and therefore all of them are in 3NF.

STOCK (B#	P#	QB	LT	RL)
210	30	5	10	5
211	30	10	10	5
225	50	7	7	6
231	81	3	15	10
232	81	12	15	10

Figure 6.7 A relation showing
transitive dependence on lead time (LT)
and reorder level (RL) on the bin number
(B#) through the part number (P#)

To demonstrate transitive dependence, let us consider a relation STOCK (figure 6.7) containing Bin number, Part number, Quantity in the bin, Lead time and Reorder level, abbreviated as B#, P#, QB, LT and RL respectively. We assume that one or more bins represented by their bin numbers are needed to hold the parts of a part number and that a bin may not hold parts belonging to more than one part number. If B# is the candidate key then this relation is not in 3NF, since the nonprime attributes LT and RL are not directly dependent on B#. They are dependent on P#, which is dependent on B#.

The quantity QB in the bin is of course directly dependent on B#. There is no repeating group in the relation and the nonprime attributes do not show any partial dependence on the key B# and therefore this relation is in 2NF. We convert this into third normal form by splitting as shown in figure 6.8.

Transitive dependence causes update problems similar to those caused by partial dependence listed earlier. Therefore all relations must be expressed in 3NF. An *optimal* third (or second or first for that matter) normal form is defined as the minimum number of relations that can express the original unnormalised relation.

As a final example of normalisation we shall extend the relation CORD of figure 6.4 by adding two new domains, Branch number (B#) and the Location area of the branch (LC). We assume that each branch is capable of supplying all items and that there can be more than one branch in the same location

STOCK1 (B#	P#	QB)
210	30	5
211	30	10
225	50	7
231	81	3
232	81	12

STOCK2 (P#	LT	RL)
30	10	5
50	7	6
81	15	10

Figure 6.8 The relations of figure 6.7 in 3NF,
the indirect dependence being removed

area. Customer orders are processed at the head office and the branches are asked to supply items depending on convenience, stock position and so on. In other words, the choice of a branch is dependent on the order for an item code, O# + IC (candidate key), but independent of the item code alone.

The new relation COR (O# C# CN IC UP QO B# LC) is shown in figure 6.9. It is unnormalised, since it contains the repeating group (IC + UP + QO). Its normalised version is shown in figure 6.10 where it is divided into two relations, CUSTOMER and COR1. Relation CUSTOMER does not show any partial or transitive dependence of nonprime attributes and hence is in 3NF. However, in relation COR1 the nonprime attribute UP is only partially dependent on the candidate key (O# + IC). This is removed in figure 6.11 by splitting it into two

COR (O#	C#	CN	IC	UP	QO	B#	LC)
1	241	H. PRATT	A10	5	10	15	LUTON
			C13	3	20	12	YORK
			P15	7	18	30	LONDON
2	250	M. HALL	A10	5	15	15	LUTON
			B16	12	2	25	LONDON
			B20	8	1	25	LONDON
			C13	3	5	12	YORK
3	241	H. PRATT	B16	12	11	15	LUTON
			B21	2	15	30	LONDON

Figure 6.9 An unnormalised relation

CUSTOMER (O#   C#   CN)

1	241	H. PRATT
2	250	M. HALL
3	241	H. PRATT

COR1 (O#   IC   UP   QO   B#   LC)

O#	IC	UP	QO	B#	LC
1	A10	5	10	15	LUTON
1	C13	3	20	12	YORK
1	P15	7	18	30	LONDON
2	A10	5	15	15	LUTON
2	B16	12	2	25	LONDON
2	B20	8	1	25	LONDON
2	C13	3	5	12	YORK
3	B16	12	11	15	LUTON
3	B21	2	15	30	LONDON

Figure 6.10 Normalised form of the relation in figure 6.9

relations, PRICE and COR2. Relation PRICE is in 3NF, since it does not display any transitive dependence on nonprime attributes, but relation COR2 is not. Its nonprime attribute LC is not directly dependent on the candidate key O#; LC is dependent on B#, which is dependent on O#. This dependence is eliminated in figure 6.12, thus generating four relations in 3NF from a single unnormalised relation.

The relations we have so far considered have only a single candidate key. To show the effect of a second candidate key we add a new domain, Part name (PN), to the relation STOCK2 of figure 6.8, assuming that there is one-to-one correspondence between PN and P#. In this new relation, STOCK2 (P# PN LT RL), the nonprime attributes LT and RL are directly dependent on both the candidate keys P# and PN separately. There is no partial dependence nor is there any repeating group and hence this relation is in 3NF.

In discussing the problems of the repeating groups earlier, we mentioned that they destroy the ordering independence of the domains in the group. We may restate the problem as the destruction of the mutual independence of the domains, since the domains in the $(n + 1)$th occurrence of a repeating group would not exist unless there were an nth occurrence. The transitive dependence also occurs owing to mutual dependence of the nonprime attributes. Taking these together we may define a relation in 3NF as a relation where each of the nonprime attributes is fully dependent on every candidate key, but they themselves are mutually independent.

CUSTOMER (O#	C#	CN)
1	241	H. PRATT
2	250	M. HALL
3	241	H. PRATT

COR2 (O#	IC	QO	B	LC)
1	A10	10	15	LUTON
1	C13	20	12	YORK
1	P15	18	30	LONDON
2	A10	15	15	LUTON
2	B16	2	25	LONDON
2	B20	1	25	LONDON
2	C13	5	12	YORK
3	B16	11	15	LUTON
3	B21	15	30	LONDON

PRICE (IC	UP)
A10	5
C13	3
P15	7
B16	12
B20	8
B21	2

Figure 6.11 The relation of figure 6.9 in 2NF

A relation in 3NF does not necessarily guarantee protection from update anomalies mentioned earlier. Consider for instance the data of a consultancy company which keeps a number of experts to advise clients on subjects such as insurance, investment and taxation. We assume that there can be more than one expert on the same subject, but the same expert cannot deal with more than one subject. Moreover a client receives advice on one subject from only one expert, although he may receive advice on another subject from another expert. Their data are shown in relation ADVICE containing Client name (CN), Subject name (SN) and Expert name (EN) as shown below.

ADVICE (CN	SN	EN)
A. JAMES	INSURANCE	F. PHELAN
A. JAMES	TAXATION	G. HOLT

L. HARRIS	INSURANCE	Z. ACKER
R. MARX	INVESTMENT	P. BRAGG
R. MARX	TAXATION	G. HOLT

The candidate key of this relation is (CN + SN), since both are necessary to identify EN uniquely. (Because there is only one unique expert who advises a particular client on a particular subject, the expert is identified if the client and the subject are known.) This relation is in 3NF; nevertheless, the data on Z. Acker as an insurance expert will be lost from the data base in the event of an update brought about by the cessation of L. Harris as a client. The problem arises because EN is fully functionally dependent on (CN + SN), while SN is functionally dependent

CUSTOMER (O#	C#	CN)
1	241	H. PRATT
2	250	M. HALL
3	241	H. PRATT

ORDER (O#	IC	QO	B#)
1	A10	10	15
1	C13	20	12
1	P15	18	30
2	A10	15	15
2	B16	2	25
2	B20	1	25
2	C13	5	12
3	B16	11	15
3	B21	15	30

BRANCH (B#	LC)
12	YORK
15	LUTON
25	LONDON
30	LONDON

PRICE (IC	UP)
A10	5
C13	3
P15	7
B16	12
B20	8
B21	2

Figure 6.12 The unnormalised relation COR of figure 6.9 in 3NF

on EN. The update anomaly is eliminated by splitting the relation ADVICE into two other relations in 3NF as follows.

AD1(	CN	EN)
	A. JAMES	F. PHELAN
	A. JAMES	G. HOLT
	L. HARRIS	Z. ACKER
	R. MARX	P. BRAGG
	R. MARX	G. HOLT

AD2 (	SN	EN)
	INSURANCE	F. PHELAN
	INSURANCE	Z. ACKER
	INVESTMENT	P. BRAGG
	TAXATION	G. HOLT

This shows that the presentation of a relation in 3NF is not enough. Perhaps the definition of third normal form should be improved to exclude the possibility of such update anomalies. Note that in relation AD1 there is no nonprime attribute; (CN + EN) is the key. In relation AD2, the key is EN.

6.3.4. Data Representation

Relations can be used to represent data showing all types of relationships. The relations of figure 6.12 can be used to show an $1:N$ relationship with three levels of hierarchy as shown in figure 6.13.

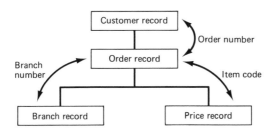

Figure 6.13

The records (tuples) in the hierarchy are related by keys such as order numbers, branch numbers and item codes, rather than pointers. No distinction is made between tree, net or cyclic net structures; the user is free to use any relation as the owner or member as necessary during processing. This relieves the data structures from the entangled web of pointers and saves the DBA much pain.

The proliferation of foreign keys required to sustain the relationships, does not necessarily lead to data redundancy, since the physical representation of relations can be different.

The network relationship between four students and three courses of section 3.2.3 can easily be represented by three relations STD, CRS, and SCL, corresponding to student, course and link records of figure 3.12. We assume that the student records contain students number (S#), student name (SN), and age (AGE), and the course records contain course number (C#), course name (CN), the university year in which the course is given (YR) and the maximum number of students that can take the course (MX). Relation SCL, linking students and courses, includes an attribute MK for the examination marks obtained by a student in that course (figure 6.14).

STD (S#	SN	AGE)
S1	A. ADAMS	21
S2	P. WARD	25
S3	T. REMUS	20
S4	G. BENN	22

CRS (C#	CN	YR	MX)
C1	COMPUTER SCIENCE	1	25
C2	MATHEMATICS	2	20
C3	ACCOUNTANCY	1	30

SCL (S#	C#	MK)
S1	C1	50
S1	C3	65
S2	C1	40
S2	C2	70
S2	C3	48
S3	C1	82
S3	C2	51
S4	C1	67
S4	C3	77

Figure 6.14 The M:N relationship of students and courses
of section 3.2.2 is represented by three relations

The loop structure discussed in section 5.2.4 can also be easily represented. In fact we do not need a relation for the link records there (see figure 5.7); only two relations, one for the part number records and the other for the relationship records, are required since we can access one from the other through the domain of the part number keys.

We shall close this section by listing the advantages of expressing a relation in third normal form.

(1) It simplifies the tabular structure and provides easy means for the representation of data relationships.

(2) It increases data access capability and hence reduces the need for restructuring the relations, thereby enhancing data independence.

(3) It frees relations from the undesirable update problems arising out of insertion, deletion and amendment.

6.4 DATA MANIPULATION

Relational algebra provides the basic means of data retrieval and update in a relational data base. It is based on the standard operations of the set theory, and can be used to construct a procedural data manipulation language as has been done in some pre-Codd relational models. However, Codd took a different approach.[5] From relational algebra he developed a predicate calculus called relational calculus and he used this as the basis for a relatively non-procedural language called Data Sub-language (DSL) Alpha. Alpha is easier to use, and yet it retains all the manipulative powers of relational algebra. This is the prime advantage of DSL Alpha over the algebraic languages. However, is not suggested that DSL Alpha should be the only DML; we can, and indeed we may, construct other data manipulation languages based on either relational algebra or relational calculus.

This section is devoted to the discussion of relational algebra, relational calculus and DSL Alpha. As we shall see, their retrieval power is virtually unlimited, but it is necessary to emphasise that all three operate on relations in 3NF, which are logical data structures; they do not specify how actual data from a physical data base are to be extracted to construct the required relations. This is an implementation problem that we shall discuss briefly in the next section.

6.4.1 Relational Algebra

Relational algebra operates on one or more relations and produces a new relation as the result. The operations are expressed in a system of notation and they can be used to retrieve information from one or more relations or to update a tuple of a relation. We shall describe here six operations of which the first three--*union, intersection* and *difference*— are traditional set operations; the other three— *projection, join* and *division*—are less common.

Union

The union of set A with set B, denoted as A ∪ B, is the set of all objects without repetition. This can be used to insert a new tuple to a relation, for example,

$$\text{CRS} \cup \{\text{"C4" "PHYSICS" 3 20}\}$$

will insert the tuple{ C4 PHYSICS 3 20} to relation CRS in figure 6.14. In these examples alphanumeric values are represented within double inverted commas.

Intersection

The intersection of set A with set B, denoted as A ∩ B, is the set of all objects belonging to both A and B. This can be used to find a duplicate tuple between two relations.

Difference

The difference of set B from set A, denoted as A − B, is the set of all objects belonging to A but not to B. This can be applied to delete a tuple; for instance

$$\text{CRS} - \{\text{"C3" "ACCOUNTANCY" 1 30}\}$$

To amend a tuple, we must first delete it with a difference operation and then insert the amended tuple by a union operation.

Projection

Projection is the selection of one or more named domains from a relation in a specified order, followed by the elimination of duplicate tuples from the resulting relation. (In fact in all operations used in relational algebra, duplicate tuples are removed since they are not allowed in a relation.) We shall use the notation R[A B C] to denote the projection of domains A, B and C in that order from relation R. Some examples are given below from the relations of figures 6.12 and 6.14.

CUSTOMER[C#	CN]	STD[S#]	CRS[YR	CN	MX]
241	H. PRATT	S1	1	COMPUTER	25
250	M. HALL	S2		SCIENCE	
		S3	2	MATHEMATICS	20
		S4	1	ACCOUNTANCY	30

Join

A join is the combination of two relations with a common domain. The join of relation A with relation B, denoted as A*B, produces a relation R that consists of all the possible tuples obtained by concatenating each tuple of A with all tuples of B that have the same value under the common domain. A tuple of an original relation is excluded from the resultant relation if its value under the common domain is not shared by a tuple of the other relation. The resultant relation contains all the domains of both the original relations, the common domain appearing only once. Consider two relations A(DOCTOR PATIENT) and B(PATIENT DRUG) as given below.

A(DOCTOR	PATIENT)	B(PATIENT	DRUG)
FARID	EINSTEIN	EINSTEIN	A17
KELVIN	NEWTON	EINSTEIN	A18
MAXWELL	EINSTEIN	FERMI	S13
DALTON	FERMI	LEIBNITZ	K25

Their join R = A*B is

R(DOCTOR	PATIENT	DRUG)
FARID	EINSTEIN	A17
FARID	EINSTEIN	B18
MAXWELL	EINSTEIN	A17
MAXWELL	EINSTEIN	B18
DALTON	FERMI	S13

The join R of relations STD and SCL of figure 6.14 is

R(S#	SN	AGE	C#	MK)
S1	A. ADAMS	21	C1	50
S1	A. ADAMS	21	C3	65
S2	P. WARD	25	C1	40
S2	P. WARD	25	C2	70
S2	P. WARD	25	C3	48
S3	T. REMUS	20	C1	82
S3	T. REMUS	20	C2	51
S4	G. BENN	22	C1	67
S4	G. BENN	22	C3	77

For operational convenience, in all subsequent join operations, we shall assume th common domain to be the rightmost domain of the first relation and the leftmost domain of the second relation; this can be ensured if necessary by a suitable projection operation. Join in conjunction with the projection operation provides a very useful tool for the manipulation of relations. This is shown in the following examples.

(1)   Extract the tuple containing information on P. WARD from relation STD
       of figure 6.14

$$STD \; [S\# \; AGE \; SN] * \{\text{“P. WARD”}\}$$

its result is

$$S2 \quad 25 \quad P. \, WARD$$

We have taken the projection of relation STD following the convention
proposed above. The brackets{ } are used to enclose constants, that is, the
values of a tuple, the alphanumeric entries being shown within double
inverted commas. Since we are interested in alphanumeric value P. WARD,
we have used it as the common domain in the form of a unary relation with
a single tuple, that is, a constant.

(2)   Find the name of the student who scored 82 in his course examination

$$((STD[SN \quad S\#]) * (SCL * \{82\} \,)) \, [SN]$$

Its result is T. REMUS. The brackets ( ) are used to specify the priorities
of operation.

Division

We may divide a binary relation by a unary relation if the domain of the unary
relation is also a domain of the binary relation. The result of such a division is a
unary relation containing the uncommon domain of the binary relation. An
attribute value of the uncommon domain of the binary relation is selected for
the resultant relation, if its associated entries in the common domain contain all
the values of the divisor domain. Consider a binary relation DT and three unary
relations DI, DJ and DK as given below.

DT(S#	C#)	DI(C#)	DJ(C#)	DK(C#)
S1	C1	C1	C1	C1
S1	C2		C2	C2
S1	C3			C3
S1	C4			
S2	C1			
S2	C3			
S2	C4			
S3	C1			
S3	C2			

Denoting division by / (slash) and the resultant relation by R, we have

DT/DI = R(S#)	DT/DJ = R(S#)	DT/DK = R(S#)
S1	S1	S1
S2	S3	
S3		

For operational convenience in division, as in join, we shall assume the rightmost (that is, the second) domain of the dividend as the common domain. All algebraic operations will be evaluated from right to left giving precedent to the projection operation over join and division, the priority over projection being indicated by ordinary brackets ( ). Using these conventions, we shall now show some examples of data retrieval from the relations of figure 6.14.

(1)   Find the name of the student who took all the courses

(STD[SN   S#] * SCL[S#   C#]/CRS[C#])[SN]

The result is P. WARD.

(2)   Find the names of the students who took course C1

(STD[SN   S#] * SCL[S#   C#]/ {"C1"})[SN]

The result is

A. ADAMS
P. WARD
T. REMUS
G. BENN

(3)   Find the names of the students who took computer science

(STD[SN   S#] * SCL[S#   C#]/CRS[C#   CN]/ {"COMPUTER SCIENCE" })[SN]

The result is the same as in (2) above. We can perform this manipulation by a join operation instead of a division as shown below

(STD[SN   S#] * SCL[S#   C#] * CRS[C#   CN] * {"COMPUTER SCIENCE"})[SN]

A number of other operations such as composition and restriction is defined by Codd, but those given above are sufficient for data manipulation.

Relational algebra can be used for a procedural language as suggested earlier. It is extremely powerful and is device independent, since the queries are based on the values of the data items rather than their positions. However, the construction of an algebraic expression for a query is very tedious, even though the technique can quickly be learnt. In addition, the nature of a query is not obvious from the algebraic expression unless it is patiently worked out. These tend to increase the chances of errors in the queries. Relational calculus is designed to improve this situation.

6.4.2 Relational Calculus

In relational algebra the user specifies the detailed procedures for extracting information, whereas in relational calculus the user defines what he wants, leaving the system to work out the procedure required. The expression of a relational calculus has two parts, a target list which consists of a list of the wanted elements separated by commas, and a logical expression, called a predicate or qualification, which defines the wanted elements in terms of the relations from which they are to be extracted. It is written in the form

Target list : Predicate

to be interpreted as: extract the elements in the target list such that (or where) the predicate is true.

A wanted element in the target list can consist of all the values of a domain in a relation or a single value of a domain corresponding to a tuple, or alternatively all the values of a relation or a tuple. These four types of element are specified in the following four ways.

$$\left.\begin{array}{l}\text{Relation name}\cdot\text{attribute name}\\\text{Tuple variable}\cdot\text{attribute name}\\\text{Relation name}\\\text{Tuple variable}\end{array}\right\}\text{for all values}$$

The following notations are used in constructing a predicate.

∃	There exists
∀	For all
∧	Logical AND
∨	Logical OR
¬	Logical NOT
$=\neq<>\leqslant\geqslant$	Standard comparison symbols

We shall now construct relational calculus expressions for some queries including those expressed earlier in relational algebra.

(1) Extract the tuple containing information on P. WARD (from the relations on figure 6.14).

$$\text{STD} : \text{STD.SN} = \left\{\text{“P. WARD”}\right\}$$

to be read as: extract all the domains of relation STD where the value of the domain student name of relation STD is equal to P. WARD.

(2) Find the name of the student who scored 82 in his course examination.

$$\text{STD.SN} : \exists\, \text{SCL}(\text{SCL.S\#} = \text{STD.S\#} \wedge \text{SCL.MK} = 82)$$

to be read as: extract the domain SN of relation STD such that there exists a relation SCL that has a common domain S# with relation STD and has a domain MK with a value 82.

(3) Find the names of the students who took the course COMPUTER SCIENCE.

$$\text{STD.SN} : \exists\, \text{SCL}\, \exists\, \text{CRS}(\text{SCL.S\#} = \text{STD.S\#} \wedge \text{SCL.C\#} = \text{CRS.C\#}$$
$$\wedge \text{CRS.CN} = \left\{\text{“COMPUTER SCIENCE”}\right\})$$

(4)   Find the names of the students who took all the courses.

$$STD.SN : \forall CRS \exists SCL(CRS.C\# = SCL.C\# \wedge SCL.S\# = STD.S\#)$$

Note that for all relations that are not specified in the target list, the notation $\exists$ (there exist) or $\forall$(for all) appears in the predicate. Each of these relations must be linked to a target relation directly through a common domain or, in the absence of a common domain, indirectly through the common domains of a sequence of other relations, thus providing a path to the target relation. Each such link constitutes a condition in the predicate and is expressed by an equality sign between the two specified common domains. In addition, other conditions specifying the characteristics of some domains or tuples of the relations can also be included in the predicate as required. All conditions in the predicate are joined by logical $\wedge$, $\wedge$ or $\neg$(AND, OR or NOT) symbols, thus making it a logical expression whose value can be either true or false.

6.4.3 Data Sub-language Alpha

The proposed DSL Alpha, as noted earlier, is directly based on relational calculus. The language and its syntax are still in an expository stage to be adjusted to suit the specific host language requirements.

A central concept in DSL Alpha is a workspace defined as a buffer area interfacing the data base with the application program. There are important differences between a workspace and a User Working Area (UWA) of the Codasyl model. An application program can own a number of workspaces, but only one UWA. In addition, a workspace can be established almost anywhere – in the computer memory, on discs, or even at a remote terminal. DSL Alpha transmits data between the data base and a workspace, treating the workspace as a relation.

As a relation, a workspace can be used as an operand, like any other relation in the data base, to construct new relations. Data in a workspace is accessible by the host language statements of an application program.

DSL Alpha, like relational calculus, operates on a relation at a time, but data transmission between the data base and a workspace (either way) can be effected in two modes as follows.

(1)   Piped mode: control is returned to the user after each tuple is transmitted.
(2)   Non-piped mode: control is returned only when the whole relation is transmitted.

Alpha Commands

An Alpha command has the following structure

       Command   Workspacename   (Target list):   Predicate

The workspace is a user-defined data name. The target list and the predicates are formed in exactly the same way as in relational calculus, except that a few additional facilities can be included in the form of qualifiers on predicates or library functions (see later). The following commands have been proposed.

GET : Construct the defined relation in a workspace from the data base.

PUT : Insert tuples into the data base from the workspace.

DELETE : Delete all the tuples of a relation from the data base, but retain its entry in the data base directory.

DROP : Drop all information about this relation from the data base including its entry in the directory.

UPDATE : Modify a relation or a tuple of the data base to reflect the changes already made in the workspace.

HOLD : Warning to the system for concurrent users that a relation or a tuple will be modified.

RELEASE : Cancellation of HOLD.

OPEN : Transmit tuples rather than relations (initiates a piped mode).

CLOSE : Close transmission of tuples (terminates a piped mode).

Use of DSL Alpha

Let us consider a few examples of the use of DSL Alpha using a workspace WS.

(1)   Retrieve relation STD (figure 6.14) from the data base to the workspace.

GET WS (STD)

The result would be all the domains of relation STD as in figure 6.14, but if the user wishes to reorder the domains, or to extract only some of the domains, he may for instance specify

GET WS (STD.SN, STD.S#)

which will retrieve only the domains SN and S# in that order.

(2)   To extract the information from the data base in accordance with the queries (1) to (4) of relational calculus discussed earlier, just add GET WS before those expressions and enclose the target list in brackets ( ).

A relation already retrieved can be amended by using HOLD and UPDATE command, for example

HOLD WS (STD.AGE) : STD.SN = {"G. BENN"}

Add, say, 2 to AGE by a host language statement, and then

UPDATE WS

Qualifiers on Predicate

Information can be extracted in ascending or descending order of selected attribute values by specifying an UP or DOWN qualifier in the predicate, for example: Get the names of the students who got more than 45 marks in course C1 in ascending order of their age

$$\text{GET WS(STD.SN)} : \exists \text{SCL(SCL.S\#} = \text{STD.S\#} \wedge$$
$$\text{SCL.C\#} = \{\text{``C1''}\} \wedge \text{SCL.MK} > 45) \text{ UP STD.AGE}$$

Library Functions

The following library functions are proposed for DSL Alpha.

COUNT	To count the number of non-redundant tuples of an attribute.
TOTAL	To sum the values of an attribute.
MAX } MIN }	To find the maximum or minimum value of an attribute.
AVERAGE	To find the average of the values of an attribute.
TOP (N,A) } BOTTOM (N,A) }	Logical variable set up to indicate whether a specific value of an attribute A is the Nth largest or Nth smallest.

A few examples follow.

(1) Find the number of students in relation STD

$$\text{GET WS(COUNT(STD.S\#))}$$

(2) Find the total marks obtained from relation SCL

$$\text{GET WS(TOTAL(SCL.MK))}$$

DSL Alpha is undoubtedly a very powerful language, but it is unlikely that a user would ever need all its facilities. The language is non-procedural compared with the Codasyl DML, mainly to the extent that it permits retrieval of a whole relation in a non-piped mode, whereas the Codasyl DML allows only one record at a time. In retrieval capacity, it retains all the power and flexibility of relational algebra,[6] but provides greater ease in writing and understanding. Compared with other data manipulation languages, DSL Alpha commands are certainly complex, but then DSL Alpha provides greater facility in data retrieval, the degree of complexity in the command being directly dependent on the complexity of the retrieval request. With a little practice, most programmers should be able to master this language and enjoy its basic simplicity and power.

DSL Alpha as conceived is entirely independent of storage structures and access paths. It does not incorporate any facility for privacy or concurrency controls. However, it is assumed that locks can easily be implemented on relations or domains with great effectiveness.

6.5 FACILITIES AND PROSPECT

In this section we shall discuss the user facilities that a relational data base is supposed to provide, and its implementation problems and future prospects.

6.5.1 Data Consistency

As mentioned at the beginning of this chapter, the preservation of data consistency was a chief motivating force behind Codd's proposal for the relational model. He has defined data redundancy in the relational context and suggested certain checks to prevent data inconsistency.[3]

According to Codd there are two classes of redundancy – strong and weak. A group of relations is strongly redundant if it contains at least one relation with a projection that can be derived from other projections in the group. Consider for instance a relation for customer account called CACT containing customer account number (A#), customer name (CN) and his outstanding balance (BL) as shown below.

CACT(A#	CN	BL)
A1	H. PRATT	2340
A2	M. HALL	400

If this relation is stored in the data base which also contains relation CUSTOMEF of figure 6.12, then these two relations together would constitute a strongly redundant group since CACT[CN] = CUSTOMER[CN].

Strong redundancies can be detected and the redundant domains can be subsequently removed, but the elimination of all strong redundancies from a data base may not always be desirable, since the removal of such redundancies from an old semiobsolete relation can involve change of an old application program which uses the now redundant domains of the old relation (see also the next subsection).

A group of relations is weakly redundant if it contains a relation which has a projection that is identical with a projection of some joins of other projections of relations in the group. Weak redundancies, if they exist, are inherent in the data and cannot be removed.

To ensure data consistencies arising out of redundancies, Codd has proposed certain checks which the system can invoke as necessary, but to be effective, such checks have to be performed after every insertion, amendment and deletion, which can be time consuming.

6.5.2 Data Independence

Data independence is regarded as the chief attraction of the relational model. In a formatted data base, the access paths supported are totally dependent on the design of the relevant data structures, whereas in a relational data base the access is free from any such considerations. All relations are expressed in 3NF, and any domain or tuple there can be accessed irrespective of their ordering in the relation.

Furthermore, relations can be combined if necessary, thus facilitating search involving more than one relation.

In the relational model no specific proposal has been made to support Sub-schemas. The description of the data base in 3NF would constitute a Schema. A Subschema can be designed to contain a subset of relations, including new relations made up of Schema relations. The following reasons show the need for Subschemas in the relational model.

(1)   In the event of the restructuring of a data base, an old relation can become obsolete, thus invalidating the old application programs which must be protected against such changes. The protection can be provided in some cases by admitting strong redundancies in the data base, but the proliferation of strong redundancies can easily make a data base cumbersome and inefficient. The problem can be solved by introducing Subschemas which will maintain an invariant set of relations irrespective of the changes in the Schema.

(2)   In a relational data base, an application programmer has unlimited freedom in searching through the whole data base for a specified data item value. However, in practice this freedom has to be controlled by the DBA to avoid excessive processing costs, since it is easy for an application programmer to design a complex predicate which would require the scanning of the entire data base several times over to produce a result. Subschemas can be used to impose restrictions in such freedom when necessary by constraining search only to the part of the data base included in the Subschema.

6.5.3 Other Facilities

Simplicity

The concept of relation provides a means of representing all types of data relationships using simple tables. Each relation is self-contained without needing any pointers to show its relationships to other relations. This removes a great load from the DBA who, in a formatted system, is faced not only with the heavy task of constructing the right datasets, but also with the linkages of the records in the datasets stipulating access paths.

Flexibility and Restructuring

Relations provide multiple access paths through foreign keys. If necessary, additional access paths can be provided subsequently through new relations containing the keys of the old relations as foreign keys. The updating of data in a relation is quite simple, as shown in some of the examples in section 6.4.1. Relations can be combined or broken down into other relations with great ease — this reduces the problems encountered by the DBA in restructuring.

Data Manipulation

We have already discussed the advantages of the proposed DSL Alpha for data manipulation.

Optimisation, Concurrency and Protection

No specific proposal has been made for performance optimisation, concurrent usage facilities and data protection. Codd recognises them as important issues needing further investigation.[7] The relations provide good facilities for enforcing privacy controls, since the sensitive domains can be grouped together into relations with privacy locks, which allows application of very selective privacy controls. Apart from the problems of data consistency discussed earlier, no other suggestions have been made for integrity control. The implementors are expected to provide backup and recovery facilities. Difficulties can be expected in the implementation of the concurrent usage facilities if tuple level locks are envisaged.

6.5.4 Implementation

Some pre-Codd relational data bases have been implemented.[2] They are more or less experimental and simplistic, and are incapable of meeting the needs of a large commercial organisation. Some of these data bases use only binary relations, while none of them employs relations in 3NF. However, the retrieval language used is similar to those (that is, algebra, calculus and DSL Alpha) proposed by Codd.

Codd's relational model is elegant and user orientated, but the facilities proposed can only be materialised by solving a series of complex implementation problems. Apart from the concurrency problems mentioned earlier, there is also a need for the optimisation of physical data organisation and the implementation of the algebraic commands. Since each attribute is accessed directly by value, the overall performance would be critically dependent on physical data organisation on the storage devices. It is essential to consider all possible file structures along with pointer organisations discussed in chapter 2. Facilities need to be built in to select data where possible from index tables as in inverted files, without having to retrieve all the relations in the predicate from the data base. This will improve retrieval efficiency considerably. The advent of cheap associative memory and magnetic bubble memory is likely to be helpful.

Data manipulation commands in the relational model are expressed directly or indirectly as a series of algebraic operations on relations. Given a command, the execution speed is very sensitive to the order in which the algebraic operations are performed. For instance, projection before join is faster than join before projection. In joins involving three relations, it is faster if the smaller two are joined first. The detail is complex and depends on many factors requiring investigation. There is also a case for batching complex requests involving common algebraic operations wherever possible. Because the cost of a complex query can be very high, especially if it requires scanning many relations, there should be some means of warning the user by indicating an estimated cost, and providing an alternative facility to batch the request, should the user wish it.

At the present state of hardware development, the implementation of the relational model with all its facilities is likely to result in an unacceptable running cost. Some 90 per cent of users do not need a relational data base;[8] their requirements can adequately be met with a relatively cheaper formatted model. If we ask whether the remaining 10 per cent of users are prepared to bear the high overheads of a relational data base, the answer will be yes from some users and no from others, which implies a rather limited user market for a relational system. However, there are two factors which would probably improve its future prospects. The first one is the increasing software and decreasing hardware development cost. A relational system will reduce systems development cost due to data independence and ease in systems design and programming. Therefore in the future a relational data base may become economically attractive. The second factor is future hardware developments, which could reduce the cost difference between the formatted and the relational data bases to an insignificant level. Until such a time arrives, the use of the relational data bases will be very restrictive.

EXERCISES

The three case studies given as exercises in the previous chapter are repeated here in questions 10, 11 and 12 for relational solutions. The reader may find the comparison between these two types of solutions, Codasyl and relational, instructive.

1. Normalisation reduces all complex relationships among the attributes of an entity record to $1:N$ form. Explain how.

2. Proliferation of foreign keys is likely to lead to data redundancy. Do a project with four relations and show how this redundancy can be avoided in storage.

3. Although the relations in Codd's relational model are in 3NF, the temporary relations created in the workspace by a join operation may not be in 3NF. Construct examples to show it.
   Does it matter if the relations in the workspace are not in 3NF?

4. Construct a relation in 3NF that does not guarantee protection from update anomaly.

5. Represent the loop relationship shown in figure 5.6 in 3NF.

6. Express the record types DEPARTMENT and JOB-TITLE of the sample Schema (section 5.3.5) in 3NF.

7. The candidate keys are used to determine whether a relation is in 3NF, but are they required for accessing a relation?

8. Discuss how privacy and integrity controls can be imposed on relations. (See sections 19.3, 20.2 and 20.3 of reference 2.)

9. Design a retrieval language based on relational algebra.

10. Design a relational Schema (that is, construct the necessary relations) for the problem described in exercise 11 chapter 5. Then write both relational algebra and DSL Alpha expressions for the following.

(a)   To find the names and addresses of those customers who are due to be invoiced on a day number held in a data name DAYN.
(b)   To find the details of the customer orders (item code, dates and quantities each day) for these customers.
(c)   To find the prices of the items as needed for invoicing these customers.

11. Design a relational Schema for the problem described in exercise 12 of chapter 5. Write relational algebra and DSL Alpha expressions to do the following.

(a)   Extract the mileage attribute of a car from the data base for updating it with new mileage after the car is returned by a customer. Assume that the customer number and the order number are known.
(b)   Assuming that a booked car is broken down, find the other cars of this model, of the next more expensive model and of the next cheaper model, the registration number of the broken car being held in a data name REGN.

12. Design a relational Schema for the problem described in exercise 13 chapter 5, and then find from this Schema the subordinate and superior components of a component whose code is held in a data name COMPC.

REFERENCES

[1] D. L. Childs, *Proc. IFIP Congress 1968* (North Holland) p. 162. R. E. Levein and M. E. Maron, *Communs Ass. comput. Mach.,* 10 (1967) p. 715.
[2] For brief descriptions of these systems, see C. J. Date, *An Introduction To Data Base Systems* (Addison-Wesley, New York, 1975) chapter 8.
[3] E. F. Codd, *Communs Ass. comput. Mach.,* 13 (1970) p. 377.

[4] E. F. Codd, *Normalised Data Base Structure: A Brief Tutorial,* IBM Research RJ935, November 1971.

E. F. Codd, *Further Normalisation of the Data Base Relational Model,* IBM Research RJ909, August 1971.

[5] E. F. Codd, *A Data Base Sublanguage Founded on the Relational Calculus,* IBM Research RJ893, July 1971.

[6] E. F. Codd, *Relational Completeness of Data Base Sublanguages,* IBM Research RJ987, March 1972.

[7] E. F. Codd, *Recent Investigations in Relational Data Base Systems,* IBM Research RJ1385, April 1974.

[8] C. W. Bachman, quoted in *Computer Weekly,* April 8, 1976.

7 The State of the Art

Many Data Base Systems are available today, some being developed by the manufacturers, others by the software houses and other interested parties. The manufacturers' products are naturally geared to their own machines; those produced by others are usually suitable for a variety of machines. Apart from this machine dependence, there is also a wide variation in the facilities these products offer. Some of these products are better than others in some respects, while worse in other respects; some are complex while others are simple, and some appeal to the larger users while others are suitable for smaller users. Despite this diversity, there is some cohesion with respect to the basic data structures employed and, from this structural consideration, we can divide the products into the following four major groups.

Set structure : Codasyl proposal

                  DMS 1100, IDMS, DBMS–10, IDS–II, etc.

Hierarchical : All IBM products

                  IMS, DL/1, etc.

Inverted :   ADABAS, SYSTEM 2000, etc.
Net :   TOTAL

Needless to say, these four groups belong to the formatted class of data bases. In the relational class, as mentioned earlier, we do not as yet have any commercially available products that provide all the facilities of the relational model. However, there is a number of prototype and experimental systems. The largest is at Peterlee and it was developed by IBM for the Greater London Council.[1] It has 60 megabytes of data spread over about 50 relations. The access language used is based on relational algebra. The system is still in the development stage—the optimisation of command execution and storage allocation (section 6.5.4) is being studied, and privacy control and concurrency facilities are yet to be added. The other relational implementations are on a much smaller scale, with variable retrieval facilities being offered. Since none of these products is fully developed with all the relational facilities, we shall not discuss them any further. The rest of this chapter will therefore be devoted to the formatted data bases: we shall examine the products listed above in the first three sections with a summary comparison chart in the last section.

7.1 CODASYL-TYPE PRODUCTS

At present there is a number of commercially available Codasyl-based products, and of these the four listed earlier appear to be more widely known. IDS-II is a newcomer, announced in the United Kingdom by Honeywell in April 1976 as a successor to its earlier product IDS, now called IDS-I (section 1.1). The present version of IDS-II incorporates only a subset of the Codasyl proposal and it is expected to be improved in the future by the inclusion of the other specifications of the proposal. DBMS-10 is available from 1973 for the DEC 10 computers and is reported to be a good system. The other two packages, DMS 1100 and IDMS, are well established and have already captured a sizable share of the market. We shall discuss them both briefly in this section concentrating mainly on their distinctive features.

7.1.1 DMS 1100 of Univac[2]

Univac has been active in data base development from an early period, and over the years it has produced a number of Data Base Systems. Its principal product is DMS 1100 which was released in late 1971, and which now has over 120 installatiohs in different parts of the world. Based on a subset of the 1971 DBTG proposal, DMS 1100 was developed for the 128K word Univac 1100 series computers under the Exec 8 operating system. It can be operated on both batch and on-line modes, but it does not have its own communication package – the user may write his own. The control system of DMS 1100 can support several independent Schemas transparent to the application programmer, who can access the data base using Cobol, Fortran and PL/1 as the host languages.

Data Base Organisation

The present version of DMS 1100 does not support any Subschema which is expected to be provided in a future version. Areas, sets and records are defined in the Schema as in the Codasyl model. The user gives to each record a unique data base key made up of area number, page number and the record number on the page. In set description, singular sets with SYSTEM as the dummy owner and direct entry to the member records of a given set by index tables are not supported; but non-embedded pointer arrays (section 2.6.3), called *pointer array set mode,* can be specified for speedy access to the set members. The other major omissions are the absence of the CHECK, ENCODING/DECODING and ON clauses. Virtual data items are not supported. The physical storage is either sequential, chained or direct under user control. The storage organisation is specified by an extended DDL which acts both as the Schema DDL and DSDL.

   In the absence of a Subschema, the Schema records required by an application program are specified in the program in a special Section under the Data Division.

The records can be accessed using the data base key or other Codasyl facilities. The currency indicators and most of the DML command of the Codasyl model are supported. The use of the data base is controlled by two additional commands, IMPART and DEPART. A run-unit must register itself with the DBCS by issuing an IMPART command before it can use the data base. A DEPART command is employed to terminate the registration, that is, to leave the DBCS.

Other Characteristics

Data independence provided by the DMS 1100 is average. Binding takes place at the compilation time, thus recompilation of the programs is required in the event of a Schema change. The user has some control on page size, buffer allocation, but no utilities exist for performance optimisation, although some usage statistics are generated.

Locking for concurrent usage is permitted at the area and the page level. An area may be opened in the protected or exclusive mode as required, the locks being released when the areas are closed. Alternatively a run-unit may lock a page by issuing a KEEP command on reading a record. (A FREE command nullifies a KEEP.) All run-units are queued for data resources, and if there is any queue for data resources, no fresh run-unit is allowed to register with the DBCS. If all the run-units registered with the DBCS are queued for data resources, then the system recognises this as a deadlock, which is then released by undoing the updates of the run-unit with least number of updated pages. Both before and after images, called before and after *looks*, are used.

No privacy control is allowed below the area level. Data validation facility is non-existent (no CHECK clause). The absence of the ON clause prevents the user detecting error conditions in a convenient form. Recovery facilities are provided with checkpoints and before and after look files. The data base can be recreated in part or whole as necessary from backup files.

Data base procedures are not supported nor is there any query language facility. A data dictionary as such is not provided, but information on data items can be obtained using specified utilities. In general, utilities available are rather inadequate. The performance of DMS 1100 is described as reasonable but not spectacular. An improved version with the Subschema facility is expected to be released in the future.

For its 9000 series computers, Univac has purchased IDMS to be marketed under the name DMS 90.

7.1.2 IDMS of the Cullinane Corporation[3]

The Integrated Data Base Management System (IDMS) was developed by the Goodrich Chemical Company of Ohio, as an implementation of a subset of the

1971 DBTG proposal for use in the IBM 360 and 370 series. It took an experienced team only about four man-years to build the basic system which became operational in 1972. A year later the system was passed to the Cullinane Corporation for marketing, development and support responsibility. Subsequently ICL and Univac bought rights to develop it for their own computers — ICL for their 2900 series, and Univac for their 9000 series. Needless to say, IDMS has proved to be a successful product: by now there are about 40 IDMS installations. For the PDP11 series of computers, another version of IDMS has been developed.

IDMS supports both batch and on-line processing, the main host language permitted being Cobol, but it can also be accessed by programs written in PL/1, Fortran and Assembler. IDMS does not have its own communication package, but it provides interfaces to a number of well-known packages such as CICS, INTER-COM and Task-Master. The run-time computer memory required is only 50K bytes + Application programs. However, for the Schema compilation, 150K bytes are needed. The system is built around a data dictionary, which constitutes the central facility containing the descriptions of physical storage, Schema, Subschema and other information.

Data Base Organisation

As in the Codasyl specification, the Schema consists of entries for areas, sets and records, an area being defined as a logical rather than a physical subdivision of the data base containing the occurrences of various record types. The notable omissions are the absence of facilities for singular sets, non-embedded pointer arrays, direct entry to the member records of a set by index tables and the CHECK, ENCODING/DECODING and ON clauses. Virtual data, certain duplicate checking and set selection facilities are also absent.

A Device Media Control Language (DMCL) is used to describe the storage organisation of the data base. A file is defined as the physical subdivision of the data base into which the areas are mapped. A file consists of an integral number of pages. The storage organisation is designed to provide efficient access to data at the cost of the storage space. Transfer between the data base and the memory takes place in units of pages.

The Subschema facility and the main DML commands, including all the currency indicators, are provided, but no facility exists for currency suppression. Cobol host language programs are passed through a DML processor prior to compilation. The binding between the Schema and Subschema takes place during Subschema compilation; thus recompilation of the Subschema is required in the event of a Schema change. Access to the data base is controlled by the DMCL object module and the object Subschema which contains the necessary Schema information. The role played by the data dictionary is similar to the one described in section 4.4.1 for a centralised data dictionary (figure 4.3).

Other Characteristics

The logical independence is restricted to the selection of the wanted records and sets, and the data items within a record. The data items can be reordered, but cannot be regrouped or reformatted. The Subschema data independence is therefore minimal.

The system collects and analyses usage statistics, but no utility exists for storage reorganisation. However, storage space is allocated dynamically, collating the space released by record deletions for subsequent use.

For concurrent usage, locks are provided at the area level in accordance with the Codasyl recommendation; the user is relied upon to declare all the areas before starting an update. Another serious limitation is the inability to use the same DML command concurrently by two run-units, because the routines for the commands are not written in re-entrant code. The result is that if two run-units wish to use the same DML command, one of them must wait in a queue until the other has finished the execution of the command, and this slows down concurrent processing considerably. However, a re-entrant routine is machine dependent, and therefore its absence increases the portability of IDMS, but the loss of efficiency in concurrent usage outweighs this gain in portability. Clearly concurrent usage facilities in IDMS are unsatisfactory. Future versions, particularly the one for the ICL 2900 series,[4] are expected to provide improvement.

Privacy locks are provided at area, set and record levels in the Subschema but, like DMS 1100, it does not provide any data validation facility. Checkpoints and before and after images are available for recovery purposes. In addition all changed areas are dumped and can be used for the reconstruction of the whole data base or its parts as necessary in the event of a failure.

The absence of support for data base procedure and the ON clause, along with the lack of data validation facility should be regarded as drawbacks. The inability to access member records directly is another serious handicap for large sets requiring direct access. Some utilities are provided, notable among them being the report generator called CULPRIT, which uses the data dictionary. Additional utilities for restructuring and reorganisation of the data base and a query language are necessary. Cullinane is prepared to incorporate additional facilities in accordance with user response, all changes being within the Codasyl specification.[5]

Despite its shortcomings IDMS has become popular very quickly. This is indicated by the decision of ICL and Univac to abandon their own products in its favour. The greatest virtue is its portability; besides which it is well tested—and it works. It also secured a boost for being the first Codasyl-based system for IBM hardware. The small run-time memory required by IDMS is often cited as an added attraction, but it should not be forgotten that this is achieved only by omitting a number of important facilities (such as direct access to set members, adequate provision for concurrent usage) which consume a lot of memory.

7.2 HIERARCHICAL-TYPE PRODUCTS

IBM is the major developer of Data Base Systems based on hierarchical tree structures. It has a large number of products, the most famous one being IMS. Another popular IBM product is DL/1 which offers a subset of IMS facilities. In this section we examine IMS in some detail, and at the end make comments on DL/1.

7.2.1 General Features of IMS[6]

The Information Management System of IBM was originally developed for the Rockwell International Corporation of California. Its first version IMS/1 was released in 1969 followed by another version called IMS/2. The system has been improved gradually over the years by the addition of new features. Its latest edition, known as IMS/VS (VS for Virtual Storage) came out in 1974. It has several versions of its own, the larger versions providing greater facilities. IMS can be operated in both batch and teleprocessing mode, and it is designed for the larger members of the IBM 360 and 370 series. The memory required just for the resident routines of IMS/VS is about 220K bytes; the minimum memory size required varies from 384K bytes to 768K bytes, depending on the version. An additional 256K bytes are needed to support the remote terminals.

IMS can be used by programs written in Assembler, Cobol and PL/1. Instead of a single data base, it supports a number of what are called physical 'data bases', which together constitute a data base. Each physical 'data base' consists of all the occurrences of a single tree structure whose description, together with its mapping into the storage device, is known as Data Base Description (DBD). A logical 'data base' is a subset of a physical 'data base' and is defined in a Program Communication Block (PCB) in accordance with user requirements. A PCB also includes the mapping of the logical into the physical 'data base'. The set of all PCBs for one user is known as a Program Specification Block (PSB). This cannot be shared, although two PSBs may contain the same data. A single language called Data Language/One (DL/1) is used as DDL and DML.

IMS is the principal IBM product and it has over 500 installations. IBM has invested vast sums of money in the system and is pleased with its success. This perhaps explains IBM's reluctance to implement the Codasyl proposal. In the following subsections we shall describe the characteristics of this product in some detail. Additional facilities provided by the Virtual Storage edition will also be pointed out in appropriate places.

7.2.2 Data Base Organisation

In IMS the basic unit of access is a segment. This is defined as a collection of data items within a record. Only IMS/VS permits variable-length segment types. Data is represented in a tree showing one-to-many relationships between segment types. The segment at a node is called the parent, and those at the branches the children. The occurrences of a segment type are known as *twin segments*. A tree may consist of 1 to 255 segment types with a maximum of 15 levels. One occurrence of the whole tree is known as a 'record', and all the occurrences of a tree constitute a physical 'data base'.

Physical Data Structure

To illustrate the IMS data structure, we consider a physical 'data base' containing the data of health centres belonging to a health board. Each centre has a number of doctors and nurses, and each doctor has a number of patients. We may represent the data by a tree containing four segment types as shown in figure 7.1.

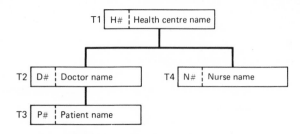

Figure 7.1 Tree structure for IMS

We have assumed that every segment type contains a key for the identification of the twins. The keys are represented here by H#, D#, P#, and N#. Depending on its position in the tree, each segment type is given an exclusive type number by the system, which we have indicated here by T1, T2, T3 and T4. One occurrence of this tree for health centre number H1 is shown in figure 7.2a. This 'record' is presented sequentially in figure 7.2b, which shows that an IMS 'record' is really a conventional record with a variable number of repeating groups. The physical 'data base' consists of all such 'records' − one 'record' per health centre. The tree used for a physical 'data base' is known as a physical tree to distinguish it from a logical tree, which is defined as a subset of a physical tree used in a PCB; all the occurrences of a logical tree constitute a logical 'data base'.

If two physical trees share a common segment type, then data redundancy is avoided by including it physically (that is, as a physical child) in one tree, and by maintaining a child pointer to it from the appropriate parent in the other tree. This segment type is then said to be a logical child of a logical parent in the second tree. A physical tree can have as many logical children as necessary, but all of them must be specified in DBD. If a segment type is included in a tree as a logical child, all the subordinate segment types of this logical child are also automatically included there. If a patient in our example is allowed to be treated by a number of

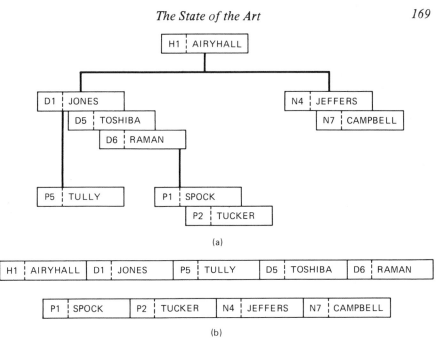

(a)

(b)

*Figure 7.2 (a) A physical 'record' (note: Dr Toshiba does not have a patient);
(b) sequential presentation of the physical record*

doctors, then the same patient segment will appear as the child of all the relevant doctor segments, thus introducing redundancy. This redundancy can be avoided by creating a separate physical tree for the patient segment type alone, and then including it logically as required in the original tree. However, the inclusion of logical children can slow down the processing, and therefore it is necessary to trade off between retrieval speed and the complexity in update due to redundancy.

IMS permits the direct representation of only tree structures, but, by using the concept of logical children, other structures, including network, can be constructed. In IMS/VS *secondary indices* to access the segments in a different order can be created to reduce the response time of specific operations in large trees, but their presence usually slows down processing in other operations.

Logical Data Structure

A PSB consists of a collection of logical trees, each representing a subset of the physical tree and including the logical children of the physical tree, if any. It is a subset only to the extent that we may omit one or more segment types of the physical tree — except the root segment which must be present. No other freedom is allowed. If a segment type is excluded from a logical tree, all its subordinate segment types are also excluded. Conversely if a segment type is included, all its superior segment types providing the hierarchical sequence to the root segment must also be included. This restricts the freedom to exclude the unwanted segment types. Furthermore, if a segment type appears in the logical tree, all its twins are automatically included. This again limits the freedom to select only specified occurrences of a segment type, without being lumbered with all its occurrences. No new access paths can be defined. However, the access paths are transparent to the user, who does not know what is specified in DBD.

7.2.3 Storage and Retrieval

In IMS a segment can be accessed only by following the hierarchical path embedded in the tree, which we shall define here in terms of a hierarchical key (not an IMS term) consisting of the segment type numbers and the successive parent keys. For patient TUCKER of our example, the hierarchical key is T1H1T2D6T3P2, where Ts identify the segment types and H1 and D6 are the keys of the successive parents as explained earlier. We can access an individual 'record' occurrence of the 'data base' — in fact the root segment — sequentially in order of the hierarchical key by scanning or directly, either through an index or by hashing. From each parent a child can also be accessed either sequentially or through pointers. Depending on these means, IMS provides the following four types of access method within the hierarchical scheme.

> HSAM   :   Hierarchical Sequential Access Method
> HISAM :   Hierarchical Indexed Sequential Access Method
> HIDAM :   Hierarchical Indexed Direct Access Method
> HDAM   :   Hierarchical Direct Access Method

In HSAM, 'records' and the segments within a 'record', are stored sequentially in hierarchical key order as shown in figure 7.2b. Magnetic tapes are ideal for this type of storage. For the other three access methods, 'records' must be stored on discs.

In HISAM, each root segment is accessed by an index, but the segments within a 'record' are accessed sequentially as in HSAM. All segments of a 'record' are stored in physical blocks chained in hierarchical key order. Within each block the segments must be stored in the hierarchical key order, thus requiring reorganisation of storage in the event of insertion of new segments. In HIDAM, like HISAM, the root segments are accessed through an index, but access to the subordinate segments is provided by pointers in two ways as follows.

(1)   By hierarchical pointers: all occurrences of a given segment type within a 'record' can be linked in the ascending and, optionally, the descending order of the hierarchical key. If such linkages are specified for a segment type, its last occurrence is automatically given a pointer to the first occurrence of the next segment type, unless the end of the 'record' is reached. Unlike HISAM, the segments here need not be stored in the physical device in order of the hierarchical key, since hierarchical sequence is determined by the pointers.

(2) By parent–child–twin pointers: all the twins of a given segment type under the same parent can be linked by one- or two-way chain; each twin has a compulsory pointer to the first and an optional pointer to the last occurrence of every child segment type under it. In addition, a pointer to the parent segment type can also be specified (figure 7.3).

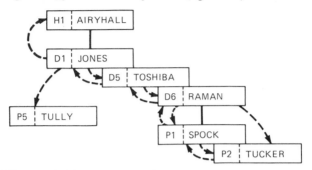

Figure 7.3 Parent–child twin pointers for doctor and patient segments of the record in figure 7.2a

Only one of these two options can be specified for a given segment type, but the different segment types of the same tree can have different options. In figure 7.3 we have shown the access paths for only two out of four segment types of the tree. Access to the segment for JONES from the root segment will be determined by the pointer option of the root segment.

In HDAM, the root segments can be accessed by using a hashing algorithm and the subordinate segments can be accessed through pointers, as in HIDAM. In both HIDAM and HDAM, the root segments are also connected by one- or two-way chain.

IMS/VS (and not the other editions) provides Virtual Access Storage Method (VSAM), in which a device-independent approach is used for HISAM, HIDAM and HDAM. The variable-length segment types are permitted only with VSAM.

These access methods are transparent to the application programmer who is only concerned with the logical tree, and requests for segments as necessary, without specifying the retrieval mechanism. The system selects the access methods, which are mapped into a PSB during its compilation. The efficiency of access clearly varies depending on the nature of the query. It is the task of the DBA to choose the right access methods for optimal performance. We should perhaps point out here that the retrieval speed in IMS is known to be slow. The inability to access a child directly from a parent, and the need to trace the whole hierarchical path for any subordinate segment, must be viewed as the major obstruction to speedy access.

Data Language/One

Apart from specifying various clauses necessary to describe DBD and PSB, DL/1 provides the following basic commands for data manipulation

GET UNIQUE   : To retrieve a unique segment directly.
GET NEXT   : To retrieve a segment sequentially.
GET NEXT WITHIN PARENT: To retrieve sequentially under current parent.
GET HOLD NEXT   : To warn the system for REPLACE and DELETE.
REPLACE   : To replace the data of an existing segment.
DELETE   : To delete a segment. Note that if a segment is
                          deleted, its subordinate segments are also deleted.
INSERT   : To insert a new segment to a predefined parent.

7.2.4 Other Characteristics

Data Independence and Optimisation

IMS does not permit access to data item values, a segment being the smallest unit
of access. Addition or deletion of data items to a segment type would normally
require changes in the application program using that segment type. If a programmer needs a new logical relationship among the segments of a tree, the
physical tree must be redesigned to include them, through logical children if
necessary. The physical 'data base' has to be reloaded and all relevant PSBs recompiled. However, the existing application programs need not be changed.

The application programmer has no freedom in defining the access paths best
suited to his need, but this loss of freedom has provided access transparency,
which permits the alterations of access paths without affecting the programs. Block
sizes, pointer options to access the subordinate segments in HIDAM and HDAM,
and the hashing routines for HDAM can be modified independently of the
programs.

Subject to certain restrictions, it is possible to replace one access method by
another, for example, HISAM by HIDAM, without affecting the application
programs. Some utilities are provided to produce usage statistics for the purpose.
IMS is very sensitive to tuning, but the tuning facilities provided are inadequate.
Deleted segments are usually left in the 'data base', to be removed subsequently
by the appropriate utilities. Although IMS is claimed to provide evolutionary
facilities, its data structure (tree) is rather rigid, making it difficult to incorporate
changes. This applies in particular to the insertion of new segment types, which
often involves the recreation of the entire 'data base', depending on their points of
insertion in the tree.

Concurrency and Data Protection

IMS/VS provides facilities for concurrent usage through what it calls program
isolation features. Four types of access are permitted — retrieve without lock,
retrieve with lock, single update with lock and exclusive locks for multiple up-

dates. Run-units are automatically queued and the system maintains state graphs for all exclusive locks. A detected deadlock is released by returning to a previous state through before images. Updates are consolidated into the data base only when the after image buffer is full, but separate protection exists against the copying of this inconsistent state into the backup files.

All changes are logged and the copies of both before and after images are retained on backup files, but in the event of failure, the entire 'data base' must be reconstructed, since IMS does not permit reconstruction in parts.[7]

Checkpoints are maintained and detailed recovery procedures provided. The reliability of IMS is reported to be good, but not wholly satisfactory.[7]

Privacy control is available in the form of a password from a terminal. Once the password is accepted, the user can access any part of the data base. In a PSB, segments can be given specific protection against retrieval, deletion, amendment and so on.

Comments and Criticism

In IMS, data duplication is avoided by creating a separate 'data base' for the duplicate segments as explained earlier, but generally this will slow down processing. IMS supports excellent teleprocessing facilities and it has its own native communication facility. User experience suggests[8] that the running costs of the batch and teleprocessing modes are more or less the same, although the manual data preparation cost is substantially higher for the batch mode. IMS provides query language and data dictionary facilities, both of which could, however, be improved. No data base procedure is supported, except for the hashing routines.

IMS is a large and complex system. Its overheads are very high and its processing speed is low, 50 per cent of storage space being used for pointers and control fields. The sequential processing for producing reports and dump is particularly slow. According to users,[7,9] up to 90 per cent of the CPU time can be taken up in executing the IMS routines, as against the processing of the actual data. Cost apart, IMS appears to be the best system for those organisations where on-line processing is the prime motivation; it is particularly unsuited to applications where frequent changes to the data structures are needed.[7]

Due partly to an early start and partly to the vigorous marketing policy of IBM, IMS is currently the most popular large DBS. However, this secure position is now being gradually eroded through the arrival of the other products, particularly Codasyl-based systems with their promise of good facilities at lower cost. In a recent survey[7] of 100 data base users, IMS had the lowest rating on nearly all counts, the other products involved being ADABAS, TOTAL, IDMS and SYSTEM 2000. It would appear that many users today are reluctant to be hooked to a particular manufacturer's product.[10] The long-term future of IMS is less assured now than it has been in the past.

7.2.5 DL/1 of IBM

Data Language/One is a relatively recent (December 1973) IBM product. It is really a subset of IMS, and the latest version provides the same data structure and access facilities, but uses less memory (minimum required about 125K bytes). It can be used in the IBM 360 and 370 series with Virtual Storage Operating System. However, it does not provide any query language, data dictionary, report generator, checkpoint or restart facility. Concurrent usage and the means to generate usage statistics are not supported either. It does not have any communication facility of its own, but this can be provided through another IBM product called CICS. IBM is marketing DL/1 very actively, and now claims to have over 110 installations.

7.3 INVERTED AND NET STRUCTURED PRODUCTS

ADABAS (pronounced as *aid-a-base*) and SYSTEM 2000 are the more well-known products which utilise inverted structures for data organisations. Both are very similar in design and in the facilities they offer. We shall here describe ADABAS and later point out the major differences of the SYSTEM 2000. TOTAL is based on a two-level net structure and forms a class of its own. It is most popular with the small users and has the largest number of installations. Its major features will also be examined in this section.

7.3.1 ADABAS of Software AG[11]

Adaptable Data Base System, or ADABAS, was developed by Software AG of Darmstadt, West Germany. Its first version appeared in 1971, and by now it has over 80 installations in Europe and the United States. Recently a number of British organisations, including British Rail, have decided to use ADABAS.

ADABAS can be operated in both batch and teleprocessing mode, the host languages provided being Cobol, PL/1, Fortran and Assembler. It uses inverted filing technique and supports both a data manipulation language and a query language. The minimum memory required is about 160K bytes and it can be installed in IBM 360, 370 and Univac 9000 series. For British Rail, an ICL 2900 version is being developed.

Data Base Organisation

An ADABAS data base is divided into two separate areas, known as Data Storage and Associator. The data records are stored in the Data Storage area, and their inverted index, mapping and linkages (showing record relationships) are kept in the Associator. The data base can support up to 255 individual files, which can be extended to 65 000 with a minor modification.[12] A file is shared between Data

Storage and Associator, its basic constituents being: data records, field definition entries (that is, record description) and inverted index.

Data records are stored in Data Storage as compressed variable-length records omitting blank fields, leading zeros in numeric fields, and trailing blanks in alphanumeric fields. The space saved in Data Storage due to data compression is claimed to be 50 per cent on average and in some cases up to 80 per cent. Each record is given a unique internal identifier, called the Internal Sequence Number (ISN). A single file can hold up to nearly 17 million records belonging to one or more record types. A record type may contain up to 500 data items, 200 of which can be descriptors, that is, user-defined keys for accessing the record.

Field definition entries and the inverted index tables are kept in the Associator along with other control information. An Associator has the following four components.

(1)   *The field description table:* contains field definition entries such as data name and picture clauses for all the record types of the data base.
(2)   *Storage management table:* maintains the mapping of the Associator with Data Storage. Storage control blocks are also set up here.
(3)   *Address converter:* holds the lookup table for ISN and the physical address.
(4)   *Association network:* contains the inverted index for the descriptors and file coupling, showing the relationship between records of two related files. An entry in the inverted index consists of a value of the descriptor followed by a list of the relevant ISNs. In a file coupling, the records of a file can be linked with bidirectional pointers to those of another file through a common descriptor. Two internal inverted index tables, one for each file in the coupling, are produced for accessing records in the two files through the same descriptor value. The common descriptor value thus acts like the foreign key of the relational model, and unless it is included in the records, the file cannot be coupled with others. For instance, to represent a network relationship between course and student records in ADABAS, it is essential to include either the course keys in the student records or the student keys in the course records. As in the relational model, no explicit owner or member record is globally defined in ADABAS, leaving it to the user to declare any record as the owner in the DML commands according to his requirements. The members of an owner can be accessed both directly and sequentially as necessary from the ISNs of the common descriptor value obtained through the internal inverted table. A single file can be coupled to 80 other files. All data relationships except loops can thus be represented through coupling. For loops it is necessary to process the related records in the same file through explicit keys.

Since the Associator is both logically and physically distinct from Data Storage, its content can subsequently be changed without affecting the Data Storage portions or the application programs. This ensures flexibility and data independence. The technique used here is roughly equivalent to separating the set entries (that is, record relationships) from the Codasyl Schema and imposing them subsequently on the Schema as an additional interface. However, unlike set descriptions, we cannot define new record relationships in ADABAS unless the relevant common descriptors are included in the records in Data Storage.

Data Manipulation

An application program wishing to use an ADABAS data base has to define its own user working area in a desired format where all data base records for the program are held. Access to the data base is gained by a call statement specifying the intended command, for example

CALL ADABAS (READ DATA)

whereupon the requested DATA will be placed in the user working area.

The basic commands supported by ADABAS are FIND, READ, UPDATE, ADD DELETE, OPEN, CLOSE and CHECKPOINT. The FIND command is used for logical searches subject to some selection criteria, which can be formulated in terms of descriptor values, using logical operators such as AND, OR and NOT. This command locates the record from the Associator network by automatically using the most effective search algorithm out of a number maintained by the system. A member record is obtained by a FIND COUPLED command which must stipulate the name of the member file and a descriptor value or a range of values.

An individual record of a file can be read directly. A group of records in a file can be accessed in the physical sequence order of their storage, or in a logical sequence order of a specified set of descriptor values. New records can be added without any problem, the Associator being automatically updated. If a substantial number of records needs insertion, a utility can be used to expedite the process. DELETE and UPDATE commands are used as necessary. The CHECKPOINT command facilitates checkpoints during execution under program control. The OPEN/CLOSE commands signal the beginning or the end of an application.

The query language supported by ADABAS is called ADASCRIPT. It is very powerful and permits the formulation of queries in 'natural English'. Data can be retrieved from only one file by a query, although the descriptors used in the selection criteria can be taken from five files. A report generator, named ADAWRITER, is also provided to select, format and print information from the data base.

An added attraction in ADABAS is its phonetic search capability, which permits retrieval of items on the basis of sound pattern rather than the actual spelling. By invoking this facility a program can find a record for MEYER even if the name is spelled as MEIER or MAYER.

Data Independence and Optimisation

ADABAS provides a great deal of data independence. An application programmer may define his record by only a subset of the original (Schema) data items of the record. He may also change the format of the data items and reorder them as necessary. Data items are bound at execution time, thus reducing the need for program recompilation.

The isolation of the specification for record relationships into a separate interface (the Association network) permits storage reorganisation and changes in the record relationships without requiring alterations in the application program, unless the changes in the record relationships directly affect the program. However, in the absence of a Subschema, the application program does not have an independent local view of the record relationships in the data base, and if new relationships are required they have to be explicitly defined in the Association network.

A fair number of utilities is provided for the reorganisation of the data base, although the facilities for the collection and analysis of usage statistics are rather poor. New files can be created, the old ones deleted, or an existing file can be altered by the addition or deletion of data items. File couplings can be modified and the descriptors can be inserted or deleted. New record relationships can also be created by first inserting the necessary common descriptors in the original records in Data Storage. The data base can be expanded to accommodate more data without having to reload it. The space allocation is dynamic, the released space after deletions being automatically consolidated and reused.

Concurrency and Data Protection

ADABAS supports concurrent usage as mentioned in section 4.2.3. The concurrent user can lock records in a predefined sequential order to avoid deadlocks, but facilities to resolve deadlocks by rollback are also provided. A HOLD command is available for locking records.

Privacy protection is provided against unauthorised access and updates separately at record type and data item levels. Facilities for encoding records are also supported. The system provides 15 levels of read and write protection. Data base auditing facility is also available.

Apart from checkpoints, ADABAS permits the dumping of the data base with the facility for subsequent reloading. Changes files on all updates are kept for use during data base recreation. Automatic restart is available. A number of reports are generated, giving information on storage space utilisation, file descriptions, coupling, checkpoint and restarts.

Comments and Criticism

Multilayered index tables are employed to speed up access. Using special routines and procedures, ADABAS is able to support both fast retrieval and update, the improvement in update speed being particularly remarkable in view of the known update problems of inverted files.

ADABAS users appear to be fairly satisfied with their products. Their only major complaint concerns the inadequacy of documentation. The system is easy to install and use, and it requires minimum file conversions. It is an efficient and flexible system, and eminently suitable for medium-large users.

7.3.2 System 2000 of MRI Systems[13]

SYSTEM 2000 was developed by the MRI Systems Corporation of Texas in 1970. It is a host language system supporting Cobol, PL/1, Fortran and Assembler. It requires a minimum memory of about 160K bytes and can be installed in IBM 360, 370 series, Univac 9000 series and a few other computers, including CDC 6000. It supports both batch and on-line processing and has over 70 installations.

As a product, SYSTEM 2000 is remarkably similar to ADABAS in data structures, capabilities and facilities, except that no data compression facility is available. It is based on inverted file structures like ADABAS, the major structural difference being in the representations of record (repeating groups in the terminology of SYSTEM 2000) relationships. Whereas ADABAS employs a network structure, the SYSTEM employs a hierarchical tree structure. The more recent versions allow the DBA to change the hierarchical structure to optimise performance without affecting the application programs. Again, like ADABAS, SYSTEM 2000 supports a good query language, in addition to a data manipulation language. However, it is a retrieval-oriented system providing four methods of data manipulation. Basic access is used in batch mode for interrogation and maintenance where a group of user commands is analysed before making a single pass of the data base. Immediate access is provided for interactive processing, with procedural access for the host languages and non-procedural access for report generation.

The data independence provided is similar to that for ADABAS. The latest version provides reorganisation facilities. Concurrent usage is allowed by locking the records of a given type. Privacy is controlled by a master password for entering the data base, and a series of other passwords for retrieval, updates, and so on, of data items. Checkpoints and restart facilities are also available. The choice between ADABAS and SYSTEM 2000 is often a difficult one.

7.3.3 TOTAL of Cincom Systems[14]

TOTAL was developed by Cincom Systems Incorporated of Ohio, in early 1969. It is based on a relatively simple architecture and it can be installed in a large variety of computers (e.g. IBM, Honeywell, Univac, NCR) requiring a minimum memory of 8K to 30K bytes. The data base can be accessed by host language programs written in Cobol, PL/1, Fortran, RPG or Assembler. It is one of the most successful products and has more than 750 installations. It permits both batch and on-line processing, being able to support ENVIRON/1, which is a communication package developed by Cincom.

Data structure in TOTAL is based on one-to-many relationships between two sets of records. The data base is described in Data Base Generation (DBGEN), which consists of entries made by a Data Base Definition Language (DBDL) for elements (defined as a collection of data items), records, files, linkage path and buffer. The first application program is normally used to load the data base. To access the data base, an application program has to issue a CALL statement with parameters which invoke the necessary DML procedures. An element is the basic unit of access.

Data Base Organisation

TOTAL permits two types of file, known as datasets. One of these is for single entry or master (that is owner) records, and the other is for variable entry or subordinate (that is member) records. A variable entry record may belong to more than one master record thus establishing a net structure. Each member record must contain the key of its owner record, which is linked with all its member records by a two-way ring called the linkage path. No member pointers are provided. A master record can be accessed directly, but the subordinate records can only be accessed through their linkage path. A variable entry dataset can support up to 2500 different record types, but all records of a dataset, irrespective of record types, must be of the same length. The restriction imposed by the two-level data structure can be overcome by establishing multiple master datasets, one for each relationship and any number of subordinate files at each level. A hierarchy of up to 2500 levels can thus be constructed.

The application program wishing to access the data base requests the required service through a CALL statement, followed by a list of parameters which includes the DML command (such as read master record), system communication locations (see section 4.6), master record name, elements wanted and input-output buffer. If a subordinate record is required, its linkage path must be given.

No query language is supported by TOTAL.

Other Characteristics

Elements and record types can be added to or deleted from the data base without affecting the application programs which are bound to the elements within a record at run time. This reduces the need for recompilation. However, an application program cannot define new datasets or new linkages, and if such changes are required, the data base has to be recreated. The application program is independent of the storage structure, but not of the logical structure, since the user has to specify the linkage path along with DML command. Therefore any modification of the logical structure requires recompilation of, if not changes to, the application program.

No usage statistics are kept, but the system is self-optimising as regards storage utilisation. Concurrent usage is allowed, although no facility for the resolution of deadlock is provided. Run-units are limited to locking a file or a single record at a time. A report generator called SOCRATES is also available. Checkpoints and before and after images are employed for automatic restart. The system permits periodic dumping of the data base, which can be used for its recreation. No privacy protection is provided, but the user can invoke special data base procedures for the selected elements.

In TOTAL the data structure is relatively rigid, data independence is poor, utilities are inadequate and optimisation facilities are lacking. It is a small package catering for relatively smaller applications where the sophisticated facilities are less important, as shown by its popularity and the absence of user complaints. As a result, TOTAL's grip on the small user market is likely to continue for a while since there is not yet any serious attempt to dislodge it.

7.4 SUMMARY

The earlier sections and the summary comparison chart to follow are presented on the basis of information available to the author in the beginning of 1976. The packages described are being continually enhanced with new facilities, and in the past six months a number of such changes has been reported. Univac has improved the technique for the deadlock detection in DMS 1100 and is about to announce a new version of DMS 1100 with Subschema facilities: data independence, tuning utilities and privacy control facilities have been enhanced, and a query language, communication interface and report generator added. The routines for the DML commands of the IDMS for the ICL 2900 series have been rewritten in re-entrant code. [4] However, many of these changes were anticipated. The most dramatic news is the changes in the number of installations, the new figures for DMS 1100 being 300 and for TOTAL 1400. The corresponding figures for the other products are not yet available. By the time this book is published many other changes will probably have taken place. This is always the problem in writing about data base packages: it is like trying to shoot at a moving target viewed through a pinhole which shows only the present position.

EXERCISES

1. Compare the relative advantages of DMS 1100 and IDMS for your organisation.

2. ADABAS is becoming very popular and some installations prefer ADABAS to the Codasyl implementations. Discuss the relative merits and describe situations where ADABAS can be an advantage.

3. Construct IMS trees to represent the relationships of figures 5.3 and 5.5b, c and d without data duplication. (Hint: Use the concept of logical children.)

4. Compare the access facilities of IMS with those of the Codasyl model.

5. Data structure in IMS is too rigid to meet the requirements of an organisation with rapid change of data relationships (such as a production department). Discuss (Check the changes that can be permitted in an IMS tree without recreating the data base from an IMS manual.)

6. Describe an environment where TOTAL would be more suitable as a DBS.

7. For a comparison of the facilities of different models, the reader is recommend to try to solve for each model the three case studies described in exercises 11, 12 and 13 of chapter 5.

REFERENCES

[1] Implementation of Relational DBMS: Panel discussion National Computer Conference, Anaheim, California, 1975.

[2] Univac Publications on DMS 1100.

[3] The United Kingdom distributor for IDMS: SCICON, Sanderson House, 49-57 Berners Street, London W1P 4AQ.

[4] Private communications from ICL.

[5] *Proceedings of the Implementation of Codasyl Data Base Management Proposals* held in October 1974 (British Computer Society, 1975).

[6] IMS manuals from IBM; IMS/VS, General Information Manual GH20-1260-0.

[7] *Data Base Systems,* Infotech State of the Art Report, 1975 p. 139 and pp. 167-77.

[8] D. A. Jardine: *Data Base Management Systems* (North Holland, Amsterdam, 1974) p. 8.

[9] *Computer Weekly* (6 February 1975) quoting Des Lee, Secretary of IBM Computer Users Association.

[10] B. Davis, *Data Base Management Systems: User Experience in the USA* (National Computing Centre Publications, 1975).

[11] The United Kingdom distributor: ADABAS Ltd, 484 Burton Road, Derby.

[12] *Datapro 70:* ADABAS, report number 70E-757-01, November 1974.

[13] MRI Systems Corporation, Austin, Texas.

[14] The United Kingdom distributor: Cincom Systems International SA, Nicholson House, Nicholson Walk, Maidenhead, Berkshire.

Comparison Chart

Subject	DMS 1100	IDMS	IMS	DL/1	ADABAS	SYSTEM 2000	TOTAL
Vendor	Univac	Cullinane	IBM	IBM	Software AG	MRI	Cincom
Year of make	1971	1973	1969	Dec 1973	1971	1970	1969
Estimated installations	120	40	500	110	80	70	750
Minimum memory required	—	50Kb	512Kb to over 1000Kb	125Kb	160Kb	160Kb	8Kb to 30Kb
Machine	Univac 1100 series	IBM360/370, ICL 2900, Univac, etc.	IBM360/370	IBM360/370 with VS	As in IDMS	As in IDMS and more	Many
Data structure	Set	Set	Hierarchical	Hierarchical	Inverted + Network	Inverted + Hierarchical	Net
Host language	Cobol Fortran PL/1	Cobol (PL/1 Fortran Assembler)	Cobol, PL/1 Assembler	As in IMS	Cobol, PL/1 Fortran Assembler	As in ADABAS	As in ADABAS plus RPG

Query language	Yes	No	Good	No	Excellent	Excellent	No
On-line support	Yes	Yes	Yes	Can be added	Yes	Yes	Yes
Data independence	Fair	Fair	Fair	Fair	Fair	Fair	Poor
Optimisation facilities	Fair	Fair	Good	Poor	Good	Fair	Poor
Privacy control	Good	Good	Fair	Fair	Good	Good	Poor
Integrity control	Fair	Fair	Good	Fair	Fair	Fair	Poor
Checkpoint/Restart	Yes	No	Yes	No	Yes	Yes	Yes
Concurrent usage	Yes	Yes	Yes	No	Yes	Yes	Yes
Data dictionary facility	Fair	Good	Fair	None	Fair	Fair	Under development
General data base procedures	No	No	No	No	No	No	No
Report generator	Yes	Yes	Yes	No	Yes	Yes	Yes

8 *Data Base Implementation*

The introduction of a data base as the central reservoir of data affects the user organisation in a number of ways. For example, it changes the organisation's attitude to data requirements and management, it creates new authorities and it brin̨ in new skills. It also enforces greater coordination between the various user departments and demands stricter adherence to standards. A good implementation scheme should include adequate provision to tackle these problems, in addition to having plans for system developments and scheduling of resources. Much of this would be planned and controlled by the DBA, on whose ability will largely depend the success of the venture—provided that the right DBS is selected in the first place. In this chapter we shall discuss these issues, starting with a general discussion in section 8.1 followed by the role of the DBA in section 8.2, the data base selection criteria being examined in section 8.3. To round off the discussion we shall present some user experience in section 8.4.

8.1 AN OVERVIEW

As discussed in chapter 1, data base offers many advantages to the users, but it is an expensive investment and without careful plans and extensive preparation, the success is likely to be elusive. The groundwork starts as soon as a decision to inst̨ a Data Base System is taken. This decision is a difficult one being dependent on a complex set of factors, many of which are unknown. It is often said that a data base does not save money, but it can make more money. To what extent it is abl̨ to make more money by improving the company performance depends on the present and the projected requirements and anticipated growth; top management is usually in the best position to make the decision. Once the decision is taken, the data-processing department must begin preparations in earnest.

The first task is to produce a set of selection criteria based on an assessment of the organisation's present and projected needs. Freedom to select a DBS is often constrained by the hardware availability; this is particularly true for the DBSs supplied by manufacturers. The DBSs vended by the software houses are usually more flexible and they can be implemented on a range of computers. The computer-independent DBSs are obviously preferable, since the computer can then be changed if need be without having to change the DBS as well.

Data bases should be developed gradually with an evolutionary approach, so that the user can then learn from his experience and improve subsequent performance. The alternative is a simultaneous changeover of all the relevant systems from conventional files to data base with the attendant risk of a catastrophe. Ideally only one system should be added to the data base at a time, and when this is performing satisfactorily, another should be added. The first system is the most difficult because the user cannot rely on previous experience; its implementation should therefore be regarded as exploratory and adequate provision should be made for mistakes and unexpected surprises.

A fallacy appears to exist in the minds of some people that, since a data base is supposed to provide data independence, the old conventional programs would not need rewriting when changed over to a data base environment. This is wrong. Firstly the data independence available varies from nothing to a great deal, depending on the DBS. Secondly, as discussed earlier, data independence attempts to provide immunity only to the application programs of a data base from the changes in the same data base. Generally, all conventional programs will require redesign and rewriting, optionally to take advantage of the data base facilities, and compulsorily to meet the data base requirements with regard to data validation, data manipulation, integrity controls, privacy codes and so on. In addition, because the old input and output files will no longer be available, the processing requirements of a program will also be affected. It is difficult to see how in these circumstances the rewriting of programs can be avoided.

The most underestimated task in implementation is that of the conversion of the conventional files to the data base, due mainly to the presence of duplicate and inconsistent data. It appears deceptively easy at first sight, but as the work progresses the magnitude of the problem gradually unfolds with all its ramifications. User experience singles this out as a main cause for late implementation (see section 8.4.3).

To administer the data base it is necessary to employ a data base administrator (DBA). He should be an experienced person and should preferably be involved from the beginning. In a data base environment, there is also a need for a coordination committee, formed from representatives of the user departments, to coordinate all activities and to resolve conflicting needs of the users. This committee should usually be chaired by the DBA, and he should have sufficient authority to take decisions where the user departments are unable to agree. Details of the functions of the DBA are discussed in the next section.

Attention should be paid to the training requirements of the staff, including the DBA, the systems analysts, the programmers and the operators. Any slip here is likely to show up later as implementation delay. It is likely that the vendor of the DBS would assist in providing some reorientation course.

The reorientation course should be designed not only to teach the staff new skills, but also to reorientate their outlooks as dictated by the needs of the data base. It particularly affects the systems analysts and the programmers whose traditional roles are significantly altered by a data base. For instance, in a data base environment, the systems analyst need not concern himself with the design of files, allocation of storage space and so on. Instead, he has to concentrate on choosing the right dataset with appropriate access paths and the most convenient host language. He must pay attention to a number of new problems such as additional data validation, integrity control, privacy control and concurrent usage, and also learn to take advantage of the multiplicity of access paths available. His task will be more involved if Subschema independence is lacking.

The programming task is generally simpler in a data base environment, since sorting, multiple updates and collating information from multiple files are unnecessary. However, the programmer will be subject to stringent controls in regard to coding, data validation and program testing. His choice of datanames will be somewhat restricted, since the reserved word list will include contributions from DDL and DML in addition to the host language words.

8.2 DATA BASE ADMINISTRATOR

In a conventional system, files belong to the relevant user departments. It is they who are responsible for the accuracy, consistency and up-to-dateness of data in the file, although regular maintenance on their behalf is normally carried out by the data-processing staff. In a data base where all company data are centrally held, no single user department can be responsible for it. Instead this responsibility is exercised by the data base administrator[1] on behalf of the whole company with a view to preserving the interest of both current and future users. In addition, the DBA is also responsible for creating, expanding and improving the data base and for providing user facilities. For a small data base, the function of the DBA can be performed by an individual as a part-time job, but for a large data base, the function can require the full-time services of a team, often involving as many as 10 people.[2] To be effective, the DBA should represent a senior position with sufficient authority to arbitrate disputes between the user departments on data base usage, and to impose decisions in case of deadlocks. He should also be accepted as the final authority in all matters relating to the management of the data base.

The function of the DBA should include the following activities:[1,3] creation of the data base, performance optimisation, data protection, specification and enforcement of standards, and coordination and the provision of the user facilities.

8.2.1 Creation

To create a data base the DBA has to analyse and assess the data requirements of the users. He must examine the existing data, their representation and usage statistics, and from these he can determine the logical datasets required and the access paths that need to be provided for each dataset. He has to design a Schema and a Storage-schema; he must allocate pointers, decide on efficient pointer organisations and record placement techniques, and specify linkages, overflows and buffers, to optimise overall performance. It is a demanding job, needing all the skills and knowledge of the DBA. When the Storage-schema is ready, the DBA has to load it with data as the final act of creation. As stressed earlier, the DBA should adopt an evolutionary approach during creation.

8.2.2 Performance Optimisation

The DBA must regularly carry out clean-up operations to release space occupied by the deleted data, and reorganise the existing data in the primary and overflow areas to increase effectiveness by taking advantage of the free space made available. He must also analyse the usage statistics collected, interpret them and re-organise the Storage-schema for optimal performance. The extent to which performance optimisation can be carried out on a regular basis depends on the facilities provided by the DBS.

8.2.3 Data Protection

The specification of privacy locks, data validation requirements, checkpoint requirements and backup files have to be provided by the DBA. For the purpose of privacy locks the DBA must define data ownership, the owner department being responsible for access authorisation. The owner department should stipulate the level of privacy protection required and should supply the list of authorised users to the DBA. The access codes to highly sensitive data should ideally be known only to the relevant authority in the owner department and not to the DBA, who should simply establish the privacy locks in accordance with the requirements of the owner department (see also section 4.3.2). For shared data units, ownership may be exercised jointly by several user departments.

The DBA is clearly responsible for recovering the data base after failure. Some of the recoveries may be automatic, while others would require human intervention. The DBA must also ensure that the necessary backup files are maintained.

8.2.4 Standards

Another major responsibility of the DBA is the specification and enforcement of standards. Some of the areas where standards are required are: data validation, update, program testing, privacy codes, Subschema specification and documentation.

As mentioned in section 4.3.1, data validation is the key to integrity control. To ensure the validity of data, the DBA should specify detailed checks and incorporate them into standards for strict compliance. For more common types of data validation, he should develop data base procedures wherever possible for the use of the application programmers. Ideally all validation requirements, along with data base procedures to be invoked, if any, should be stipulated in the data dictionary.

The prescribed validation checks should also include checks required for the elimination of inconsistencies arising out of data update, in particular, insertion and deletion. In the absence of reliable concurrent usage facilities, standard operational procedures must be laid down to preserve data integrity.

Program testing has to be thorough, and it should be rigidly controlled to a standard. The DBA should provide a test data base—particularly for update programs. Allocation of privacy locks and access code should likewise be standardised. There is also a clear need for establishing standardised procedures for Subschema specification and generation.

Finally all user programs, systems, Subschemas, and so on, must be properly documented, so that in the event of errors or subsequent modification, it is easy to find the required information.

8.2.5 Coordination and User Facilities

The DBA must act as the controlling element between the data base and the users. The user departments and the systems analysts will need to communicate with him frequently. To ensure smoother operations amid conflicting user needs, it is advisable, as suggested earlier, to form a coordination committee consisting of the user departments as the members. Here the users should be able to vent their grievances, suggest improvements and approve future plans. The committee should act both as a safety valve and as a radar system. The role of the DBA as the arbitrator and decision-maker in the case of user disputes has already been pointed out. The DBA must of course provide all user facilities, some of which have already been mentioned. To extend the use of data base facilities, he should encourage new users and cater for their needs; for this the DBA should be closely associated with all new system developments in the organisation so that he can advise on the various aspects of data base usage and estimate the additional facilities needed. All aspects of a data base should be properly documented for the benefit of the users. In this respect, a data dictionary can be very useful.

8.3 DATA BASE SELECTION

A data base is an expensive product and it represents a substantial investment for any organisation; unless it is chosen carefully it can turn out to be a 'white elephant'. It involves a major decision based on a few hard facts and many soft speculations. Consequently the chances of pitfalls are greater. However, selection is an expensive process, but it is an entirely justifiable cost in view of the extensive commitment the user has to make.

As a first step, the user organisation must set up a selection committee, which should immediately embark on the assessment of the current and projected requirements of the organisation. If in-house expertise is not available, outside experts should be called in. Having established the requirements, tenders should then be invited from the data base vendors. In the initial evaluation phase most Data Base Systems should be eliminated on the basis of the user requirements, leaving two or three products for detailed evaluation in the final phase where a comparative study of the characteristics, performance and support facilities of the products should be made in relation to user requirements. A set of selection criteria follows, covering aspects to which attention should be paid.

(1) Processing cost
(2) Expansion and reorganisation cost
(3) Software cost
(4) Storage cost
(5) Ease of installation
(6) Ease of systems design
(7) Ease of programming
(8) Error diagnostics
(9) Host languages
(10) Query language
(11) Remote terminal support
(12) Optimisation facilities
(13) Data independence
(14) Concurrent usage facilities
(15) Redundancy control
(16) Integrity control
(17) Recovery facilities
(18) Privacy control
(19) Program testing facilities
(20) Data base procedures
(21) Data dictionary
(22) Utilities
(23) Aids to data base administrator
(24) Portability and compatibility
(25) Hardware requirements and flexibility
(26) Vendor's support
(27) Documentation
(28) Changeover cost

The estimation of processing cost is vitally important, since it can vary widely from one DBS to another for a particular application. The only available means is benchmark testing by creating a small representative data base for the purpose. There are, however, problems in benchmarking. Apart from the difficulty of defining and creating a representative data base, there is an additional complication, due to the dependence of the test performance on both intrinsic and extrinsic characteristics of a DBS. The extrinsic characteristics are the user's knowledge of the DBS, his skill and variable parameters such as the memory size and buffer size. It is known that at given values of parameters like memory and buffer size, one DBS may perform much better than another. To reduce the effect of these user controlled parameters, the tests should be repeated varying the parameter values but using the same computer. A less corrigible source of error, however, is the extent of the user's experience in the product in question. There is no direct means of correcting this; all that can be done is to take it into consideration in the final analysis. In general the result of the processing cost evaluation has to be treated with caution. Because of these problems and uncertainties, some organisations are reluctant to estimate processing cost, but there are others who believe it to be a useful exercise for reducing the margin of error.

The estimation of processing cost, being costly and demanding, should be made only for the products on the final short list. The actual method used in evaluation will depend on the application and its complexity. To illustrate the problems involved, we shall briefly describe here the technique used by the Government of Ontario in selecting a DBS for their payroll/personnel system.[4] In this selection technique the processing activity was broken down into three separate functions—loading, updating and report generation, and for each function the following were estimated

> x = number of times the function is performed
>   in a year
> y = number of record accesses per function
> z = cost per record access per function

The product xyz gave the annual processing cost per function.

At a more detailed level the loading cost was resolved into three factors—the initial loading cost, expansion and reorganisation cost and backup file generation cost. The update function was also divided into daily updates from transactions, biweekly updates and annual accounting updates. The reports to be printed were divided into five categories—weekly, monthly, quarterly and two types of annual report, depending on the number of records required to be accessed to generate a report.

To estimate the cost of expansion it is necessary to add new data items, record occurrences, record types and datasets into the representative data base and ascertain the loading cost.

The estimation of reorganisation cost involves finding the man-hours and computer time required to analyse and interpret collected usage statistics and to reorganise the Storage-schema for tuning. Depending on the utilities available, it can be a major cost item. The storage requirements, and hence the storage cost, can be estimated from the knowledge of the user requirements and the information supplied by the vendor. The software cost would obviously be quoted by the vendor. Some DBSs are easier to install than others, depending on the complexity of the DBS selected. All sophisticated DBSs are complex, but all equally complex DBSs are not necessarily equally sophisticated. Often there is a choice, and if there is, it should be exploited. TOTAL, ADABAS, and SYSTEM 2000 are easier to install, but IMS and Codasyl-type DBSs are more difficult, requiring greater skill.

The ease in systems design emanates partly from data independence and partly from the access paths and data structures supported by the DBS. Subschema independence, the complexitities of DML commands and the additional work required by the programmer to ensure data integrity, determine the ease in programming. The binding procedure used will affect the frequency of compilations required. Adequate error diagnostics—not only in programming, but also in all aspects of data base operations—are essential for efficient performance of the system. The host languages supported, and the relative ease of their use, are obviously crucial factors in data base selection. The importance of a query language and the associated end user's facilities, will depend on user requirements, but in considering this it is necessary to bear in mind the possible future need for a remote terminal.

As stressed in section 4.1, the facilities for evolutionary development and performance optimisation are vital for a good data base. Items 13 to 22 in the selection criteria list have also been discussed at considerable length in chapters 3 and 4. The utilities to support the DBA have been covered in chapter 4 and in the previous section of this chapter.

The size of the computer memory required to operate a data base is an important consideration, and must clearly lie within a prescribed limit. Ideally the DBS should be portable so that the user can change computers if necessary. Without this portability a user can get locked into a particular hardware system without any hope of future extrication except at high cost, since the DBS has to be changed as well. Another important feature is the compatibility of a DBS; too many DBSs are available without there being any compatibility between them. This has the disadvantage of bonding a user to a particular product 'until death them do part'. For long-term development, it is desirable to aim for a suitable Codasyl-type DBS. When the ANSI specifications for a standardised DBS become available, one of them should of course be chosen (see section 9.3).

The user should also examine the extent of vendor's support and documentation available for the product. The vendor is likely to provide pre-installation support quite readily otherwise the user may not buy the product. Therefore focus should be more on post-installation supports, including the nature of the maintenance contracts offered by the vendor. The level and the quality of documentation available should likewise be checked thoroughly before a decision is made. User experience suggests the lack of adequate documentation as a major source of frustration. Depending on the aids available, the cost of changeover to the data base can vary. The changeover cost should be taken into consideration before arriving at a final decision.

Lastly, in selecting a DBS, it is better not to be a pioneer since the risk is great. It is also advisable to check with other users of the product, preferably those with similar problems. This last exercise can reveal startling information on many unsuspected fronts.

8.4 USER EXPERIENCE

There is a dearth of published material on user experience of data bases. What is available is often scanty, reflecting the lack of sustained experience because the technique is relatively new. User experience presented here is largely based on the following three works: *Data Base Management Systems* edited by D. A. Jardine,[5] *DBMS: User Experience in the USA by B. Davis,*[6] and *Data Base Management* by I. Palmer.[7] The first book consists of the proceedings of a SHARE conference held in 1973 where a number of users presented papers on their experience. The second book is a report of a survey carried out on 21 American companies in 1975 by the National Computing Centre of Britain. In the third book, an appendix is devoted to a survey of 8 British companies in 1972.

User experience, for the most part, is a reflection of the DBS being used. In other words many of the problems encountered are a direct consequence of the characteristics of the DBS in question. Since we have mentioned these DBS-dependent problems in the previous chapter during the discussion of the individual products, we shall here restrict our treatment of user experience to data bases in general, ignoring the DBS-dependent features. The following aspects of user experience are pertinent: motivation, selection and facilities, development and maintenance, and administration and user skill.

In reading through these pages, it should be borne in mind that this material is drawn from the experience of the early users, some of which may now appear naive.

8.4.1 Motivation

It would seem that in the majority of the cases data duplication, leading to data inconsistency and the attendant maintenance cost of the existing systems, were the primary reasons for changing to data bases. The inflexibility of the existing system to cope with the growing volume of data and the increasing demand for information, often played important roles in the decision. In some cases the need for integration of the related systems and also the need for standardisation, along with a desire to minimise program development and maintenance cost, acted as the prime movers. In a few cases the need to provide better and speedier management information was given priority, the facilities to support on-line systems also being regarded as important deciding factors. The evolutionary aspects of data base development, and the ease in systems design and programming afforded by a data base generally contributed in tilting the balance in favour of the change. Some users believed that ease in systems design and programming would lead to increased productivity in systems development, and would thus reduce data-processing costs. Some users also expected substantial savings in storage requirements, and hence cost, from the elimination of data redundancy.

8.4.2 Selection and Facilities

The majority of organisations used their in-house expertise to select data bases. In a few cases, the need of a single user system (as against the need of the organisation as a whole) or the superficial knowledge of a particular DBS, subordinated all other considerations. In most cases, however, the experience of other user organisations played an important part in the selection procedure. The quality of evaluation used varied from being casual to fairly thorough, involving anything from one week to three years. The reason for the casual evaluation probably lies in the fact that at the time there was a lack of any established selection procedure.

In most organisations, some preliminary evaluation is carried out in the initial phase, reducing the number of contending products to 2 or 3; then a detailed evaluation is made using a variable number of criteria including some form of benchmarking.[4,6]

Until recently most of the users, although reluctant to select manufacturer's products, and despite pressure in some cases, have shown a general lack of appreciation for compatibility of Data Base Systems. The advantages of a Codasyl-type DBS in providing compatibility and possible future standardisation were mostly ignored. In some instances users were not even interested in the need for future improvement of their DBSs by the vendors. This is shown by their selection of DBSs from vendors whose financial viability they suspected. In such cases the users safeguarded themselves by acquiring special legal rights over the coding and the documentation, against the financial collapse of the vendors.

Although most users of the surveys did not use any comprehensive set of selection criteria, such as the one presented in the last section, they nevertheless recognised the need for the following as a result of their post-installation experience.

Data redundancy control
Data dictionary
Data independence
Data protection
Test data base
Data base procedure
Automatic recovery facilities
Utilities, in particular, report generator
Query language and end user facilities
Concurrent usage facilities

The control of data redundancy was of course, in many cases, the main reason for changeover; therefore users' concern at its inadequacy is to be expected. Users learned to give priority to data independence, since this led to increased productivity through ease in systems design and development. Some users even constructed additional interfaces to increase data independence. Execution time binding (for data items in ADABAS and elements in TOTAL) proved to be very helpful, since it reduced the need for repeated recompilation after alterations. Some users introduced additional facilities for data validation and consistency checking and generated test data bases. The absence of data base procedures was also recognised as a drawback.[5] Some users were particularly affected by the lack of automatic recovery facilities, since they had to restart the system manually after every minor fault, which occurred quite frequently. Some users installed dual processors to improve reliability.

The inadequacy of performance evaluation facilities was an anathema to most users. Some users collected usage statistics, but found it difficult to analyse them and to reorganise the data base; bold users went ahead and reorganised the data base despite difficulties, with worthwhile outcome. One user claimed to have reduced the running time of a program from 9 to $1\frac{1}{2}$ hours.[6]

8.4.3 Development and Maintenance

As might be expected, the experience in the development and maintenance of data bases varied widely, depending on the characteristics of a particular product. However, most organisations adopted an evolutionary approach adding one system to the data base at a time. After an initial settling-down period, they noted increased productivity in systems development as a result of relative ease in data base expansion, systems design and programming. Some organisations claimed reductions in development and maintenance time between 25 and 70 per cent. Savings were also reported, in one case up to 90 per cent, in the volume of data processed, resulting apparently from the elimination of sorts, sequential updates, and so on. According to some users, data compression was also found to reduce processing time, since more data were stored in the same volume. Claims made on the reduction of data redundancy varied from a few to up to 50 per cent. Savings of up to 30 per cent in storage requirement were reported by one user, through a home-made DBS. This probably resulted from the combination of data compression and redundancy control.

The experience of most organisations seemed to converge on an underestimation of the initial development efforts and costs; this seems to be due to the following reasons.[6]

(1) Underestimation of manpower required.
(2) Problems in program specification largely due to the lack of experience.
(3) Underestimation of file conversion task mainly due to the proliferation of redundant and inconsistent data.

(4) Underestimation of the extra load imposed by the addition of on-line systems.

However, in most cases the situation recovered quickly as experience was gained and understanding of the DBS developed. The users agreed that with improved staff training, they could have avoided some of these initial problems.

Most organisations were generally satisfied with the performance of their data base, and were pleased with the new-found ability to respond quickly and efficiently to the demand. Contrary to popular expectation, there was in most organisations apparently a remarkable absence of inter-departmental politics, which often plagues progress in data sharing. Experience showed that, compared with conventional data processing, a data base environment demands greater emphasis on the following areas

Advanced planning
Documentation and standards
Program and systems testing
Coordination and communication
Control in resources—both time and cost

8.4.4 Administration and User Skill

Reviewing the situation over the past few years, there appears to have been a wide variation in the attitude towards the DBA. In some organisations no specific individual was given this function, while in some others the data-processing manager himself assumed the role. There is no doubt that the size of the enterprise has something to do with this. Experience shows that the higher the position of the DBA in the organisation, the more effective is the role he can play, but in some instances this has led to organisational problems. Most organisations reported difficulty in finding the right man for the job, although they were content to let his duties and responsibilities evolve with the growth of the data base. The majority of organisations established user committees to coordinate the demands of the user departments. The roles of such committees were mostly restricted to general coordination and supervision rather than to the actual scheduling of jobs and the allocation of priorities. The reason for this was partly to prevent the more vociferous members from taking advantage of their more reticent colleagues.

The skill required of the systems analyst depends on the nature of the package used, a greater skill being required for a data base without any data independence than for one with data independence. No information on skill versus data independence is available, but it is however generally agreed that data base environment demands systems analysts of better calibre than might otherwise be required. Experience has also seemed to show that the skill of a data base programmer need not be very high.

EXERCISES

1. Prepare an implementation schedule for changing over to a DBS in your organisation.

2. Prepare a scheme for the evaluation of DBSs for your organisation.

3. Describe the role a DBA can play in your organisation.

REFERENCES

[1] *Joint GUIDE-SHARE Report on DBMS Requirements*, November 1970.

[2] P. L. Peck, *Data Base Design and Implementation* (Online, Uxbridge 1974), p. 13.

[3] *Codasyl DDL—Journal of Development*, June 1973.

[4] Comparative Evaluation of ADABAS and System 2000 for the Integrated Payroll/Personnel/Employee Benefits Application and Associated Reports, Government of Ontario, March 1974 (private communication).

[5] D. A. Jardine, *Data Base Management Systems* (North Holland, Amsterdam, 1974).

[6] B. Davis, *Data Base Management Systems: User Experience in the USA* (National Computing Centre Publications, 1975).

[7] I. Palmer, *Data Base Management* (Scicon, London, 1973).

9 *Future Development*

Data base technology is barely 10 years old and is still in the early stage of development, but is has already made a great impact on data processing. A growing number of people are now using data bases and there is no doubt that this trend will continue, most probably with an accelerated pace due to decreasing hardware and increasing software costs. However, data bases are slow in processing and consequently costly in operation. The breakthrough here is likely to come from the current researches in storage technology, particularly in associative memory. In fact the widespread use of the relational model, with all its powerful facilities, crucially depends on such a breakthrough. But is the relational model capable of meeting all our future data base requirements? To the academic, the answer is a resounding 'yes'. And yet to researchers in IBM, where the relational model was conceived and is still being nourished, the answer appears less clear cut. One of their team led by M. E. Senko has already proposed another model called Data Independent Accessing Model (DIAM). This is a serious proposal and certainly deserves careful examination. Future development will also be affected by standardisation in data bases where work has already begun. In this chapter we shall consider these issues, beginning in section 9.1 with an examination of future storage development, followed in section 9.2 with a look at the DIAM model. The progress in standardisation will be discussed in section 9.3, with a conclusion in section 9.4.

9.1 STORAGE TECHNOLOGY

We shall discuss the development in storage technology in three areas and assess their relevance to data bases. The areas are: laser memory, bubble memory and associative memory.

Both laser and bubble memory are being designed for secondary storage, whereas associative memory can act as the primary memory, with the capability of accessing an item by value rather than by its physical address. It is this associative memory that is likely to have the biggest impact on future data bases.

9.1.1 Laser Memory

In a laser memory the information is sorted, with the help of a laser beam, on a special plate in the form of a hologram of binary bits. For retrieval the information is reconstructed from the hologram by exposing it to a suitably prepared laser beam.[1,2]

The input information is passed through a special device which converts the electric pulses into light and reorganises it in the form of a matrix of binary bits. This matrix, modulated with a laser beam, is allowed to create a hologram on a section of a specially prepared plate by physical deformation of its surface. To retrieve the information thus stored, the section is exposed to another laser beam, which reconstructs the stored information as a hologram on a photo-detector array for conversion into electric pulses. To erase information, the surface of the section concerned is melted to the unrecorded state by a stronger laser beam. The currently available plates can support several thousand such record/write/erase cycles before replacements are required. One disadvantage of such storage is the need to recreate a whole section for each amendment or deletion.

In a prototype laser memory under construction for NASA,[2] the surface is divided into 400 sections (20 $\times$ 20) for a total storage capacity of 6.5 megabytes. The writing and reading speeds are expected to be 1 and 13 megabits per second respectively. Note that it takes longer to write than to read and, in consequence, laser memory is more suitable for read-only storage.

A modern fast disc has an access time of 5 to 20 milliseconds with a data transfer rate of about 8 megabits per second, and it has a storage capacity ranging from 10^7 to 10^8 bits. The larger discs can hold between 10^9 and 10^{10} bits, with an access time ranging from 20 to 300 milliseconds. Compared with these figures the expected achievements of the prototype laser memory are not dramatic, but the scope for improvements is large. Surface capacity of up to a trillion (10^{12}) bits of information and higher access rates look feasible. Moreover the laser memory is likely to be considerably cheaper than discs.[2] However, it is unlikely that the laser memory will have any direct effect on improving the performance of a data base, except that it may provide cheaper secondary storage for archiving old data.

9.1.2 Magnetic Bubble Memory

Magnetic bubbles may be described as tiny magnets (dipoles) floating in a suitable magnetic medium. These dipoles are made to act as binary bits.[3,4]

Dipoles are created on thin film or sheets of certain magnetic material by applying a low magnetic field perpendicular to the surface. As the field is increased the surface gradually breaks down into tiny cylindrical magnets which float like bubbles in a sea of reverse magnetisation. The bubbles can be propagated along predefined tracks with the help of auxiliary magnets of special shapes, whose forces of attraction and repulsion are used to guide the bubbles. Techniques exist to detect, create, annihilate and deflect the bubbles; no moving parts are involved. Each bubble represents a binary bit and is driven through a read/write mechanism called *read/write gate*. The logical operations can be performed by deflecting a bubble from one track to another. This allows data manipulation on the bubbles, as in a computer memory.

It is interesting to compare bubble memory with disc storage. In both, information is stored by magnetisation, but in bubble memory, the magnetisation pattern moves along the medium rather than the medium itself moving. An additional point is that logical operations can be performed on the bubbles but not on discs. At present a storage density of 10^5 to 10^7 bits per cm^2 with an access time of 20 milliseconds has been achieved in magnetic bubble memory. An access time of less than 1 millisecond with a storage density of 10^9 bits per cm^2 appears feasible.[4] This compares very favourably with discs, whose performance statistics were given earlier. One problem, however, is the production cost of bubble memory, which at present is very high.

Since the magnetic bubble incorporates both memory and data manipulation on the same medium, it can become very useful to data bases.

9.1.3 Associative Memory

As indicated earlier, associative memories are special types of processor which can access words in the memory by their content rather than by their address, hence it is also known as content-addressable memory. Basically it is a processor which can perform an operation simultaneously on all the words of the memory. Its concept first appeared in the literature about 15 years ago. Ever since, various ideas have been put forward to translate the concept into reality, and now several prototypes are available, but they all are too expensive for large-scale use.[5,6]

The present technique in associative memory involves slicing every word into bits, and carrying out parallel operations on the same bit position of every word in the memory. By repeating the operation successively from the first to the last bit of a word, the entire content of the memory is processed. This is known as *bit slice mode*. Recently byte slicing has also been suggested.

To demonstrate the principle involved, we shall consider an example. Suppose we have loaded in the memory a file with fixed-length records, each containing name and address of people as shown in figure 9.1. We wish to search for those people who live in Aberdeen and whose surname starts with the letter D. To do this the associative memory will require two special registers—a *comparand register* and a *mask register*—each having the same length as that of a record in the file. The comparand register will be loaded with the letter D and the city name ABERDEEN in the appropriate positions, and the mask register will be loaded with 1s in the positions of interest and 0s (space is used here) otherwise, as shown in figure 9.1. The mask register is intended to mask all the unwanted positions in the memory. All the records in the file will be searched simultaneously for a match with a content of the comparand register, starting at the leftmost bit

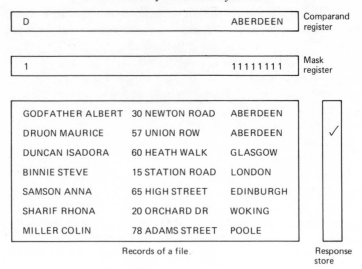

Figure 9.1 Associative memory

position. The masked positions will be ignored. The result of the search will be indicated in the response store by means of a pointer directing to Maurice Druon. This record can then be removed for further processing.

We produce here some performance characteristics of associative memory based on a theoretical model.[6] For ordinary search, the ratio of the number of interrogations into the memory required by sequential processing to that required by associative processing was proportional to the logarithm of the list being searched. For a multiconditional search this ratio was 50 to 1. For a list of 16 items the ratio for update was 30 to 1. It was also estimated that, for a data base, a sequential memory would take about 2 to 4 times more storage compared to that of an associative memory, primarily because of the need for directories when using memories of the sequential type.

The impact of an inexpensive associative memory on data processing in general, and data bases in particular, can hardly be overestimated. The greatest advantage will accrue from the facility for parallel search, which will considerably cut down the time spent in the selection of items. Apart from cost, there are at present two other handicaps which need attention. Firstly data have to be loaded in the associative memory from the secondary storage before they can be searched. High-speed data transfer and large associative memory would hopefully resolve this problem. The second problem concerns the need for fixed-length records in the associative memory for parallel searching. In a data base this may result in wasteful storage. Use of delimiter may solve this problem, but it would reduce the searching speed.

Currently a few prototype associative memories are available but the cost is excessive. Perhaps future research will help produce cheaper types.

9.2 DATA INDEPENDENT ACCESSING MODEL

In 1973 M. E. Senko, E. B. Altman, M. M. Ashrahan and P. L. Fehder[7] of IBM proposed a new model for a data base called *Data Independent Accessing Model* (DIAM), which is expected to provide a high degree of data independence. In this model the data of the real world are presented in four successive levels of abstraction, known as the *Entity Set Model, String Model, Encoding Model* and *Physical Device Level Model*, as shown in figure 9.2. Using entities and their properties, an Entity Set Model is created to represent the world of reality and is meant to be independent of the storage representation of data. Application programs can access the data base at this level through a *Representation Independent Accessing Language* (RIAL). Alternatively an application program can enter the data base at the String Model level through a *Representation Dependent Accessing Language* (RDAL), but in this case the program will not be protected against the changes in the data base.

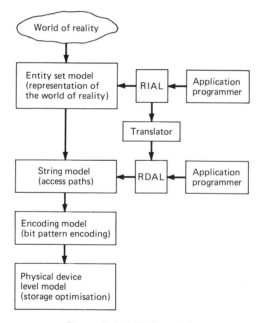

Figure 9.2 DIAM model

In the String Model, attribute values (that is, data item values) are grouped together into various physical data structures called strings, the same attribute value appearing in more than one string. Access paths are provided to each string, thus allowing more than one means of finding an attribute value. An application program entering the data base at this level must stipulate the access paths to follow; and therefore it has to be changed in the event of a reorganisation of the String Model. In the Encoding Model, the strings generated in the previous model are encoded economically into bit patterns. The Physical Device Level Model facilitates efficient management of the physical storage space.

9.2.1 Entity Set Model

We mentioned in section 3.1 that an attribute can be used either as the identity attribute or as a role attribute, depending on the choice of the entity. In recognition of these two aspects, each attribute in this model is given two names—an *Identity Name* (not a DIAM term) and a *Role Name*. This is explained in the following example. Let us consider an entity record set made up of three attributes—employee, manager and job title—as shown in figure 9.3.

Employee	Manager	Job Title
Jack Lynch	Nicola Brown	Programmer
Habib Ehsan	Nicola Brown	Systems Analyst
Neal Lewis	Tom Jackson	Salesman

Figure 9.3 Entity records

If we assume employees as the entities, then both manager and job title are role attributes, and as such we give them role names, say, MANAGER and JOB-TITLE respectively. A value of attribute manager is a person such as Nicola Brown who can be an entity as an employee, and therefore we associate an Identity Name EMPLOYEE with attribute manager. Similarly we might be using the values of attribute job title as entities to find information on job titles and therefore, to include this possibility, we also associate an Identity Name, say, JOB, with attribute job title.

Two separate names for the two aspects of an attribute are provided so that a user can refer to the attribute by a naturally meaningful name of the aspect in which he is interested. The names EMPLOYEE and MANAGER for attribute manager serve such a purpose, but sometimes the same name can describe both the aspects equally well; if so, two distinct names are really unnecessary. For instance we could have used JOB-TITLE for both the Identity and Role Names of attribute job-title. Another example is the attribute employee of figure 9.3, where we can use the same name EMPLOYEE as both Identity and Role Name. Alternatively we can use EMPLOYEE and EMPLOYEE-NAME for Identity and Role Name respectively.

In DIAM, the Identity Names are termed *Entity Name Set Name*, or *Name Set Name* for short. The entity names of the entities belonging to an entity set are said to constitute an *Entity Name Set* or just *Name Set*; the name given to the Name Set is Name Set Name, whose values are the entity names belonging to that Name Set. Every attribute in the Entity Set Model is qualified by its Name Set Name and Role Name written in the form: Name Set Name/Role Name/Attribute Value.

We can therefore write the three entity records of figure 9.3 as shown in figure 9.4.

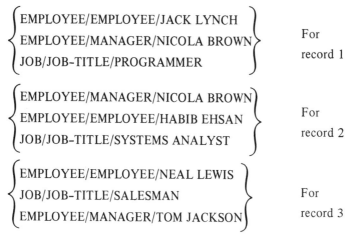

$$\left\{\begin{array}{l}\text{EMPLOYEE/EMPLOYEE/JACK LYNCH}\\ \text{EMPLOYEE/MANAGER/NICOLA BROWN}\\ \text{JOB/JOB-TITLE/PROGRAMMER}\end{array}\right\} \quad \begin{array}{l}\text{For}\\ \text{record 1}\end{array}$$

$$\left\{\begin{array}{l}\text{EMPLOYEE/MANAGER/NICOLA BROWN}\\ \text{EMPLOYEE/EMPLOYEE/HABIB EHSAN}\\ \text{JOB/JOB-TITLE/SYSTEMS ANALYST}\end{array}\right\} \quad \begin{array}{l}\text{For}\\ \text{record 2}\end{array}$$

$$\left\{\begin{array}{l}\text{EMPLOYEE/EMPLOYEE/NEAL LEWIS}\\ \text{JOB/JOB-TITLE/SALESMAN}\\ \text{EMPLOYEE/MANAGER/TOM JACKSON}\end{array}\right\} \quad \begin{array}{l}\text{For}\\ \text{record 3}\end{array}$$

Figure 9.4 Entity description set

In an entity record set, the entity records do not have to appear in any specific order; the attribute values within an entity record are also ordering independent, every attribute value being identified by a Name Set Name and Role Name. However, this freedom in DIAM is more apparent than real, since the strings defined in the String Model for access paths use specific orderings (see later).

In DIAM a many-to-one relationship is represented by including the second entity as an additional attribute in the entity record of the first entity. Figure 9.3 shows a many-to-one relationship between attribute employee and manager. Obviously these entity records can also be used to provide the one-to-many relationship between manager and employee. Many-to-many relationships can be represented by using link records exactly in the same way as for the Codasyl model.

The terms used in Entity Set Model for entity record and entity record set are *Entity Description* and *Entity Description Set*. The name given to the Entity Description Set is *Entity Description Set Name*, or *Description Set Name* (DSN) for short. DSN is roughly equivalent to a record type name.

The Entity Set Model provides the global data structure, independent of the storage consideration. An application program entering the data base at this level is also independent of the access paths and storage structure. Addition, deletion and amendments of attributes, Entity Descriptions or Entity Description Sets can easily be handled without affecting the application programs.

9.2.2 String Model

In this model, three types of physical data structure, called strings, are created from the attribute values of the Entity Set Model as follows.

(1)   An *atomic string* (*A-string*) is formed from a collection of attribute values in a specified order. A number of A-strings can be constructed from the same entity record, and the same attribute value may appear in more than one A-string. Except for this data duplication, A-strings are similar to the segments of IMS.

(2)   An *entity-string* (*E-string*) is formed by connecting specified A-strings of the same type in a specified order and it may contain some or all the A-strings of the same type. It corresponds to a collection containing the occurrences of a segment type, except that an E-string need not contain all the occurrences. The order of appearance of the A-strings can be specified as a function of the Role Names. The same A-string may participate in more than one E-string.

(3)   A *link-string* (*L-string*) is a collection of A-strings, E-strings and other L-strings belonging to the same entity, and is somewhat similar to the hierarchical 'record' of IMS. A particular A-string, E-string or L-string can belong to a number of L-strings and can be accessed through a variety of access paths—sequential, indexed or direct.

Each string is assigned a name and the correspondence between the Name Set Name/Role Name and string name is maintained by appropriate tables. Each A-string is physically represented in the storage device thus permitting multiple copies of the same attribute value in the data base.

Since a particular attribute value can appear in a number of strings, it can also be accessed in a number of ways. Therefore the system must select the optimal access path, if the application program enters at the Entity Set Model level, by using RIAL. Alternatively a program may enter the system at the String Model level by using RDAL, which specifies the access paths to be employed. The problem of finding the best access paths for programs using RIAL is equivalent to the translation of RIAL into RDAL in an optimal manner, and this may prove to be very costly in terms of the processing speed.

The accessing languages RIAL and RDAL have not as yet been described in any detail and thus it is difficult to write much about them here. From the material presented in the paper by Senko *et al.*, it would seem that a RIAL user will construct his local entity record set from a subset of attributes belonging to a global entity record set (that is, an entity record set in the Entity Set Model). He may sequence the attributes as necessary, and specify conditions to exclude unwanted entity records. It would also appear that the freedom to form a single entity record set with attributes from two or more global entity record sets will be denied to him. The user may, however, construct as many entity record sets as necessary, each from a global entity record set, the relationships between the entity records of any two local sets being determined by the presence of explicit role attributes in the entity records. These linking attributes would act like the foreign keys of the relational model.

As mentioned earlier, the selection of an optimum access path is likely to decrease the processing speed significantly. However, the processing speed can be improved if we accept a reasonable, but not necessarily optimal, access path. For instance, we might choose a path that has the minimum number of nodes (in the context of a hierarchy). A higher relative accuracy can be provided by weighting the nodes and selecting the path with least total weights. If a user employs a particular hierarchical relationship among entity records too often, presumably the DBA would construct an L-string for him.

In RDAL, the user is dependent on the strings, and must extract explicitly the strings he needs. At this level, the user interface is somewhat similar to that in IMS. Any program that uses RDAL has to be changed if the strings it accesses are altered in the event of the reorganisation of the String Model for improving the access performance of the RIAL users.

In both RIAL and RDAL, the system will have to cope with update problems arising from data duplications.

9.2.3 Encoding and Physical Device Level Models

As mentioned earlier, the Encoding Model provides means of encoding the strings into binary bits in an efficient manner, whereas the Physical Device Level Model is intended to facilitate optimum utilisation of storage space required for the encoded A-strings through the specification of block sizes, overflows, and so on.

9.2.4 Summary and Conclusion

Summarised below are the salient points of DIAM, using standard data-processing terms wherever possible.

(1) In DIAM every data item is given two names for user convenience.
(2) A user can enter the data base either in a representation independent (RI) or a representation dependent (RD) mode. Data independence is provided for the RI users.
(3) An RI user is free to construct his local record types using only a subset of the data items in the global record type. He may specify the order in which the data items should appear and impose conditions to exclude unnecessary occurrences.
(4) For an RI user, the record relationships are determined by the explicit keys present in his local records.
(5) Access paths are transparent to an RI user. Three types of string—A-string, E-string and L-string—roughly corresponding to segment, the occurrences of a segment type, and 'record' of IMS, are provided to facilitate the representation of a wide variety of access paths, such as sequential, indexed and direct. Data duplication is allowed in the strings. This generates a new problem of finding a reasonably efficient access path and this consequently

slows down update, as well as access speeds. The strings can be restructured as required to optimise the access performance of the RI users, without requiring any change in their programs.

(6)   An RI user is independent of changes in the data base, unless the change directly affects the data of his interest.

(7)   An RD user accesses the strings of the data base. He may extract as many strings as he needs. For him the data relationship is provided by the string structures. If the strings are restructured, RD programs will have to be changed.

(8)   Storage economy in DIAM is provided at two levels, both independent of the application programs. Firstly all A-strings are coded optimally into bit pattern, and secondly, storage space is managed optimally, thus reducing overall storage requirements. Only A-strings are physically stored, and they may include data duplication.

DIAM is not founded on any rigorous theoretical considerations; it is an empirical model based on experience. It is designed to mirror as far as possible the natural data relationships that exist in the real world, and thus provide convenience for users. In contrast, the relational model reduces natural data relationships into two-dimensional tables, while the Codasyl model lies somewhere in the middle of these two approaches.

Many of the features of DIAM are similar to those of IMS, and, in a sense, it is an improved version of IMS/VS. In place of segments, DIAM uses strings, and in place of a single access method, DIAM can support an unlimited number of access methods. However, this multiplicity of access paths in DIAM generates path selection problems, leading to slow retrieval speeds.

Data duplication allowed in DIAM would slow down updates and use extra storage space. It would also make the enforcement of privacy and integrity control during concurrent usage more difficult, since the same piece of data could appear in many A-strings. Moreover, the DBA will have great difficulty in designing the strings needed to meet the access requirements of all users in an efficient manner.

Recently Senko[8] has proposed a new version of DIAM called DIAM-II, the original version described above being known now as DIAM-I. In DIAM-II, the Entity Set Model is replaced by what is called an Infological level, where data items are presented in pairs (as binary relations), each pair containing the identity attribute and a role attribute of an entity record. For instance, the entity records of figure 9.4 would be presented in DIAM-II as two binary relations—(EMPLOYEE MANAGER) and (EMPLOYEE JOB-TITLE)—assuming employee to be the identity attribute. If there is more than one identity attribute of interest, then there has to be one such set of binary relations per identity attribute, and this introduces a proliferation of identity attributes. This infological level is likened to the Schema, and it can be entered by a RI user through a non-procedural language called FORAL. A Subschema level, named End user level, is added on the top of the infological level, permitting access by programs written in pro-cedural languages such as Cobol and PL/1, and also by FORAL.

The String Model is renamed as the Access path level, the original three types of string being replaced by two new types: I-strings, for the construction of seg-ment types, and T-strings to form A-set types (section 3.2.4) from these I-strings. Both I-strings and T-strings are logical collections, and hence the same attribute may appear in more than one string. The other two models remain unchanged, and are called Encoding level and Physical device level, instead of Encoding Model and Physical Device Level Model.

The proposition of DIAM-II should be interpreted as an indication of the difficulties of implementing DIAM-I, and it could well mean the abandonment of DIAM-I by its designers. DIAM-II bypasses some of the problems of its predeces-sor, but it also creates some of its own—for instance, it suffers from all the in-conveniences of the relational DBSs based on binary relations, which are prolifera-ted with duplicate attributes, and hence unsuited to the needs of large users.

9.3 STANDARDISATION: THE ANSI-SPARC MODEL

We mentioned in section 5.1.2 that responsibility for the standardisation of Data Base Systems rests with appropriate national authorities. In the United States, this responsibility is exercised by the American National Standards Institute (ANSI) through its Committee on Computers and Information Processing, known as X3. In November 1972 the Standards Planning and Requirements Committee (SPARC) of ANSI-X3 set up a study group, called ANSI-X3-SPARC/DBMS study group, to specify a model for a standardised DBS. This study group (also referred to as ANSI-SPARC or just ANSI study group) coordinates its activities with the relevant authorities of other countries, and also with the Codasyl standing committees (PLC and DDLC) responsible for data base activities. A number of organisations are common members of these Codasyl committees and the ANSI-SPARC study group.

ANSI does not intend to develop any data base languages; its purpose is to specify the overall architecture and the characteristics of a standardised DBS. The specification will include the interfaces and the components of the DBS and the facilities it should provide. Any DBS that conforms to these specifications would qualify as a standard DBS.

The study group produced an interim report[9] in February 1975. This is a large document, parts of which are ill-defined, imprecise and very confusing. The final report is not expected for a number of years, and therefore a standardised DBS is unlikely to be marketed before the mid 1980s. We shall present below the main feature of the ANSI-X3-SPARC model as it appears in the interim report.

The architecture of the ANSI model will be based on three schemas—concep-tual, external and internal—which roughly correspond to the Schema, Subschema and Storage-schema discussed in the earlier chapters. The conceptual schema would describe only the entities and their properties in the real world, without any reference to the world of machine. The entries in the conceptual schema would include data items, records and datasets, but not Picture clauses, access paths or other storage-dependent clauses. A conceptual record type may share data items with other conceptual record types (thus the same data item appears in more than one record type), and can be defined, if necessary, as a hierarchical tree, as in IMS. Records can be grouped into sets, as in the Codasyl model. In addition a conceptual schema may also contain record types which are not stored.

The external schema (Subschema) entries would include data items, Picture clauses (or equivalent), records, datasets, and so on. A record type in the external schema must be a subset of a given conceptual record type—data items can be omitted or reordered, but new record types from two or more conceptual record types cannot be created. If a new record type is required, it has to be defined in the conceptual schema. External schemas would be mapped into the conceptual schema, which would in turn be mapped into the internal schema, external schemas being protected from the changes in the internal schema. Direct mapping of external schemas into the internal schema would also be permitted if required for faster access, but such mapping would naturally reduce data independence for the external schemas and the application programs involved.

The internal schema must specify the physical organisation of all data including data items, records, datasets, their pointers, indices and access paths, with a view to optimising performance, response time and storage space requirements. It would also specify record placements, virtual data, block size and overflow. It would be possible to represent a conceptual record in the internal schema, either as a single physical record, or as several physical records. The conceptual record can be stored as a free-standing record, as a node of a tree structure, or as a repeating group within a higher level physical record.[10] A conceptual schema may contain entries for records that are not represented in the internal schema. There are other similar optimisation facilities that can be used in the internal schema for data items, datasets and indices.

The conceptual schema is expected to facilitate the evolution of data declaration by allowing the splitting of an entity record into several entity records, sometimes known as *entity splitting* or *attribute migration*, to cater for the growing volume of data. Such entity splitting should not require remapping of the existing external schemas. The mapping should be based on the attributes and, so long as the attributes exist, their migration to new entity records should not affect the external schema binding.

Entity splitting in the conceptual schema need not be immediately incorporated into the internal schema, but when it is incorporated, it may not necessarily be directly represented, since it could involve the re-optimisation of the internal schema structure, including the declaration of new virtual data. It would depend on the kind of changes proposed.

The ANSI-SPARC model would provide both host language and query language facilities, and would permit the creation of external schemas to support the facilities of Codd's relational model (see also the next section). Data independence is a prime feature of the model, and it is provided by the three schemas, each schema being insulated against changes in the other two, as outlined in chapter 3. The model also includes a data dictionary as a central facility (section 4.4.1).

The ANSI specification as detailed in the interim report is at variance with the present Codasyl approach; but it is most likely that a subset of a future Codasyl model (the Codasyl approach being evolutionary) would meet the ANSI specification and would thus become a standard model. In this connection the parallel between the Codasyl Cobol and ANSI Cobol is instructive.

9.4 CONCLUSION

Developments in data bases have been rapid, and for a time there was a mushroom growth of data base packages of every kind and size. The Codasyl proposal has helped to check this diversification by providing a common framework for data base development. As mentioned earlier, all major manufacturers except IBM are now committed to implement the Codasyl specifications; indeed, some have already done so. This has opened up the new possibility of a data base network, linking a family of data bases and supplying, if required, data jointly to the same application program. We are likely to witness an increasing number of such *distributed systems* in the future.

Of the four major Codasyl-based products available, DMS 1100 contains only a subset of the Codasyl specifications; an improved version is expected shortly. IDMS has implemented a small subset of the specification, but because of its portability and availability on IBM hardware, it has made quite an impact in the market. IDS-II was released only recently, so it is too early to assess user reactions to it. The current version contains only a small subset of the Codasyl specification, but an eventual full implementation is reported to be Honeywell's long-term aim. The widespread use of DBMS-10 is constrained by the market of the DEC 10 computers.

IMS is clearly the most popular large DBS, but its heyday is probably over, since it is facing increasingly harder competition from other products, particularly the Codasyl-based DBSs. The tendency among many users to move away from the exclusive manufacturer's products, and also the slow processing of IMS founded on outdated data structures, are likely to erode IMS's popularity. However, IMS has a very large lead over other products, and IBM will no doubt come out with a successor long before this lead evaporates. This new product could be an implementation of the ANSI-SPARC specification.

ADABAS and SYSTEM 2000 have relatively simpler but very effective data structures. These two products are easy to understand, install and use. As products they are less sophisticated than IMS or those based on the Codasyl specification, but they suit admirably the needs of many medium-large organisations. For smaller organisations, TOTAL has proved to be the most successful product.

There is little doubt, however, that the Codasyl-based products will capture an increasingly larger share of the market. Nevertheless, products like ADABAS, SYSTEM 2000, TOTAL, IMS, DL/1 will probably continue side by side during the next 10 years or so. It is likely however that their influence will diminish when standardised Data Base Systems, following the ANSI-SPARC specifications are available—perhaps in the mid 1980s.

A prediction for the long-term future is more difficult to make. There appear to be four models—Codasyl, ANSI, DIAM and Relational—which may be considered. Codasyl has adopted an evolutionary approach, and therefore the model will change with time. It is most likely that in the future a subset of the Codasyl specifications will satisfy the ANSI requirements, and this standardised DBS will dominate the market.

The prospect of a widescale usage of DIAM-I appears less likely. Data independence and access facilities provided in DIAM-I are less than those in the relational model, where it is possible to construct a relation from many other relations and access any data item value in the data base directly, with the capability of using data item values of other relations as conditions. The contemplated accessing language (RIAL) in DIAM does not appear to cater for such powerful facilities. Furthermore, from the DBA's point of view, the relational data base would be easier to design and develop. Therefore DIAM-I does not seem to be a strong contender as a DBS of the future. The specification of DIAM-II appears to be an admission of the difficulties of DIAM-I. Using data structures founded on binary relations, DIAM-II can hardly compete as the future DBS, since binary relations are unsuitable for large data bases.

There is also a difference of opinion concerning the future of the relational model. Some see it as the data base model of the future, while others are less optimistic, mainly because of implementation problems discussed in chapter 6. There is yet another possibility[11]—the relational structure can perhaps be used as an additional global or local view of data stored for a formatted data base. For instance, a Codasyl-type data base could have, in addition to its Schema, a relational Schema or Subschema where all data would be shown as logical relations. This could provide powerful query facilities for users. In fact Codasyl is interested in a relational Subschema facility, as is the ANSI-SPARC study group which has already proposed relational external schema as a standard facility of its model. Despite this interest, it must be said that the problems of implementing such an interface are many and its feasibility is by no means assured.

EXERCISES

1. Compare the data structure and the access facilities of DIAM-I with those of IMS, and explain why DIAM-I can be regarded as a superset of IMS.

2. Compare the ANSI-SPARC model with the present Codasyl model. (Consult reference 10.)

3. Discuss the problems of constructing a relational interface to the Codasyl model.

REFERENCES

[1] D. Vilkomerson, *et al. Proc. AFIPS Conf.* 33 (1968) p. 1197.

[2] M. Cashman, *Datamation,* 19 (1973) p. 66.

[3] J. Lucas and R. Lock, *New Scient.* 58 (1973) p. 81.

[4] A. Chang, *Proc. AFIPS Conf.* 43 (1974) p. 847.

[5] R. Linde, *et al., Proc. AFIPS Conf.* 42 (1973) p. 187.

[6] P. B. Berra, *Proc. AFIPS Conf.* 43 (1974) p. 1.

[7] M. E. Senko, *et al., IBM Syst. J.* 12 (1973) p. 30.

[8] M. E. Senko, 'DIAM as a Detailed Example of the ANSI-SPARC Architecture' *Proc. of IFIP TC-2 Working Conf. on Modelling in DBMS* held at Freudenstadt, Germany, 1976 (North Holland, Amsterdam)

[9] *ANSI–X3–SPARC/DBMS Study Group: Interim Report,* February 1975.

[10] C. W. Bachman, *Proc. AFIPS Conf.* 44 (1975) p. 569.

[11] Symposium on Implementing Relational Data Base Systems, University of Southampton, March 1976 (unpublished discussion).

Answers to Selected Exercises

CHAPTER 5

1. Answer NO.

4. Since any record described in the Schema can be a member of every dynamic set type, every record of the data base has to be provided with this extra pointer space, and this increases overheads.

5. In an *M:N* relationship, a record can be related to an unlimited number of records of the other type, and the Schema does not know at the time of compilation how much pointer space to allocate. Link records remove this uncertainty by ensuring that a record cannot appear more than once in any set type. From the set membership entries, the Schema can then determine the maximum number of pointers for a record of a given type.

6. Hints: By introducing some sort of predicate or other means to describe conditions in the set entry.

7. If in the Schema A owns B and B owns C, then in the Subschema we should be able to have A owns C, although it is not defined in the Schema.

11(a) *Schema* (The capital letters in brackets in the record descriptions below are data names used later in the DML commands.)

(1) Customer Order Record (COR)
Customer no. (CN)/Item code(IC)/Daily quantities for 62 days.
Location Mode Calc, Key = CN + IC.
(2) Item Detail Record (IDR)
Item code(IC)/Description/Price(PR)/Weight/Size.
Location Mode Calc, Key = IC.
(3) Sales Information Record (SIR)
Item code/Monthly sales for 24 months.
Location Mode Calc, Key = Item code.
(4) Van Information Record (VIR)
Van no. (VN)/Van capacity.
Location Mode Calc, Key = VN.

(5) Customer Accounts Record (CAR)
Customer no. (CN)/Name and Address (NA)/Route no. /
No. of times delivered/YTD sales/YTD payment/Balance.
Location Mode Calc, Key = CN.

(6) Day Number Record (DNR)
28 records for 28 days each with a single field (DN)
containing the day number.
Location Mode Direct, Key = DN.

SET1:   Owner SIR, Member COR.
SET2:   Owner DNR, Member CAR, in the ascending order of the customer
        number.
SET3:   Owner CAR, Member COR.
SET4:   Owner SYSTEM, Member SIR, in the ascending order of the item code.
SET5:   Owner SYSTEM, Member IDR, in the ascending order of the item code.
SET6:   Owner SYSTEM, Member VIR, in the ascending order of the van
        number.

11(b) Assume the day number as read into the data name DAYN.

    FIND DNR   DB–KEY DAYN.
    FIND   FIRST CAR WITHIN SET2 .

B20.

    GET CAR.
    FIND FIRST COR WITHIN SET3 .
    IF ERROR–STATUS > 0,
        DISPLAY "NO ORDER FOR CUSTOMER", CN;
        GO TO B40.

B30.

    GET COR.
    MOVE IC IN COR TO IC IN IDR.
    FIND ANY IDR.
    GET IDR.

(Now process by Cobol as necessary and then get the next COR.)
    FIND NEXT COR WITHIN SET3.
    IF ERROR–STATUS = 0, GO TO B30.
    DISPLAY "END OF ORDERS FOR CUSTOMER", CN.

B40.

    FIND NEXT CAR WITHIN SET2.
    IF ERROR–STATUS = 0, GO TO B20.
    DISPLAY "END OF CUSTOMERS FOR DAY", DAYN.

12(a) *Schema*

(1) Car charges Record (CCR)
Model(MD)/Fixed daily charge(DC)/Mileage charge.
Location Mode Calc, Key = MD.

(2) Car Detail Record (CDR)
Car registration no. (RN)/Date purchased/Mileage (ML)/
Daily bookings for 120 days, each containing the order number if booked.
Location Mode Calc, Key = RN

(Note these 120 fields for bookings should be treated as a circular buffer to reduce updates.)

(3) Customer Accounts Record (CAR)
Customer no. (CN)/Name and Address(NA)/YTD sales/
YTD payment/Balance.
Location Mode Calc, Key = CN.

(4) Order Completion Record (OCR)
Customer no. (CN)/Order no. (ON)/Miles driven/fixed daily charge/
Mileage charge/Car registration no. (RN)/Start date/Finish date.
Location Mode Calc, Key CN + ON.

(Daily and mileage charges or something in lieu of are necessary for this record, since a customer can be charged at the rate of the next cheaper model rather than the one actually used.)

SET1:   Owner SYSTEM, Member CCR, Prior processible, members in the
        ascending order of the fixed daily charge.
SET 2: Owner CCR, Member CDR, Linked to owner.
SET 3: Owner CAR, Member OCR.
SET 4: Owner SYSTEM, Member CAR, in the ascending order of the customer
        number.

12(b)1 Assume we have read the customer number and the order number of the car into the data name CUSTN and ORDN respectively.

        MOVE CASTN TO CN IN OCR.
        MOVE ORDN TO ON IN OCR.
        FIND ANY OCR.
        GET OCR.
        MOVE RN IN OCR TO RN IN CDR.
        FIND CDR.
        GET CDR.
        Update by Cobol and then,
        STORE CDR.

12(b)2 We have used below the data name NEWRN to hold the registration number of the newly selected car.
A10.

        MOVE SPACES TO NEWRN.
        MOVE OLDRN TO RN IN CDR.
        FIND ANY CDR.
        FIND OWNER WITHIN SET2.

A20.

    PERFORM B-SEARCH SECTION.

    IF NEWRN NOT = SPACE, GO TO A40-PROCESS.

    FIND NEXT CCR WITHIN SET1.

    IF ERROR-STATUS > 0,

        DISPLAY "NO NEXT CAR–END OF SET";

        GO TO A30.

    PERFORM B-SEARCH SECTION.

    IF NEWRN NOT = SPACE, GO TO A40-PROCESS.

    NOTE TWO PRIOR COMMANDS ARE NECESSARY.

A30.

    FIND PRIOR CCR WITHIN SET1.

    FIND PRIOR CCR WITHIN SET1.

    IF ERROR-STATUS > 0,

        DISPLAY "NO PRIOR CAR–END OF SET";

        GO TO A50.

    PERFORM B-SEARCH SECTION.

    IF NEWRN = SPACE, GO TO A50.

A40.-PROCESS.

    Process if any

A50.

    EXIT.

B-SEARCH SECTION.

B10.

    GET MD IN CCR.

    FIND FIRST CDR WITHIN SET2.

B20.

    GET CDR.

Now search for a free car by Cobol instruction; if found

    MOVE RN IN CDR TO NEWRN, and GO TO B40.

If not found continue as follows

    FIND NEXT CDR WITHIN SET2.

    IF ERROR-STATUS = 0, GO TO B20.

    DISPLAY "NO FREE CAR, MODEL", MD.

B40.

    EXIT.

13(a) *Schema*

(1)   Component Information Record (CIR)

    Component code (CC)/Quantity in stock/Reorder level/Standard

    manufacturing time/Price.

    Location Mode Calc, Key = CC.

(One record per component.)

(2)   Component Explosion Record (CER)
Superior component code (SUPC)/Subordinate component code (SUBC)/
Quantity of the SUBC in the SUPC.

(One record per superior/subordinate pair—as in the REL records of figure 5.7.)

(3)   Component Link Record (CLR)
Component code (CC)/Hierarchy code/Data base key of a CER containing
this component code.

(Two CLRs per CER, one for each component of the pair—as in the LINK Records
of figure 5.7. Hierarchy code = 1 or 2, depending on whether the component
code of this CLR appears as the superior or the subordinate component in the
CER of this data base key.)

(4)   Material Information Record (MIR)
Material code/Description/Quantity in stock/Reorder level/Lead time/
Price.
Location Mode Calc, Key = Material code.

(5)   Component Material Record (CMR)
Component code/Material code/Quantity of material required in the
component.

(One record per component code/material code pair.)

(6)   Supplier Information Record (SIR)
Supplier code/Name and Address.
Location Mode Calc, Key = Supplier code.

SET1:   Owner CIR, Member CLR for Hierarchy code = 1 only.
Each CIR will own all CLRs having its component code with Hierarchy
code = 1.

SET2:   Owner CIR, Member CLR for Hierarchy code = 2 only.
Each CIR will own all CLRs having its component code with Hierarchy
code = 2.

SET3:   Owner CIR, Member CMR.

SET4:   Owner CER, Member CLR.
Each CER will own two CLRs, one for each component.

SET5:   Owner MIR, Member CMR.

SET6:   Owner MIR, Member SIR.

SET7:   Owner SYSTEM, Member CIR, in the ascending order of component
code.

SET8:   Owner SYSTEM, Member MIR, in the ascending order of the material
code.

SET9:   Owner SYSTEM, Member SIR, in the ascending order of the supplier
code.

13(b) Assume an array ARR occurring 50 times in the Working-Storage Section.
Suppose that the component code is read into the data item COMPC.

MOVE 0 TO COUNT.
MOVE COMPC TO CC IN CIR.

FIND ANY CIR.
FIND FIRST CLR WITHIN SET1.
IF ERROR-STATUS > 0,
    DISPLAY "NO SUBORDINATE COMPONENTS",
    GO TO A50.
A20.
FIND OWNER WITHIN SET4.
GET SUBC IN CER.
ADD 1 TO COUNT.
MOVE SUBC IN CER TO ARR (COUNT).
FIND NEXT CLR WITHIN SET1
IF ERROR-STATUS = 0, GO TO A20.
PERFORM A40 VARYING I FROM 1 BY 1 UNTIL I > COUNT.
GO TO A50.
A40.
MOVE ARR (I) TO CC IN CIR.
FIND ANY CIR.
GET CIR.
Process as necessary by Cobol.
A50.
EXIT.

The superior components can also be found if SET1 everywhere is replaced by SET2, and SUBC by SUPC. Change also the content of the DISPLAY verb from SUBORDINATE to SUPERIOR.

13(b)2 Assume COMPC is the data name containing the code of the component.

MOVE COMPC TO CC IN CIR.
FIND ANY CIR.
A20.
FIND FIRST CLR WITHIN SET1.
IF ERROR-STATUS > 0,
    DISPLAY "NO SUBORDINATE COMPONENT",
    GO TO A50.
FIND OWNER WITHIN SET4.
GET SUBC IN CER.
MOVE SUBC IN CER TO CC IN CIR.
FIND ANY CIR.
GET CIR.
Process as necessary by Cobol
GO TO A20.

Note that FIND FIRST CLR WITHIN SET1 gives the first record of the set (in set type SET1) owned by the latest CIR accessed.

Second solution: The solution to the problem of exercise 13 given above can be improved by dropping SET4 and the component Link Records (CLRs) from the Schema given in 13(a) and redefining SET1 and SET2 there as follows.

SET 1: Owner CIR, Member CER, each CIR owning all CERs whose SUPCs are the component code of the owner CIR.

SET 2: Owner CIR, Member CER, each CIR owning all CERs whose SUBCs are the component code of the owner CIR.

In 13(b), replace all CLRs by CERs everywhere, and delete the sentence FIND OWNER WITHIN SET4 from both 13(b)1 and 13(b)2.

CHAPTER 6

3. NO, the join operation does not produce repeating groups in a tuple (check yourself). The presence of partial and indirect dependence does not matter since the update anomaly is irrelevant there.

7. Since relations are accessed by domain directly, it matters little whether this particular domain is a candidate key or not. However, the domain for the primary key is likely to be used more often for access, since it can be a foreign key in other related relations.

10. For a relational Schema treat all the record types except DNR of the corresponding Codasyl Schema given earlier as relations, and insert a new attribute, say, DN, for day number in the relation CAR.

(a)   CAR[NA DN]/DAYN

or

GET WS(CAR. NA) : (CAR. DN = DAYN)

(b)   (CAR[CN DN]/DAYN)* COR

or GET WS(COR) : $\exists$CAR(COR. CN = CAR. CN $\land$ CAR. DN = DAYN)

(c)   IDR[PR IC] * COR[IC CN]/CAR[CN DN]/DAYN

or GET WS(IDR. PR, IDR. IC) :$\exists$COR$\exists$CAR

(IDR. IC = COR. IC $\land$ COR. CN = CAR. CN $\land$ CAR. DN = DAYN)

Note that we can extract one tuple at a time using the piped mode.

11. For a relational Schema, use the record types of the corresponding Codasyl Schema given earlier as relations. Insert in the relation CDR the attribute Model (MD) as a foreign key, and in the relation CCR a new attribute, say, RL, giving the relative position of each model in the ascending order of the fixed daily charge (DC).

(a)   Suppose the customer number and the order number are held in the data names CUSTN and ORDN respectively

CDR[ML RN] * (OCR[RN ON CN] * CUSTN) [RN ON]/ORDN

or

GET WS(CDR. ML, CDR. RN):

∃OCR(CDR. RN = OCR. RN ∧ OCR. CN = CUSTN ∧ OCR. ON = ORDN)

(b) Cars of the same model

(CDR[MD RN]/REGN)* CDR

or GET MODL(CDR.MD): CDR.RN=REGN

GET WS(CDR): CDR. MD=MODL

Note that the relation CDR includes domain MD as stated above. For prior and next car, we assume that Fortran-like assignment statements given below are valid in the host language.

RELP = CCR[RL MD]/CDR[MD RN]/REGN

This will put the relative position (in order of the fixed daily charge) of the current model in RELP.

NEXT = RELP + 1

PRIOR = RELP − 1

Check by using host language instructions that the values of NEXT and PRIOR are within the permissible range. If yes, the wanted records are

(CCR[MD RL]/NEXT)* CDR
(CCR[MD RL]/PRIOR)* CDR

In DSL Alpha

GET RELP (CCR. RL): ∃CDR(CCR. MD = CDR. MD ∧ CDR. RN = REGN)
NEXT = RELP + 1
PRIOR = RELP − 1
GET WS(CDR): ∃CCR[CDR.MD = CCR. MD ∧ CCR. RL = NEXT)
GET WS(CDR): ∃CCR[CDR. MD = CCR. MD ∧ CCR. RL = PRIOR)

12. For a relational Schema, treat the record types of the corresponding Codasyl Schema given earlier as relations, except the record type CLR which is unnecessary in a relational data base. Insert the supplier code as a foreign key in the relation MIR.

Subordinate components

CER[SUBC SUPC]/COMPC)* CIR

or

GET WS(CIR): ∃CER(CIR. CC = CER. SUBC ∧ CER. SUPC = COMPC)

The superior components can be obtained by exchanging SUBC with SUPC in the above expressions.

Index